PAST
IMPERATIVES

SUNY Series in Jewish Philosophy
Kenneth Seeskin, editor

PAST IMPERATIVES

*Studies in the
History and Theory
of Jewish Ethics*

Louis E. Newman

STATE UNIVERSITY OF NEW YORK PRESS

Published by
State University of New York Press, Albany

© 1998 State University of New York

For information, address State University of New York Press,
State University Plaza, Albany, N.Y., 12246

Production by Cathleen Collins
Marketing by Anne Valentine

Library of Congress Cataloging in Publication Data

Newman, Louis E.
    Past imperatives : studies in the history and theory of Jewish
ethics / Louis E. Newman.
        p.   cm. — (SUNY series in Jewish philosophy)
    Includes bibliographical references and index.
    ISBN 0-7914-3867-8 (alk. paper). — ISBN 0-7914-3868-6 (pbk.)
    1. Ethics, Jewish—Philosophy.   2. Jewish law—Philosophy.
3. Judaism—Doctrines.   4. Bioethics.   I. Title.   II. Series.
BJ1285.N49   1998
296.3′6—dc21   97-38798
                                                                CIP

10 9 8 7 6 5 4 3 2 1

For my parents
Annette Newman
(1919–1995)
and
Marion Newman

Contents

Preface

The essays collected in this volume address a range of topics, yet address a common concern—to study Jewish ethics in the context of the history of Judaism. My goal has been not to enter into Jewish ethical debates but to analyze the terms of those debates as they have taken shape historically. Rather than contributing to the resolution of moral questions, my concern here is to explore the questions themselves and how they arise in the context of this particular religious tradition. The academic study of Jewish ethics has not been as fully developed as the study of other aspects of this religious tradition, for reasons that I discuss in the introduction to this volume. As a result, we know a great deal more about Jewish mysticism and liturgy, ritual and communal structure than we know about Jewish ethics. My goal is to advance our understanding of this important dimension of the Judaic tradition through these focused studies of selected historical and theoretical issues.

The essays included here were written over the past decade for a variety of audiences. In reviewing and revising them I have attempted to draw them together into a coherent series of studies that take up a cluster of related issues. Hopefully, in their current form they will be readily accessible to those with interests in the history of Judaism, religious ethics, comparative ethics, and Jewish studies in general. At times I have found it necessary to draw from fields in which I claim no particular expertise, including legal theory, hermeneutics, and biblical studies. It is the nature of Jewish ethics that it is closely related to many other aspects of Judaism, as well as to other disciplines. Hence, it can be understood only when it is studied through a number of lenses. I trust that this endeavor will have been successful if it opens up some previously unexplored questions and/or illuminates old issues in new ways.

In pursuing these issues over the past decade, I have been exceptionally fortunate to have received assistance from many quarters. First, I wish to thank Carleton College for the faculty development grants that supported my research during 1988–89 and 1994–95 and for the many ways, tangible and otherwise, in which this institution has nurtured my professional development over the past fifteen years. During my sabbaticals I benefited from the resources and the hospitality of the University of Minnesota Law School and the John Ireland Library at the University of St. Thomas. Much work in preparing this manuscript was done by Douglas Mork—former student, research assistant, and friend. I appreciate his diligence and dedication.

Many colleagues and friends have read my work over the years and I have learned from each of them. Their insights have stimulated me to probe issues I would otherwise have missed and to clarify points that would otherwise have remained murky. A few people in particular have been steady conversation partners and deserve special mention: Martin Jaffee, Daniel Mandil, Richard Sarason, and Earl Schwartz. Others who read and commented upon one or more of these essays include Lisa Sowle Cahill, Richard Crouter, Barry Cytron, Joel Green, Peter Haas, Barry Kogan, Riv-Ellen Prell, Mark Rotenberg, Howard Vogel, and Michael Zuckert. Collectively, their contributions to my work are reflected on virtually every page of this volume.

There are a few special mentors to whom I am particularly indebted. David Blumenthal, Eugene Borowitz, Elliot Dorff, David Ellenson, Lawrence Hoffman, and David Novak have taught me much about Jewish ethics and also about the meaning of collegiality. I am grateful to each of them for sharing their learning so generously and for expressing their support so openly.

I have been blessed with several friends who have helped me, both personally and intellectually. Sheldon Berkowitz has been an exemplary friend. His companionship and playfulness have sustained me in difficult times and enriched my life immeasurably. Paul Lauritzen and Howard Eilberg-Schwartz not only read each of these essays and gave me many valuable suggestions but encouraged my work and believed in its value even when my own faith faltered. But for the support of these three special people, this book would not have been possible.

My wife, Amy, has reawakened my sense of wonder and delight, of passion and tranquility. In sharing my life with her, I have discovered a fulfillment more profound than I have ever known before. In the deepest sense, all that I do bears witness to her devotion to me and mine to her.

I dedicate this book to my parents. My mother's memory is a source of continual blessing, as is my father's ongoing presence in my life. Together they have taught me more about Jewish ethics than any book ever could, for in so many ways they modeled the values and virtues central to our tradition. I have no words to express the gratitude I feel for all the gifts they have given me. I hope only that my love can be as powerfully present in the lives of my children as theirs has been in mine.

25 Sivan 5757
30 June 1997

Acknowledgments

Several of the chapters in this book were originally published as journal articles. I gratefully acknowledge the permission of those publishers to reprint these essays. Chapter 1 was originally published in *Journal of Jewish Studies*, vol. 40, (1989), pp. 61–88. Used by permission of the publisher. Chapter 2 was originally published in *Shofar*, vol. 9, no. 1 (1990), pp. 13–31. Copyright, Purdue Research Foundation, West Lafayette, IN 47907. Used by permission of the publisher. Chapter 3 was originally published in the *Journal of Law and Religion*, vol. 9, no. 1 (1992), pp. 89–112. Used by permission of the publisher. Chapter 4 was originally published in the *Journal of Religious Ethics*, vol. 15, no. 2 (Fall 1987), pp. 155–72. Copyright 1989 by the Journal of Religious Ethics, Inc. Used by permission of the publisher. Chapter 5 was originally published in *Journal of Medicine and Philosophy*, vol. 17, no. 3 (1992), pp. 309–27. Copyright by The Journal of Medicine and Philosophy, Inc. Reprinted by permission. Chapter 8 was originally published in *Modern Judaism*, vol. 10, no. 1 (1990), pp. 17–42. Used by permission of the publisher. Chapter 9 was originally published in Paul Camenisch, ed., *Religious Methods and Resources in Contemporary Bioethics*, Dordrecht: D. Reidel Publishing, 1993, pp. 127–43. Reprinted with permission of Kluwer Academic Publishers, 1993. Chapter 10 was originally published in *Journal of Medicine and Philosophy*, vol. 18, no. 6 (1993), pp. 549–67. Copyright by The Journal of Medicine and Philosophy, Inc. Reprinted by permission.

Introduction

This is a book not *of* Jewish ethics, but *about* it. I do not here offer Jewish moral guidance or contribute to the dissemination of Jewish moral teachings, but rather raise critical questions about the development of Jewish ethics. My goal is not to offer answers to moral questions from a Jewish perspective, but to explore what such a perspective amounts to and how it differs from other moral perspectives. This entails raising historical and theoretical questions about the relationship between Jewish ethics and theology, how contemporary Jewish ethicists have appropriated their ethical/religious tradition, and how they might do so more critically. The essays collected here do this by exploring a series of interrelated questions concerning the nature of Jewish ethics and the ways in which it has developed. Because I believe these essays represent a significant departure from most work in the field of Jewish ethics, I begin by placing them in context.

Ethics: Applied and Theoretical, Prescriptive and Descriptive

In order to explain more fully how these studies differ from most current work in Jewish ethics, we must first attend to the differences between different types of ethical discussions. Among ethicists it is commonplace to distinguish between applied and theoretical issues in ethics, sometimes marked by the terms *morals* and *ethics* respectively. Applied work in ethics is prescriptive in nature. Its aim is to provide moral guidance, to offer positions on specific moral issues, and to persuade readers that these positions are worth adopting. To the general public, ethics means precisely this effort to answer practical questions: Is abortion right or wrong? Under what circumstances can a terminal patient be disconnected from life-support equipment? When are we justified in using force, individually or as a society, to defend

1

our interests? How shall we make decisions involving triage, when we have the means to help some, but not all, of those in need? These questions are hardly new. Indeed, within classical Jewish sources we can find comments and sometimes extended discussions of these matters dating back at least to talmudic times. In recent years there has been a rapidly growing literature in the area of Jewish normative ethics. Following the trend in society at large, new moral dilemmas, many of them related to recent, dramatic developments in the area of biomedical technology, have forced upon us a range of new moral problems. A great number of books and articles addressing these moral problems have been written by Jewish authorities who speak for the tradition and interpret its teachings from a variety of perspectives. A survey of some of the best known contributors to the field reveals the considerable range of viewpoints represented—Orthodox (J. David Bleich, Fred Rosner, Basil Herring), philosophical-halakhic (David Novak), Conservative (Elliot Dorff, Seymour Siegel, Robert Gordis), and Reform (Eugene Borowitz, Albert Vorspan).[1]

In addition to this literature in *applied ethics*, there exists a substantial literature that explores what ethicists refer to as *metaethical* or *second order* questions in Jewish ethics. These are the theoretical questions that arise when we reflect on the nature of the moral judgments we make about real-life, practical situations. In the context of Jewish ethics, a number of theoretical questions have been raised: How is ethics related to law? If God's commandments determine what is morally incumbent upon us, is there any role in Judaism for the autonomous (self-legislating) moral agent? To what extent is Jewish ethics compatible with (or comparable to) other, non-religious systems of ethics? Here again, theoretical questions of this sort have a long history within Judaism. Although classical rabbinic literature by its nature tends not to employ a philosophical idiom, a number of Jewish philosophers in both medieval and modern times have grappled with these questions. In addition, midrashic literature contains a wealth of (nonphilosophical) reflection about the nature of the moral law, the relationship between moral duties and legal ones, and the moral duties of those outside the covenantal community who are not bound by God's commandments. Modern Jewish scholars have dealt with these matters as well, among them, Emil Fackenheim, Jacob Agus, Shubert Spero, Walter Wurzburger, and S. Daniel Breslauer. Given the more theoretical nature of this work, of course, it has appealed largely to a smaller, mostly academic audience.[2]

It should be noted at this point that these two realms of discourse—applied and theoretical, morality and ethics (or, as some would say, ethics and metaethics)—are never entirely independent of one another. Ethical theory always informs ethical practice, at least implicitly. So, how a particular ethicist thinks about the problem of abortion, or euthanasia, will depend at least partly on how that person thinks about legal versus moral obligation, or about the role of the autonomous self in moral decision making. Yet, it is useful to retain the distinction between applied and theoretical ethics since, of course, it is possible to discuss theoretical questions about the nature of morality itself (or of Jewish morality) without discussing specific questions of how to respond morally to particular situations. Moreover, underscoring the distinction helps all concerned to remember the very fact that all work in applied ethics does rely on some theoretical assumptions about the nature of moral judgments, whether these are made explicit or not.

At this point, it is important to note the obvious fact that *within the history of Judaism a wide range of positions on questions of both applied and theoretical ethics have been held and are preserved in Jewish literature.* Although the fact that this diversity exists has been recognized, its implications have generally not been fully appreciated. Thus, it is quite apparent that a contemporary Jewish ethicist writing about organ transplantation or the responsibilities of children to their parents or any other aspect of the moral life has a wealth of material on which to draw, and this material taken as a whole will point in multiple directions. To develop a position on "what Judaism says about . . . (fill in any specific moral issue)," then, is always to draw on this material, to interpret and synthesize it in a certain way, and to determine what one thinks it implies for the present. The same can be said, of course, for those addressing theoretical questions in Jewish ethics. The relationship between law and ethics as well as that between heteronomy and autonomy and between particular theological doctrines and moral responsibilities have been the subjects of considerable deliberation over the centuries. Judaism says a great many things about such questions, and the modern Jewish ethicist must take a position within these debates and explain how his or her interpretation of the traditional sources supports this stance. In short, to "do Jewish ethics," either applied or theoretical, is to reflect on certain questions while standing within this particular religious-ethical tradition and interpreting the many voices that have already spoken to these questions or others like them. To be a Jewish ethicist, then, is perforce to be both a participant within a centuries-long conversation and an interpreter of that conversation.

In precisely that sense, I am not a Jewish ethicist. For, while I am interested in both applied and theoretical questions, I attempt only to describe this enterprise, not participate in it. Like scholars of Jewish mysticism who are not themselves mystics and scholars of Jewish theology who do not themselves theologize,[3] there is a need for scholars of Jewish ethics whose goal is to analyze and understand this aspect of the tradition without necessarily participating in it. As in other academic pursuits, the study of Jewish ethics ought to be characterized by a historical-critical perspective and a neutral stance toward the material in question. Its aim is neither to advocate nor to evaluate Jewish ethics but simply to explain the issues as they arise in historical context. Unfortunately, much work that purports to be strictly descriptive and academic turns out on further analysis to fall short of these goals. So, for example, ostensibly scholarly treatments of the relationship between law and ethics in Judaism have not actually described the issue and explained it, but rather taken a stand within the traditional debate, defending one position against others. The fact is that, until now, there has been strikingly little genuine scholarly work on Jewish ethics.[4] The reasons behind this peculiar lacunae of historical-critical work in this field deserve to be explored, though doing so, like any attempt to explain the absence of something, entails engaging in some historical speculation.

The Modern Study of Jewish Ethics

We would not expect an academic, historical-critical approach to Jewish ethics to emerge within traditionalist, or Orthodox, Jewish circles. For traditional believers, Torah is divine and eternal, not subject to historical development in the modern sense. The entire history of rabbinic interpretation from this perspective is itself part of the "oral Torah," so that each new application of the halakha is regarded as latent within the original Torah given by God to Moses. Gershom Scholem captured this traditional understanding of revelation and tradition when he wrote, "The achievement of every generation, its contribution to tradition, was projected back into the eternal present of the revelation at Sinai. ... According to this doctrine, revelation comprises within it everything that will ever be legitimately offered to interpret its meaning. ... "[5] It follows that ethics, being part of Torah, can have no history. By the same token, all disputes and competing views within the tradition must ultimately be reconcilable, if only in the days of the Messiah.[6]

Rather, it is within the circle of liberal Jews, heirs of the nineteenth-century *Wissenschaft des Judentums*, that we would have expected to find a scholarly investigation of Jewish ethics and its historical development. To appreciate why ethics was largely exempted from critical analysis by these scholars we must attend to the special place that ethics held within their worldview and the significance it was given as against all other aspects of Jewish tradition.

Consider the context in which liberal Judaism developed. The earliest generation of modern Jewish scholars and liberal rabbis in the nineteenth century were engaged in an effort to reconceptualize Jewish theology and religious practice. Their fundamental belief was that the "essence" of Judaism could survive and even thrive in the new intellectual and social setting in which Jews lived, provided that Jews were willing to examine their own religious heritage in a new light. They believed that it was possible, using the tools of historical research, to distill that essence from the whole gamut of traditional beliefs and practices. In this way, Judaism, stripped of its inessential elements and archaic forms, would be literally "re-formed" so as to preserve the essence of its religious message while simultaneously adapting to the radically new situation of modern Jewry.

Within this reconceptualization, Jewish ethics took on unprecedented significance. For, without exception, classical reformers identified the essence of Judaism as its belief in one God and the corollary belief in the unity of "mankind." It followed that the primary religious obligation for Jews was to embrace a humanistic, universalist ethic and to work toward the realization of the biblical vision of global peace and harmony. Indeed, they regarded this universalist ethic as the message that God had entrusted to the Jewish people and that they were "chosen" to teach the world. This article of liberal Jewish faith received perhaps its most famous and forceful articulation in the Pittsburgh Platform of 1885:

> We recognize, in the modern era of universal culture of heart and intellect, the approaching of the realization of Israel's great messianic hope for the establishment of the kingdom of truth, justice, and peace among all men.

And later,

> We acknowledge that the spirit of broad humanity of our age is our ally in the fulfillment of our mission, and therefore, we extend the hand of fellowship to all who operate with us in the establishment of the reign of truth and righteousness among men.

In this formulation of Judaism, Israel's (particular) mission is to spread the (universal) moral teachings that will lead to the fulfillment of the ancient, messianic vision of global peace.

The quintessential expression of this ideal could be found in the prophetic literature. Thus, it is no surprise that the reformers returned again and again to the prophets for prooftexts that seemed to support their preference for ethics over ritual and for universalism over particularism.

> For I desired lovingkindness and not sacrifice, and knowledge of God more than burnt offerings. (Hos. 6:6)

> Though you offer me burnt offerings and your meal offerings, I will not accept them. . . . But let justice roll down like waters, and righteousness like a mighty stream. (Amos 5:22,24)

> Have we not all one father? Has not one God created us? Why do we deal treacherously every man against his brother, to profane the covenant of our fathers? (Mal. 2:10)

These passages, and others like them, reassured liberal Jewish thinkers of the previous century that their tradition remained relevant, that Judaism's religious-moral truth was timeless, and that contemporary Jews could live out the meaning of their faith within a secular society.

This view found expression in the work of every liberal Jewish thinker of the nineteenth and early twentieth century. Kaufman Kohler, arguably the first systematic liberal Jewish thinker of the period, wrote,

> Judaism is nothing less than a message concerning the *One and holy God* and *one, undivided humanity* with a world-uniting *Messianic goal*, a message intrusted by divine revelation to the Jewish people. Thus Israel is its prophetic herbinger and priestly guardian, its witness and defender throughout the ages, who is never to falter in the task of upholding and unfolding its truths until they have become the possession of the whole human race.[7]

Virtually the same thought is expressed a generation later by Leo Baeck, whose work, in turn, influenced a generation of rabbis and thinkers in America.

> Its ethical character, the basic significance which it sees in the moral action, is the primary thing in the religion of Israel. No matter at what date one may fix its origin and no matter how one may view the question of its progress, one thing is certain, that since that Israelitisch, prophetic religion began, which is the true religion of Israel, the moral law has formed its cardinal point. Ju-

daism is not only ethical, but *ethics constitute its principle, its essence and nature.*[8]

Especially worth noting is Baeck's explicit claim that historical investigations into the development of Judaism cannot change what he regards as an unassailable fact, that ethics is the essence of Judaism. In this sense, he articulates perfectly the longstanding liberal strategy of identifying ethics as the timeless core of Judaism, distinct from other aspects of the tradition (primarily, the ritual law).

This strategy of placing ethics at the center of a reconstructed Jewish religion appeared to resolve both the intellectual and social challenges of modernity. Within the intellectual sphere, Judaism's essence, the one truth that it had proclaimed throughout its long history, was in no sense invalidated by positivism's emphasis on empirical, scientific study, or by the extension of this attitude into historical-critical study of religious-literary traditions. To the extent that empiricism cast into doubt the mythological and miraculous aspects of biblical stories, the reformers could readily concede that science was to be trusted in such matters more than the Bible, without thereby sacrificing the essence of Judaism's religious truth. Moreover, they could adopt a historical perspective on the tradition, conceding that some elements were products of human creativity alone, while insisting that a kernel of divinely inspired or revealed truth was present as well. Finally, and perhaps most important, the universalism propounded by Enlightenment thinkers like Rousseau and Kant could be embraced as consistent with (or even prefigured by) the prophetic emphasis on "ethical monotheism."

On the social plane, of course, Jews who subscribed to this liberal interpretation of Judaism could in good conscience integrate into the wider society and embrace the opportunities it offered them. In fact, they could even justify their doing so as a religious obligation, insofar as their God-given mission was to spread the religious truth at Judaism's core and thereby facilitate the coming of the "Kingdom of God."[9] Thus, the end of the ghettoization of Jews, as well as their self-isolation as a discrete national group, could be viewed as but the next phase in a necessary process leading to a messianic culmination of history.

But this liberal reconceptualization of Judaism was characterized by several important features. First, it relied upon an "evolutionary-essentialist" understanding of tradition. Judaism was viewed as both evolving over time in response to historical circumstances and as possessing an essence ("core," "kernel") that remained constant and that was understood, in some sense, as divine. Second, since ethics was identified as the essence of Judaism, all other aspects of the tradition were either minimized or valued only as vehicles for its ethical message. Finally, prophetic universalism was identified as the pinnacle of Jewish ethics and, once again, all other ethical views within the tradition were either minimized or interpreted as deviations from Judaism's essentially universalist moral truth.

Given their need to view this universalist prophetic ethic as the timeless, unchanging essence of Judaism, it is no wonder that the generation of scholars and rabbis who first produced critical studies of Jewish literature did not turn their critical attention to ethics.[10] Acknowledging, as any historical-critical account must, that Jewish ethics is composed of multiple, often contradictory, views would entail displacing the universalist, prophetic ethic from its favored status as the religious truth at the core of Judaism. This, in turn, would have challenged the very strategy that they consistently employed for addressing the most pressing intellectual and social questions of their day.

And what was true for nineteenth century liberal Jewish thinkers continued to be true for the next few generations. During at least the first half of the twentieth century the same intellectual and social agenda preoccupied Jews living in western countries. Jews continued to find in their universalist ethical tradition the source of both their uniqueness and the ground of their commonality with the non-Jewish societies in which they lived. Hence it is not surprising that the academic study of Jewish ethics failed to emerge during this period, just as it had received scant attention among nineteenth-century scholars.

In the decades since the end of World War II this situation has begun to change. Some studies of Jewish ethics have appeared, as the field of Jewish studies generally has blossomed in North America and in Israel. Much of this work has been produced by scholars of Jewish law and, accordingly, has focused on the legal dimensions of Jewish ethics (the *halakha* as it relates to *mitzvot bein adam l'havero*) and on the relationship between law and ethics.[11] Some work too has been done on the ethics of specific figures—Saadia Gaon's ethics, or Maimonides' understanding of Aristotle's "Golden Mean," for example—mostly by those interested in the history of Jewish philosophy.[12] Yet, most issues in Jewish ethics have received little, if any, scholarly attention. Moreover, in contrast to other fields of Jewish studies—literature, history, mysticism, sociology, etc.—it is striking that, notwithstanding the proliferation of courses in Jewish studies in American universities, few courses are offered on Jewish ethics, and as yet no college textbook in the field exists.

So the question remains, why has a substantial body of historical research in Jewish ethics not appeared in more recent times? The answer, I suspect, can be traced in part to the current state of scholarship in rabbinics. The
academic study of rabbinic literature began with Leopold Zunz and his Wissenschaft colleagues more than one hundred years ago and continued to be
pursued actively in a small number of institutions: principally in seminaries
such as Hebrew Union College and the Jewish Theological Seminary, and at
the Hebrew University in Jerusalem. Additionally, in the past thirty years
great advances in the academic study of this literature have been made
through the prodigous efforts of Jacob Neusner and his students, among others. But the focus of these scholarly studies has been on retracing the development of this vast and complex literature, analyzing its peculiar literary
forms, and making this data accessible to scholars of religion in antiquity.
These scholars have tended to regard the study of ethics as best left to
philosophers, or perhaps theologians.

In addition, apart from academic students of rabbinic literature, the majority of those with the textual ability to read and analyze the classical sources
are rabbis. On the whole, they have been trained to think of themselves as interpreters of the tradition, and to direct their efforts to communities of living
Jews in need of moral guidance, not to producing analytic studies of Jewish
ethics. In this sense, the situation today is not as different from that in the
nineteenth century as we sometimes suppose. Modern Jews wish to anchor
their Jewish identity in something transcendent that does not continually
change with historical circumstance. Ethics would seem to be that aspect of
Judaism that can most easily be affirmed as eternally valid, even if most people would no longer appeal to the language of Judaism's "essence." And this
implies that any historical developments that have occured in Jewish ethics are
less important than basic religious-moral truths that Judaism has always
taught. At least among liberal Jews, the greater the need for ethical direction
and for placing ethics at the center of their religious identity, the less inclination there will be to study its development objectively in an academic context.

Whatever the cause, the fact remains that there are few studies that explore the history of Jewish ethics from a scholarly perspective, explain the features of Jewish ethics that make it distinctive, and examine the theoretical
underpinnings of the entire ethical tradition within Judaism. To do this in a
comprehensive way would be a monumental undertaking; the studies collected in this volume are limited in scope. They are meant to illuminate discrete aspects of the Jewish ethical tradition and to suggest some ways in

which constructive work in Jewish ethics can build on these historical and theoretical investigations.

Studies in the History and Theory of Jewish Ethics

The essays in this volume uniformly begin from the historical-critical assumption that a religious-ethical tradition like Judaism, spanning more than two millennia, has undergone enormous development. It follows, first, that Jewish ethics will exhibit significant diversity and that the goal of the scholar is to examine and explain these diverse views within the tradition, not to harmonize them or to posit coherence where none exists. This is not to deny that Jewish ethics, like the tradition as a whole, exhibits a significant degree of internal consistency over time. Arguably, there exists a certain framework of values and assumptions that have persisted over many centuries and that collectively help to define the "tradition." It is the goal of scholarship in Jewish ethics to explore and explain the unity, as well as the evident diversity, within classical sources.

To examine issues in Jewish ethics from this perspective is, once again, not to enter into the historic debates, certainly not to side with any of the traditional positions on either normative or theoretical issues. Rather, the goal is to "deconstruct" the issues, to investigate the presuppositions underlying each of the positions that traditional authorities adopted, and to uncover the common assumptions that made it possible for authorities with conflicting views to engage in a coherent conversation. In short, the purpose throughout these essays is to explore the contours of Judaism's ethical dimension and to explain why this tradition has assumed the shape it has.

Finally, the work of contemporary Jewish ethicists must also be subjected to critical analysis. Their stated goal, after all, is to stand within this religious-ethical tradition and apply its teachings to contemporary problems. But their reading of the tradition, their assumptions about how it can be appropriated, and how their conclusions can contribute to moral debate in a pluralistic society, all deserve more careful study than they have heretofore received.

These investigations of classical and contemporary Jewish ethics naturally cluster around three sets of issues and have been presented here accordingly. In the first, I explore the relationship between law and ethics (chapters 1 through 3), in the second the connection between Jewish ethics and theology (chapters 4 through 7), and in the final section the methodological issues that confront contemporary Jewish ethicists (chapters 8 through 10).

Chapter 1 presents a conceptual analysis of a much debated term in classical Jewish ethics, *lifnim mishurat hadin*. Typically this concept refers to moral actions that go beyond the requirements of the *halakha* (law) and has suggested to many that Judaism acknowledges an extra-legal ethic. Yet the precise relationship between actions designated as *lifnim mishurat hadin* and one's legal duty has been the subject of controversy for centuries. My analysis suggests that the very indeterminacy of the relationship between *lifnim mishurat hadin* and *din* (law) is a key to certain distinctive religious characteristics of Jewish ethics. Therefore, all attempts to explain this traditional concept in terms of secular concepts, such as "ethics" and "law," will invariably confuse rather than clarify the matter.

Building on this analysis, chapter 2 explores the problem of the relationship between law and ethics more generally. Modern writers have reached quite different conclusions about this question, but the debate as a whole has never been subjected to careful analysis. I argue that there is a certain paradox at the heart of traditional Judaism, inherent in its dual character as a functioning legal system and as a system of religious instruction, which necessitates that the boundary between law and ethics always be ambiguous. Failure to recognize this fact about the tradition has led scholars to conclude mistakenly that there must be some clearly defined, static relationship between law and ethics in Judaism.

Chapter 3, in turn, carries forward this analysis of the religious dimension of Jewish ethics by exploring one central theological category, covenant. Many scholars have noted that covenant entered Israelite religion via ancient near eastern notions of treaty and denoted a kind of legal contract between two parties. It has also been noted, however, that within both biblical and rabbinic sources there exists a range of covenant concepts, only some of which resemble a legal contract. I argue that, when the similarities and differences between covenants and contracts are examined, it is possible to see how diverse understandings of covenant correlate to various theoretical positions within Jewish ethics (including the relationship between law and ethics). In mapping the relationship between a theological category (covenant) and trends within Jewish ethics, this essay provides a fitting segue-way to the group of studies that follows.

Chapters 4 and 5 examine the ways in which religious beliefs shape certain moral duties in Judaism. The issue of forgiveness makes a good case in point. In the context of secular ethics, it is difficult to establish a general duty to forgive others for offenses they commit against us. Yet, distinctive Jewish religious views about the nature of a covenant community and about moral obligations as duties to God (and not only to other people) underlie the Jewish moral duty of forgiveness. In the realm of bioethics as well, Jewish perspectives are closely related to theological beliefs, especially beliefs about creation and the nature of humankind. I suggest that Jewish bioethics must be understood as a product of these religious beliefs, but that nonetheless Jewish perspectives may prove coherent even to those who do not share those beliefs.

Chapter 6 turns to an important issue in metaethics, whether there is a natural moral order distinct from either divinely revealed moral law or humanly enacted law. The concept of natural law has a long history within Roman Catholic moral theology, and the extent to which it has a place within Judaism has been the subject of significant debate among both classical and contemporary writers. My analysis of this debate suggests that the underlying issue is theological, specifically the way in which one construes the relationship between creation and revelation. Different theological positions will support different understandings of the possibility, and also the limitations, of natural law thinking in Judaism.

The final essay in this section represents an attempt to bridge the gap between the academic study of Jewish ethics and normative work in Jewish ethics. Constructing a modern Jewish ethic in the context of a historical analysis of the tradition requires that ethicists view all traditional ethical teachings as products of their own historical periods. This immediately challenges the traditional Jewish faith that ethical norms represent expressions of God's will. So the theological question arises: is there any way to develop a Jewish ethic using the tools of historical criticism and simultaneously to claim that the norms so developed are religiously grounded? I believe that there is, provided that we revise our understanding of revelation and of the way God "speaks" to us in history. Drawing on aspects of process theology, I suggest that we can conceptualize God as immanent and impersonal (rather than transcendent and personal). By the same token, we can envision Jewish moral guidance as emerging over time from our own engagement with the divine presence. Thus, Jewish ethics is grounded in history and yet reflects a genuine engagement with the divine presence, especially with the collective moral wisdom of earlier generations, which is itself understood as the product of their efforts to live in harmony with God. So a historical-critical perspective on Jewish ethics is compatible with a theological understanding of Jewish moral obligation.

The final section of the book turns to methodological questions confronting contemporary Jewish ethicists. In chapter 8 I examine the contemporary debate surrounding euthanasia and the efforts of many ethicists to construct a Jewish position on these questions out of the classical sources. I conclude that normative Jewish ethicists have failed to appreciate the full extent of their own role as interpreters of the ethical tradition, and so too the uncertainty inherent in any such process of interpretation. An analysis of this interpretive process requires that we reconceptualize the very nature of contemporary Jewish ethics and the status of the claims that ethicists make on behalf of their tradition.

Chapter 9 builds on this analysis by exploring diverse ways in which the entire enterprise of contemporary Jewish ethics can be conceptualized. I delineate three alternative approaches to reading classical Jewish texts and, corresponding to these, three ways of construing the coherence of the tradition. One's theory of modern Jewish ethics, of what it means to build upon and extend this moral tradition, depends in the end on which of these approaches to text and tradition one adopts.

Chapter 10 explores the resources within Jewish tradition for offering moral teaching to those outside the Jewish community. I suggest that, notwithstanding the fact that *halakha* is a body of teaching by and for Jews, it embodies some moral principles that are intelligible in the public domain. Jewish ethics thus can contribute, albeit in a limited way, to moral discourse in a pluralistic society. At the same time, certain Jewish moral principles may challenge secular values and prompt us to reconsider the preeminent significance that we generally attribute to autonomy and freedom as core values in our society.

In the conclusion I offer a brief programmatic statement outlining future directions for academic studies in Jewish ethics. In addition to further studies of the issues taken up here—ethics and law, ethics and theology, method in contemporary ethics—I identify several avenues for further research. These include the relationship between ethics and eschatology, focusing on the way in which a vision of the end of time gives shape and urgency to moral life in historical time. In addition, I suggest that various elements in a traditional Jewish theory of virtue might be fruitfully analyzed in relation to both the cycles of the Jewish liturgical year and the (often overlooked) narrative dimensions of the tradition. A contemporary Jewish narrative (or liturgical) ethic might be developed, and the problems and prospects for doing so are worth exploring. Finally, I propose that the history of Jewish philosophical ethics should be analyzed with a view to explaining the obstacles inherent in any effort to translate religious concepts into philosophical ones.

The title of this volume, *Past Imperatives*, is intentionally ambiguous. Jewish ethics has often been viewed as a system of moral rules bequethed to us from the past. These "past imperatives" constitute the raw material out of which ethicists in each generation produce their moral teachings. They have understood their task as that of applying these past imperatives to current situations. Yet, as I have indicated, the motive force behind these essays is that we must move beyond this conception of ethics as a set of essentially timeless imperatives toward a fuller understanding of Jewish ethics as a historically evolving expression of Jewish religious life. Once we begin to move "past imperatives," a great many questions, both historical and theoretical, suggest themselves—about the very nature of the enterprise called Jewish ethics, about the course of its development, and about its relationship to other aspects of Jewish tradition.

In conclusion, these studies, both those included in this volume and those projected for the future, are intended to enrich our understanding of the ethical dimension of Judaism, both in relation to other aspects of this religious tradition and in relation to other systems of ethics. At the same time, they are directed to those "practitioners" of Jewish ethics interested in exploring the foundations of their own work. In this way, these essays on the history and theory of Jewish ethics are meant both to illuminate where we have been and, in some small way, to suggest how we might proceed from here.

Part One

Ethics and Law

Chapter 1

Law, Virtue, and Supererogation in the Halakha

The Problem of Lifnim Mishurat Hadin Reconsidered

J ewish ethicists have devoted much attention in recent years to the question of the relationship between ethical and legal responsibilities within the Jewish tradition.[1] In particular, much discussion has focused on the question of whether Judaism recognizes an ethic independent of Jewish law (halakha) and, if so, how we should understand the relationship between this "extra-legal" ethic and the halakha. While discussions of this issue incorporate a vast range of rabbinic sources, the concept of lifnim mishurat hadin (lit., "beyond the line of the law")[2] figures prominently in the debate and, so, deserves special attention. The phrase lifnim mishurat hadin, which occurs a number of times in rabbinic literature, apparently refers to the morally praiseworthy action of doing more than the law requires or, as we would say, going above and beyond the call of (legal) duty. The very fact that the traditional sources recognize such a category suggests that Judaism does indeed recognize a type of moral action that is not embodied in the halakha. Yet, the precise status of actions designated as lifnim mishurat hadin remains very much in doubt. Some have argued that this concept reveals an implicit recognition on the part of the rabbis that the law is not invariably just, so that in fulfilling one's legal duty one does not always discharge one's moral duty.[3] Others, however, have suggested that lifnim mishurat hadin, rather than standing in opposition to the law, is in fact part and parcel of one's legal responsibility in the broadest sense.[4] Halakha, on this view, encorporates both strictly legal duties (din) and extra-legal/ethical duties (lifnim mishurat hadin). Still others have held that the concept has not been used consistently throughout the tradition, but rather evolved from a strictly moral, extra-legal standard in the talmudic period to a fully actionable legal norm in medieval times.[5] The scholarly debate about the status of *lifnim mishurat hadin* is further complicated by the fact that a variety of traditional sources can be cited in support of each of these positions.

Despite the wide range of disagreement, however, all who have written on the meaning of *lifnim mishurat hadin* readily concede the significance of the issue at hand. Indeed, one can hardly discuss the relationship between ethics and law in Judaism without coming to terms with the problem of *lifnim mishurat hadin.* This is because, in asking about the status of *lifnim mishurat hadin,* we confront the question of whether Judaism allows for the existence of an ethic "independent of the halakha." The answer to this question, in turn, will determine whether or not Jewish law embodies all Jewish ethical norms. So, at stake is the very comprehensiveness of halakha as a moral system, for we wish to know to what extent the halakha encompasses all of one's ethical responsibilities. And, given the centrality of halakha to the whole of Jewish tradition, it is apparent that one's answer to this question may shape decisively one's stance on many other legal and ethical issues that arise within the tradition.

My own discussion of *lifnim mishurat hadin* and its significance unfolds in three parts. First, I systematically review all the talmudic sources that mention the term in an attempt to discern its precise definition. Part of the confusion that has arisen concerning the meaning of *lifnim mishurat hadin,* I believe, stems from the fact that the very character of actions so designated has not been carefully defined. By looking closely at each of the contexts in which the term is used, we will be able to specify more precisely the special character of the actions that this term denotes. From the issue of definition I turn to the problem of interpretation. Here two questions are of central importance. First, what appears to be the moral significance of the term *lifnim mishurat hadin* as the talmudic sages used it and, second, how have post-talmudic authorities understood this concept and its relationship to legal norms? The answers to these questions, as I have already indicated, are varied and complex, for the textual evidence is itself ambiguous on the question of the relationship between *lifnim mishurat hadin* and law. I assess the merits of three competing positions on the status of *lifnim mishurat hadin* and then offer a new interpretation of both the ethical and legal dimensions of this concept. In the concluding section, I consider briefly the implications of this new interpretation for the issue of the relationship between law and ethics in Judaism. I shall contend that our understanding of *lifnim mishurat hadin* has significant bearing on this issue, though not in the way that scholars generally have been inclined to assume.

Talmudic Sources

The term *lifnim mishurat hadin* appears only nine times in the Babylonian Talmud, including one source that also appears in two midrashic compilations.[6] Two basic questions will guide our examination of these sources: in what context does the term appear and what sort of action does the term seem to designate? Once we have succeeded in determining the denotation of the term, we can proceed to explore its moral significance, specifically in relation to legal norms.[7]

I. Legal Sources

1. Baba Qamma 99b
   A. There was a certain woman who showed a denar [an ancient coin] to Rabbi Ḥiyya [who] told her that it was good.
   B. Later she came again to him and said to him, "I showed it [to others] and they told me that it was bad, and in fact I could not pass it."
   C. He [Ḥiyya] said to Rab, "Go forth and change it for a good one and write down in my register that this was a bad transaction."
   D. But why should he [Rabbi Ḥiyya] be different from Dankho and Issur, who would be exempt [from reimbursing a customer under these circumstances] because they needed no instruction [that is, because they are experts and so are assumed to be correct about the authenticity of the coin, even if others do not concur in their judgment]? Surely Rabbi Ḥiyya also needed no instruction [and so should not be required to reimburse the customer who could not pass the denar.]
   E. Rabbi Ḥiyya acted *lifnim mishurat hadin*, on the principle learned by Rabbi Joseph [in explication of Exod. 18:20]:
   F. "And shalt show them" means the source of their livelihood; "the way" means deeds of lovingkindness; "they must walk" means the visitation of the sick; "therein" means burial; "and the work" means the law; "which they must do" means *lifnim mishurat hadin*.

The present passage appears as part of a larger discussion that concerns whether the expertise of a moneychanger affects his liability when he makes an error. The expert moneychanger, it is argued, need not reimburse customers if he makes a mistake. The case of Rabbi Ḥiyya is introduced in order to challenge that position by offering an instance in which an expert in fact made such a reimbursement. In response to this challenge, the Talmud proposes that Ḥiyya did not act in accordance with the law, but rather *lifnim mishurat hadin*. That is, he voluntarily made good on a transaction, sacrificing his own monetary gain for the sake of his customer's, even though he was not legally required to do so.

We deal here, therefore, with the case of a privileged individual, for whom acting *lifnim mishurat hadin* means forgoing his exemption from a legal duty by conforming to the standard that applies to the ordinary person. The key elements appear to be the voluntary nature of the act and the fact that it involves greater self-sacrifice (in this case, monetary sacrifice) than is expected of a person in that situation. In addition, though the purpose of Ḥiyya's action is not explicitly stated, the fact that he acts in response to a request from a customer implies that his motivation is simply to redress her grievance. Acting *lifnim mishurat hadin*, then, entails forgoing a legal right with respect to another for the purpose of helping that person. The explication of Exodus 18:20 (F) will be dealt with in source 8 below.

2. Baba Metsia 30b
   A. Rabbi Ishmael son of Rabbi Yose was walking on a road when he met a man carrying a load of sticks.
   B. The man put them down, rested, and then said to him [Ishmael], "Help me to take them up."
   C. "What is it [the wood] worth?" [Ishmael] inquired. "Half a zuz" was the answer.
   D. So he [Ishmael] gave the man the half zuz [thereby acquiring ownership] and declared it ownerless. [By rendering the sticks ownerless, Ishmael avoids violating the law that requires one to help a person with a load]. Thereupon [the man] reacquired it [thereby again placing Ishmael in the position of one who is obligated to help with this load.][8]
   E. He [Ishmael] gave him another half zuz and again declared it ownerless. Seeing that he was again about to reacquire it, [Ishmael] said to him, "I have declared it ownerless for all

but you." {A brief discussion follows about the legitimacy of declaring property ownerless in this restricted way.}

F. Was not Rabbi Ishmael son of Rabbi Yose an elder for whom it was undignified [to help one to take up a load. If so, why did he act as if he were obligated to help the man with his load.]?

G. He acted *lifnim mishurat hadin*.

H. For Rabbi Joseph learned [concerning Exod. 18:20]:
"And thou shalt show them" refers to their house of life;
"the way" refers to deeds of lovingkindness;
"they must walk" refers to the law;
"that they shall do" refers to *lifnim mishurat hadin*.

This passage appears in the midst of a discussion of whether an elder is relieved of the obligation to help a neighbor load and unload an animal, an act presumed to compromise his dignity. The case of Rabbi Ishmael is cited to demonstrate that a sage should help a neighbor with his load. The question at (F), then, is meant to challenge this view by proposing that Ishmael was exempt from this duty. In response (G) it is suggested that, while Ishmael had no duty to help the man with his load, he chose to do so anyway, to do more than the law expected of him. Here again, the term *lifnim mishurat hadin* is employed with reference to a person who has been exempted from a general legal duty due to his exceptional status. Again, the individual in question acts voluntarily, though not necessarily at his own initiative, since his help has been enlisted by the other man. Both here and in the previous case, it should be noted, acting in this extra-legal fashion does not constitute violating any positive legal duty. Neither Ḥiyya nor Ishmael act in a way that could be called illegal. Rather, each has a right to refrain from acting in accordance with the general duty incumbent upon others, but chooses to forgo that legal right.

3. Ketubot 97a

A. The question was raised: if a man sold [a plot of land] but [on concluding the sale] he was no longer in need of this money, may his sale be withdrawn or not?

B. Derive the answer from the following case: There was a certain man who sold a plot of land to Rav Papa because he was in need of money to buy some oxen, and, as eventually he did not need it, Rav Papa actually returned the land to him.

C. Rav Papa acted *lifnim mishurat hadin* [and so his action in this case cannot serve to establish that one is legally bound to rescind a sale under these conditions.]

This passage appears in the context of a discussion about the conditions under which a contract of sale may be rescinded. If the seller makes the sale conditional upon his ability to use the proceeds for a specific purpose (for example, moving to the Land of Israel) and subsequently discovers that he cannot do so, he may rescind the sale. But what if he has made no such explicit condition, though he enters the transaction with this intent? In this case must the buyer return the property he has bought if the seller asks him for it? The case concerning Rav Papa (B) suggests that the buyer has such an obligation. But this claim is defeated (C) by the statement that, in returning the property, Rav Papa did more than the law required. Unlike the previous two cases, here we are concerned with an ordinary individual, not one who is of exceptional status and so exempt from a specific legal duty. Nonetheless, the structural elements that we noted earlier are present in this situation as well. Specifically, Rav Papa is said to act *lifnim mishurat hadin* when he voluntarily forgoes a legal right (in this case, to keep the land that has been sold legitimately to him) for the purpose of helping another individual (who wishes that he had not entered into this transaction). Once again, the act in question entails both financial loss and some measure of personal inconvenience for the person who refrains from exercising his legal right. The motivation to act in this way, though not stated in any of these texts, can only be an altruistic one. Acting *lifnim mishurat hadin* begins to emerge here as a demonstration of generosity, both financial and personal.

4. Baba Metsia 24b
    A. Rab Judah once followed Mar Samuel into a market of whole-meal vendors and asked him, "What if one found a purse here [may one keep it]?"
    B. Mar Samuel answered, "It would belong to the finder."
    C. [Judah asked,] "What if an Israelite came and indicated an identification mark?"
    D. Mar Samuel answered, "[The finder] would have to return it." (*ḥyb lhḥzyr*)
    E. [Judah objected, "You maintain] two [contradictory positions." That is, if objects left in crowded places belong to the finder (B), then how can it also be the law that it must be returned to an Israelite (D)]?

F. Mar Samuel answered, "[It should be returned]" "*lifnim mishurat hadin.*"

G. Thus the father of Samuel found some asses in a desert, and he returned them to their owner after a year of twelve months—*lifnim mishurat hadin.*

The case before us is intended to clarify one's responsibility to return lost objects to Israelites. According to Mishnah Baba Metsia 2:1, an object found in any place where there are frequent crowds belongs to the finder, because the original owner is presumed to have given it up. The finder, therefore, is exempt from the general obligation to return the lost object to its original owner. The question then arises whether this law applies even in places where the majority of people are Israelites, who are presumed to return lost property, or only where the majority of people are heathens, who are presumed not to do so. This case stands somewhat apart from those just examined in that the action deemed *lifnim mishurat hadin* is presented as a requirement, rather than as a voluntary act of generosity. This is the force of the language at D (*ḥyb lhḥzyr*), "one is required to return it." Unfortunately the text does not enable us to distinguish whether the finder is compelled to act thus as a matter of legal or of moral duty (or both). Could the man be forced to return the purse and could legal action be taken against him if he refused? If so, we would surely regard his obligation as a legal one. On the other hand, Samuel may mean simply that he ought to return the purse, even though the law does not require it.[9] This latter reading would be most consistent with the sources examined earlier, though this alone should not be allowed to prejudice our reading, as we have no assurance that the term is used consistently throughout the talmudic sources. In either case, it appears that acting *lifnim mishurat hadin* constitutes a kind of duty, whether moral or legal we cannot be sure. Nonetheless, this case, like those that preceeded, reaffirms the view that acting *lifnim mishurat hadin* will entail financial loss for the individual involved. The appended case about Samuel's father (G) offers little help in determining the denotation of the term. We can only assume, since this is nowhere stated, that one has no legal obligation to return a lost object after twelve months. In doing so, then, Samuel's father could be described as acting *lifnim mishurat hadin.*

5. Berakhot 45b

A. Raba said, "The following statement was made by me independently and a similar statement has been reported in the name of Rabbi Zera:

B. 'If three persons have been eating together, one interrupts
his meal to oblige two [that is, for purposes of saying the introduction to the grace after meals, which requires a minimum of three persons, one person interrupts his meal to
join with the other two who are ready to say grace],
C. but two do not interrupt their meal to oblige one.' "
D. But do they not? Did not Rav Papa break off for Abba Mar
his son, he [Papa] and another with him? [If so, this appears
to contradict the rule just stated at B.]
E. Rav Papa was different because he acted *lifnim mishurat
hadin.*

The question here is the extent to which a man is required to inconvenience himself for the sake of others with whom he is eating. While the general rule is that two individuals are not obligated to inconvenience themselves
for the sake of a third, Rav Papa and a companion did so anyway. They were
prepared to forgo their legal right to continue their meals uninterrupted in
order to enable a single individual to participate in a communal grace. In
doing so they acted *lifnim mishurat hadin.* While this case concerns a matter
of personal convenience alone, rather than of monetary loss, we have seen
that this too has been a common element in the cases where our term is employed. This again highlights the character of *lifnim mishurat hadin* as an act
of unexpected generosity or self-sacrifice.

II. Nonlegal Sources

Let us turn now to those talmudic sources that employ the term *lifnim mishurat hadin,* though not in the context of a legal discussion. As we shall see,
these references both reinforce and greatly augment what we have already
learned about the term and its meaning.

6. Berakhot 7a
A. Whence do we learn that the Holy One who is Blessed
prays?
B. It is written [Isa. 56:7]: "I will bring them to my holy
mountain and I will make them joyful in my house of
prayer" [lit., 'the house of my prayer.']
C. It does not say 'their prayer,' but rather 'my prayer,' thus we
learn that the Holy One who is Blessed prays.

D. What does God pray?

E. Said Rav Zutra bar Tuvia, Rav said, "May it be My will that My mercy may suppress My anger and My mercy may prevail over My other attributes, so that I may deal with My children according to the attribute of mercy and may on their behalf enter *lifnim mishurat hadin.*"

F. It was taught: Rabbi Ishmael ben Elisha says, "I once entered into the innermost part [of the Sanctuary] to offer incense and saw Akatriel Yah, the Lord of Hosts, seated upon a high and exalted throne."

G. He said to me, "Ishmael, my son, bless Me!"

H. I replied, "May it be Your will that Your mercy may suppress Your anger and Your mercy may prevail over Your other attributes, so that You may deal with Your children according to the attribute of mercy and may on their behalf enter *lifnim mishurat hadin.*"

I. And He nodded to me with His head.

J. Here we learn that the blessing of an ordinary man must not be considered lightly in your eyes.

The notion that God is capable of acting *lifnim mishurat hadin* may seem at odds with the sources examined so far. Since previous sources have led us to suppose that this phrase refers to the person who sacrifices some monetary or personal gain for the benefit of another, it is difficult to see how this could be relevant to God's actions. The connection becomes apparent, however, when one notes the association of *lifnim mishurat hadin* in this text with the quality of mercy (E,H). Just as one individual may act benevolently by relinquishing a claim against another, so too God is here urged to act generously or mercifully by suppressing the legitimate anger aroused when Israelites sin. The use of the term *lifnim mishurat hadin* ("beyond the line of the law") is in fact quite appropriate in this context, for God is being asked to forgo the divine right to punish Israel under the terms of their covenant, which, throughout biblical and rabbinic literature, is conceived as a kind of legal right. When God refrains from exercising this right of retribution against Israel, it can therefore be said that God acts more generously than is required by the terms of the covenant. It is important to note that here, as in the cases discussed earlier, God's acting in this way does not constitute a violation of the covenant, for the terms of that agreement permit God to punish Israel for its sinful behavior but do not require God to do so. God is free, as are individuals, to act more mercifully than the law expects of them, and doing so is what is meant here by the term *lifnim mishurat hadin*.

7. Avodah Zarah 4b

    A. Said Rabbi Joseph, "No one should recite the Amidah of the Musaf service on the first day of the New Year during the first three hours of the day in private, lest, since judgment is then proceeding, his deeds may be scrutinized and the prayer rejected." . . .

    B. But have you not said, "During the first three hours the Holy One who is Blessed is occupied with the Torah, [while during the second three hours God sits in judgment over the whole world?" In that case, why should one be concerned that a prayer will be rejected during the hours when God is occupied with Torah?]

    C. You may reverse [the sequence of God's activities during these two periods of the day, thereby resolving the problem just mentioned] or, if you wish, you may say it need not be reversed.

    D. [Thus, during the first three hours, when God is occupied with] the Torah, which Scripture designates as 'truth,' as it is written, "buy the Truth and sell it not" (Prov. 23:23), the Holy One who is Blessed will not act *lifnim mishurat hadin*,

    E. [whereas during the second three hours, when God is sitting in] judgment, which is not designated by Scripture as 'truth,' the Holy One who is Blessed may act *lifnim mishurat hadin*.

As in the previous text, God's acting *lifnim mishurat hadin* is discussed in the context of God judging Israel. The point of this passage is that when truth is at stake, God will scrutinize Israel's deeds most carefully. At such times God cannot be expected to act with special benevolence. By contrast, when God is engaged in judgment, which does not require adherence to a strict standard of truth, the deity may show mercy to Israel. In short, acting "truthfully" requires that God give Israelites exactly what they deserve, neither more nor less. This attitude, in the context of either divine or human behavior, is not compatible with the thrust of *lifnim mishurat hadin*, which, as we have seen, entails giving others more than they deserve by the canons of strict justice.

8. Mekhilta of Rabbi Shimon bar Yoḥai (Exod. 18:20)
    Mekhilta of Rabbi Ishmael (Masechta d'amalek, Yitro 2)

A. Eleazar Hamodai says, " 'And thou shalt show them:' that you shall show them their house of life; (some mss.: "show them how to live")

B. 'the way:' that means visiting the sick;

C. 'they must walk:' that means burial of the dead;

D. 'therein:' that means the practice of deeds of lovingkindness;

E. 'and the work:' that means the law; (Mekhilta de Rabbi Ishmael: "the line of the law;" *shurat hadin*)

F. 'that they shall do:' that means *lifnim mishurat hadin.*"

This explication of Exodus 18:20, familiar from sources 1 and 2 above, juxtaposes *lifnim mishurat hadin* with other examples of righteous behavior. In doing so, the text appears to be making two significant points about the status of extra-legal actions. First, doing more than one's legal duty is consistent with observing the law. Indeed, it is much like other deeds of lovingkindness that one performs out of a sense of compassion for one's fellows. This, of course, accords well with the view of *lifnim mishurat hadin* that emerges from the sources just examined. Moreover, this willingness to do more than the law requires is itself required by the biblical verse cited. The idea appears to be that the Torah ordains all acts of righteousness, including both fulfilling one's prescribed legal duties and exceeding these duties. This midrash then supports the view that *lifnim mishurat hadin* is obligatory in some sense. This, of course, does not necessarily imply that this is a duty actionable in a court of law. It may still be the case that one who fails to act *lifnim mishurat hadin* is liable to no punishment, just as there may be none for failing to visit the sick or to bury the dead. Rather, the point is that these are all righteous acts that, punishable or not, are part and parcel of what God expects of Israel.

9. Baba Metsia 30b

A. 'That they shall do;'—that means *lifnim mishurat hadin.*

B. [Commenting on this explication of Exod. 18:20,] Rabbi Yoḥanan said, "Jerusalem was destroyed only because they gave judgments therein in accordance with biblical law (*din Torah*)."

C. [How can this be?] Were they then to have judged in accordance with untrained arbitrators? [Surely not. So what can be the meaning of Rabbi Yoḥanan's statement?]

D. Rather say this: [Jerusalem was destroyed] because they based their judgments on biblical law [alone] and did not act *lifnim mishurat hadin.*

This last talmudic reference to *lifnim mishurat hadin* is significant in
that it provides a number of new insights into the meaning of the term.
First, this is the only source that explicitly contrasts our term with another,
in this case *din Torah*. Since other occurrences of this term in rabbinic literature can support several readings, including "biblical law,"[10] "the correct
law,"[11] and "strict law,"[12] its exact meaning in this context is not clear. What
is clear is that this standard, which in any case is an explicitly legal one, is
not as demanding as *lifnim mishurat hadin*. This reinforces what we have
gleaned from other references to the term. The most striking and unexpected point is Yoḥanan's opinion that failing to act beyond one's legal duty
could bring such dire consequences. How can we account for the view that
divine punishment would result from simply dispensing justice, that is,
judging in accordance with the law and compelling people to fulfill their
legal duties? The answer may lie, in part, in the juxtaposition of law and
lifnim mishurat hadin, which we noted in the last source. God expects people not only to uphold the law but also to be merciful and compassionate
where the law does not specifically require them to do so. The point of the
passage, then, is not that judging in accordance with the law is wrong and
so deserving of punishment,[13] but rather that this, in itself, is not all that
God expects of Israel. Rather, God expects, and earthly courts should demand, that people act more mercifully than the letter of the law requires.
The reference to the destruction of Jerusalem, then, may have additional
significance. Perhaps judging in accordance with the established law alone
is adequate in ordinary times, but during a period of great sinfulness, such
as that which preceded the destruction of Jerusalem, Israelites must show
special compassion to one another if they are to merit similar treatment
from God. In any event, the effect of the passage is to heighten greatly the
significance placed on acting *lifnim mishurat hadin*, perhaps even to the
point of making it, rather than mere observance of the law, the primary
standard of righteous behavior.

Let us stand back from this body of material now and attempt to sum-
marize what we have learned about the way in which the rabbis used the term
lifnim mishurat hadin. To be sure, not all of these texts are in complete agreement, particularly about the degree to which actions of this sort are obligatory. Nor is it our purpose here to harmonize these discrepancies in the
interests of supporting the belief that the rabbis concurred about substantive
issues when in fact they did not. Our task is to sketch as precisely as possible
those points that our sources have in common, as well as to delineate the
points of divergence.

It appears that, within the talmudic sources, *lifnim mishurat hadin* has a rather carefully circumscribed meaning. First, in every case the term is implicitly or explicitly contrasted with legal duties. This, of course, is evident from the very terminology that we have been examining. "Beyond the line of the law" must refer to an action that is both distinct from and defined in relationship to "the law." But this point is underscored, as we have seen especially in the legal sources, by the fact that the term is consistently employed in the context of discussions about whether one has a legal duty to perform some specific action. In classic talmudic fashion precedents are brought ("on this occasion, rabbi x did such and such . . .") to demonstrate that some action constitutes a legal duty. The counterclaim that this action was performed *lifnim mishurat hadin*, however, immediately defeats the suggestion that it could be a legal obligation. As we have seen, the term actually is more closely related to the notion of legal rights than of legal duties.

It would appear that the concept of *lifnim mishurat hadin* parallels most closely notions of waiver in Anglo-American jurisprudence. While the concept of waiver arises in a wide range of legal contexts, the fundamental element is "a voluntary relinquishment or renunciation of some right, a forgoing or giving up of some benefit or advantage, which, but for such waiver, a party would have enjoyed."[14] Specifically, the term denotes waiving a legal right to act, or to refrain from acting, in some specified manner. Whether we are concerned with an elder who has a right to refrain from unloading animals (but does so anyway), or a man who has a right to keep the property that has been sold to him (but returns it to the seller), the term *lifnim mishurat hadin* designates a willingness to waive voluntarily some benefit or right to which one is entitled by law. In each case, it is implied that the party who waives the right in question does so out of a concern for the other party, who would be harmed or disadvantaged if the right were exercised. In this sense, *lifnim mishurat hadin* has a moral dimension that distinguishes it from other sorts of waivers that could be exercised for any of a number of reasons, including monetary gain or self-interest. This moral dimension is present also in those sources that speak of God as the moral agent. God has a legal right, established by the covenant at Sinai, to punish Israel for its sins, a right that God may voluntarily choose not to exercise out of compassion for the people.

It follows from this basic fact that *lifnim mishurat hadin* is not an absolute, unvarying standard of action, but one that is relative to specific individuals or circumstances. That is to say, just as different people may have different legal rights, so too what is meant for them to act *lifnim mishurat hadin* will vary, depending upon the extent and nature of these rights. Thus an exceptional individual (cases 1, 2) is said to act "beyond the line of the law" when he or she waives a special exemption and acts as the ordinary person is obligated to do. If the ordinary person acted in the very same way, he or she would simply be fulfilling a legal duty, not acting *lifnim mishurat hadin*. We see then that our term refers to an individual's willingness to do more than the law requires of that particular person, whatever that may be. In this context, it is also worth noting that none of the sources establishes any upper limit on the extent of such actions. One may do only slightly more than the law requires or a great deal more and in either case one's action deserves the designation *lifnim mishurat hadin*.[15]

As we have also seen, one who acts *lifnim mishurat hadin* invariably gives up something, whether tangible property or an intangible benefit, for the sake of another. Often this loss is financial, as in the case of the money-changer's reimbursing his customer or the man returning lost property. In other cases, it is a matter of an elder's forgoing his honor to help relieve another person's burden or inconveniencing oneself while eating to enable another person to join in the grace after meals. More to the point, the personal sacrifice that invariably accompanies an act of this sort is an expression of compassion or generosity. This point emerges most clearly in sources 6 and 7, where God's acting *lifnim mishurat hadin* is explicitly associated with the divine attribute of mercy. The same attitude is implied, however, in each of the other cases as well. Most notably, it is concern for others and acting compassionately toward them that unites the list of righteous deeds—visiting the sick, burying the dead, obeying the law, acting *lifnim mishurat hadin*—that the midrashic writer associates with the injunction of Exodus 18:20.

It is particularly important to note that in no case does acting *lifnim mishurat hadin* entail violating a legal duty. That is, we speak only of cases in which one waives a legal right, never cases in which one violates a legal duty. The term then does not encompass acts of conscientious objection, for example, when one violates the recognized law out of a felt duty to a higher authority. In short, the concept of *lifnim mishurat hadin* sanctions certain actions that the law does not require but never sanctions actions that the law does not permit.

Nor does acting beyond the line of the law, as our sources have described it, imply that the law itself in these particular instances is fundamentally unjust. Again, the contrast to cases of conscientious objection is illuminating. In the latter case, one's action is prompted, at least in part, by the conviction that to perform one's legal duty would be immoral.[16] By contrast, (with the sole exception of source 9), our sources suggest that it would be morally quite acceptable for the elder not to unload his neighbor's animal or for God to give Israel the punishment she rightly deserves. Indeed, in the cases we examined, those who follow the law are not chastised; rather, those who do more than the law requires (or less than the law permits) are praised. The point, then, is not that fulfilling the law is morally wrong, but rather that those who are exceedingly righteous sometimes act in a way that transcends their (merely) legal obligation.

While the forgoing conclusions may appear self-evident, they have not been acknowledged by many who have discussed the importance of *lifnim mishurat hadin*. The following passage from Leo Landman's discussion of law and conscience in Judaism is typical of many treatments of the topic.

> The Halachah, too, took cognizance of the "higher law," that is, obedience to conscience, although the term is not found. Man was enjoined to live not only in accordance with din (law) but also in accordance with a higher moral order which could not be enforced by the bet din (court). The Sifra (Mekhilta) derived the concept of *lifnim mishurat hadin* and ordained that man must follow a way of life "beyond the line of legal justice." The Halachah, however, also saw that the "higher law" was ordained by the law itself. To live "beyond the line of the law" was not left to the discretion of an individual nor to his own sense of kindness.[17]

Such an interpretation of *lifnim mishurat hadin* has no basis in the rabbinic sources that employ that term. None of the sources examined here suggest either that *lifnim mishurat hadin* refers to the dictates of conscience in general or that such a "higher law" takes precedence over the provisions of the written law. If such a view can be found within the tradition, it is not to be associated with the term before us, which, as we have seen, refers to a much more restricted sort of moral behavior and then only within a certain context. To be sure, the willingness to waive one's legal rights out of concern for the other party may in some instances be a matter of obedience to conscience. But this is quite a different matter from identifying *lifnim mishurat hadin* with the dictates of conscience and the "higher law" in general and then proceeding, as Landman does, to argue that this term refers to "the highest degree of ethical perfection to which man may aspire."[18]

Nor do these sources support the view presented by Boaz Cohen, who argues that *lifnim mishurat hadin* refers to a principle of equity or fairness that represents one's moral duty, independent of one's actual legal responsibility in any given case.[19] In every legal system, Cohen suggests, there are occasions when the established law does not adequately serve the ends of justice. In such cases, the rabbis invoked the concept of equity or *lifnim mishurat hadin* whereby they derived one's legal duty not from strict legal principles, but from principles of ethics or justice that were independent of the written law.

While numerous hermeneutical rules are preserved in the Talmud, the overriding principles motivating their interpretations are rarely stated, nevertheless we may distinguish two paramount attitudes that determined to a large extent their interpretation, that is strict law versus equity. There were times when the sages deemed it wise to accept the *ius strictum*, and the interpretation of the law was in keeping with the letter. In other instances equity was the supreme consideration and interpretation was in accordance with the spirit of the law. The problem confronting the rabbis was the same that faced the expounders of every other code of law. "A system of law must consist of a body of invariable rules or it will neither grow nor persist, at the same time it must do substantial justice." Equity is denominated *lifnim mishurat hadin . . .* and contrasted with *shurat hadin* strict law. . . . Instances are recorded in the Talmud of scholars who yielded in matters where the law was on their side, in accordance with the principle of *lifnim mishurat hadin*. The equitable man, says Aristotle, is one who does not strain the law, but is content to receive a smaller share although he has the law on his side. . . .

While considerations of equity were undoubtedly the prime factors which actuated the rabbis to deviate from the letter or the *ius strictum*, there were other motives which were just as compelling, such as public welfare or the interest in a peaceful society.[20]

This interpretation of *lifnim mishurat hadin* is problematic, however, for it relies on the identification of that term with the concept of equity. But principles of equity, at least as they have developed in western legal systems, encompass a broad range of moral principles concerned with ensuring just remedies that the established law itself cannot provide. Yet, none of the sources we examined invoked *lifnim mishurat hadin* in the context of rectifying a past injustice, or preventing a potential inequity, that was caused by adherence to the law. In fact, as we have seen, the term occurs primarily in reference to actions that individuals take on their own initiative, rather than in obedience to judicial injunctions, as Cohen imagines. Cohen may, of course, be correct in claiming that *lifnim mishurat hadin* signifies a moral duty, as distinct from a legal one. But, if so, it is a far more restricted duty than his identification of the term with principles of equity suggests.

In contrast to these very broad interpretations, we have seen that the talmudic authorities consistently employed the term *lifnim mishurat hadin* in reference to quite specific sorts of acts within certain limited contexts. Both the definition of such an act as a waiver of one's legal rights as well as the moral praiseworthiness of acting in this way as an expression of generosity or compassion appear to have been well established by talmudic times. The sources differ only in their assessment of what I have called the "status" of such actions. That is, if we were to ask the talmudic authorities whether an action performed *lifnim mishurat hadin* was a moral duty, or a legal duty, or no duty at all but simply an act of great generosity, it appears that the answer would be unclear at best. For the sources do not speak with one voice on this issue, but rather provide the basis for several divergent interpretations of the status of such actions. Let us turn then to resolving this ambiguity, for in determining the precise relationship between *lifnim mishurat hadin* and law we stand to gain new insight into the character of Jewish ethics.

The Status of *Lifnim Mishurat Hadin*

Even a cursory review of the talmudic sources that employ the term *lifnim mishurat hadin* reveals an apparent lack of unanimity about the degree to which such action is obligatory. To be sure, none of the sources speaks directly to the question at hand and, in the absence of direct statements concerning the status of such actions, we are left to draw inferences from the claims that are made. But it is not difficult to discern within the sources at least two tendencies concerning its moral force.

On the one hand, we have the view attributed to Rabbi Yoḥanan that failure to act *lifnim mishurat hadin* brought about the destruction of Jerusalem. This surely can only be understood as implying that such actions, from God's perspective at least, were obligatory, for the result of shirking this duty is divine retribution. The notion that actions of this sort are obligatory is further reinforced by the frequently cited midrash on Exodus 18:20, which suggests that *lifnim mishurat hadin*, like the law itself, is a positive biblical injunction. Finally, in one of the cases we examined (source 4), the language of the text suggests at least obliquely that one has the obligation to do more than the law requires, not simply the option of doing so.

On the other hand, the contexts in which *lifnim mishurat hadin* is mentioned consistently portray this as an optional act. We never hear of anyone being compelled to act in this fashion, nor do the legal sources give even the slightest hint that one has a legitimate claim against a person for failing to act in this way. Even more important, as we have noted earlier, each time the rabbis refer to an action as *lifnim mishurat hadin* they do so precisely to preclude its being regarded as a legal precedent. This provides the clearest evidence that the term did not denote the performance of a legal duty in any ordinary sense. So the talmudic sources as a whole suggest both that *lifnim mishurat hadin* is obligatory (though in what sense they do not say) and that it is optional.

This very ambiguity appears to have generated among later rabbinic authorities a range of positions on the extent to which *lifnim mishurat hadin* represents a legal standard such that failure to act in this way is actionable in a court of law. As we shall see, the positions fall along a spectrum from the view (1) that these are acts of extreme piety or supererogation to the view (2) that one is legally obligated to act *lifnim mishurat hadin* just as one is required to fulfill the dictates of the written law. Between these extremes lies the position (3) that *lifnim mishurat hadin* represents a moral duty as distinct from a legal duty insofar as such actions were demanded by the "spirit of the law" though not by its letter.

The first view, that *lifnim mishurat hadin* is a form of supererogation, is championed by Maimonides in a passage from his Mishneh Torah [Code of Jewish Law]. In his discussion of proper ethical behavior, he notes that saints in ancient times sometimes deviated from the (Aristotelian) mean by being exceedingly humble or generous. This is the case, he says, with those who acted *lifnim mishurat hadin*.

> Whoever is particularly scrupulous and deviates somewhat from the exact mean in disposition, in one direction or the other, is called a saint. For example, if one avoids haughtiness to the utmost extent and is exceedingly humble, he is termed a saint, and this is the standard of saintliness. If one only departs from haughtiness as far as the mean, and is humble, he is called wise, and this is the standard of wisdom. And so with all other dispositions. The ancient saints trained their dispositions away from the exact mean toward the extremes; in regard to one disposition in one direction; in regard to another in the opposite direction. This was supererogation (*lifnim mishurat hadin*). We are bidden to walk in the middle paths which are the right and proper ways, as it is said, "and you shall walk in His ways" (Deuteronomy 28:9).[21]

For Maimonides, *lifnim mishurat hadin* represents a standard of saintly behavior characterized by extreme humility. On Maimonides' view, such actions are in no way required, for, in general, people do not have the ability, much less the duty, to become saints. Indeed, Maimonides' point in the passage just quoted is that such extreme piety is generally not even desirable. One should strive toward the mean in all one's actions and, to the extent that acting *lifnim mishurat hadin* violates this moral norm, it is to be avoided. This same view emerges, though less explicitly, in another passage from Mishneh Torah where Maimonides summarizes the law concerning the return of lost property to an Israelite (case 4 above). He notes that, "even though it (the lost object) belongs to him (the finder), one who wishes to walk in the good and upright path and to act *lifnim mishurat hadin* returns the lost object to the Israelite who identifies it."[22] Here too, it is seems that Maimonides regards actions of this sort as optional or supererogatory. It is neither a legal nor a moral obligation for the finder to return the lost object, but rather just the sort of thing that a scrupulously pious person will want to do. On this view, it seems that the primary distinction between law and *lifnim mishurat hadin* is that the former represents the standard of behavior required of all, while the latter represents the behavior that especially pious persons occasionally and voluntarily exhibit.[23]

This view of *lifnim mishurat hadin* accords well with descriptions of supererogation given by contemporary moral philosophers.[24] Supererogatory acts entail unusual self-sacrifice. As such they are the mark of "saints and heroes" whose behavior exceeds socially accepted moral norms. By definition, one can have no duty either legal or moral to perform acts of supererogation, and failing to do so, by implication, carries no negative moral judgment. This seems to be precisely the sort of moral category that encompasses *lifnim mishurat hadin*, as Maimonides describes it.

A second, radically different view is represented by those authorities who interpret *lifnim mishurat hadin* as a fully enforceable legal standard, that is, as part and parcel of the din or halakha.[25] This appears to have been the position taken by Nachmanides in his commentary to Deuteronomy 6:18, "you shall do the right and the good."

And our rabbis have a fine interpretation of this. They said, "This refers to compromise and *lifnim mishurat hadin*." The intent of this is that, initially, He had said that you should observe the laws and statutes which He had commanded you. Now He says that, with respect to what He has not commanded, you should likewise take heed to do the good and the right in His eyes, for He loves the good and the right. And this is a great matter. For it is impossible to mention in the Torah all of a person's actions toward his neighbors and acquaintances, all of his commercial activity, and all social and political institutions. So after He had mentioned many of them . . . he resumes to say generally that one should do the good and the right in all matters, to the point that there are included in this compromise, *lifnim mishurat hadin,* and the like . . . so that he is regarded as perfect and right in all matters.

The point of Nachmanides' comment is that "acting beyond the line of the law" is itself a divine commandment, just like the specific laws that one finds enumerated in the Torah. It is not mentioned explicitly in Scripture simply because it could not be, for it refers to the general principle of acting righteously, a principle whose specific applications are far too numerous to be spelled out fully in Scripture. Nonetheless, and this is the crux of the matter, the standard of righteous behavior referred to as *lifnim mishurat hadin* is no less obligatory than the law itself. It is "beyond" the law only in the very restricted sense that the content of this norm has not been indicated specifically in the written law. It follows that people who act *lifnim mishurat hadin* are not "saints," nor have they done anything extraordinary, as Maimonides would have us believe. Rather, they have simply done what God expects and what the law demands, implicitly if not explicitly. It is this position that seems to have led many medieval authorities to include *lifnim mishurat hadin* among the 613 commandments of the Torah. The implication of this view, of course, is that there is no qualitative moral distinction between *lifnim mishurat hadin* and law, for both are obligatory, both have their origin in divine imperative, and both therefore represent actionable standards that apply equally to everyone in the community of Israel.

A third view is proposed by Aharon Lichtenstein in his well known essay, "Does Jewish Tradition Recognize an Ethic Independent of Halakha?" While Lichtenstein's analysis of the issue and of the sources is often somewhat confusing, his own position appears to fall somewhere between those of Maimonides and Nachmanides described earlier. He argues on the one hand that *lifnim mishurat hadin* is an ethical norm distinct from din in the narrow sense. That is, it is not generally understood as an actionable legal norm, notwithstanding the view of some medieval authorities to the contrary. But neither is it simply a matter of optional, pietistic behavior. It is an ethical duty, an imperative for all Jews no less than the halakha itself, though not a

legal obligation in the strict sense of the term. In Lichtenstein's words, "traditional Halakhic Judaism demands of the Jew both adherence to Halakha and
commitment to an ethical moment that though different from halakha is
nevertheless of a piece with it and in its own way fully imperative.[26] The same
position is taken by J. David Bleich, who argues that "adherence to the standard denoted thereby [as *lifnim mishurat hadin*] is prescribed as normative
and binding and hence endowed with the essential attributes of Halakhah."[27]

These three positions concerning the status of *lifnim mishurat hadin*
frame the basic interpretative question of this study. Does this term refer to
acts of supererogation or to legal duties or to moral duties that do not have
the force of law? Or, as the Tosafot suggests in commenting on one of the
sources discussed earlier, does the term signify sometimes a legal obligation,
sometimes a moral obligation that is not legally binding, and sometimes an
act of supererogation?[28] Indeed, it appears that all three answers are possible,
for as we have seen, each can be defended on the basis of the texts, both talmudic and medieval, that address the question of *lifnim mishurat hadin*.

One explanation of this rather perplexing evidence has been provided by
Menachem Elon, who suggests that the category of *lifnim mishurat hadin* un-
derwent significant development between the talmudic and medieval periods.
The discrepancies among our sources then are the result of historical development. In Elon's words,

> Before us therefore is an example of a norm which in its origin was
> solely a moral-religious sanction, but became over time under certain
> conditions a full legal norm which was actionable in a court of law.[29]

Elon cites a variety of later rabbinic sources that held actions of this sort to be
legal duties in the fullest sense and which therefore carried legal sanctions
when these norms were violated. But while this seems to have been the dominant view during the medieval period, he notes that other authorities conceived such actions as expressions of special piety. This latter view, Elon
suggests, accords more nearly with the talmudic perspective according to
which these actions were morally praiseworthy, but not legally required.

> In the realm of legal rights and duties there is, in general, no sanc-
> tion of any kind to be derived from the injunction [associated with
> Exodus 18:20] to act *lifnim mishurat hadin*. It is meant to convey
> only that it is fitting that a man who is strict about his behavior
> will not determine his actions according to the letter of the law,
> but rather will behave *lifnim mishurat hadin*.[30]

The merit of Elon's view, apart from accounting for the discrepancies that we find among the sources, is that it accords with general observations by scholars of jurisprudence concerning the relationship between ethics and law. Not infrequently moral principles of justice and fairness that originate outside a legal system at a later time become integrated into the law. In this sense, while Boaz Cohen's identification of *lifnim mishurat hadin* with equity distorts the denotation of the term, it may clarify its relationship to law. For principles of equity have an ambiguous relationship to the law, one that changes as the legal system itself develops. As Ralph A. Newman writes in his comparative study of law and equity,

> Equity in its substantive aspect consists essentially of a body of principles dealing with relief from hardship; principles which are of course merely a part of the larger concept of fairness and justice upon which all law is based. Early law, which is primarily concerned with rules designed for general application, allows little room for variation in individual cases, and relief from hardship emanates from an authority external to the law itself. Viewed at this stage of the evolution of law, equity corrects the law by applying, in circumstances where the ordinary rules would lead to unwarranted hardship, considerations of what is fair and just. In this sense equity constitutes a body of principles separate from the general rules it sometimes supplements or supersedes. As law advances haltingly toward humanitarian ideals, it becomes concerned with the harshness of its effects in particular situations. Equitable solutions devised to meet the requirements of justice are received into the general law, and law and equity gradually coalesce. . . . Viewed at this stage of the evolution of law, equity is an integral part of a unitary legal system and becomes synonymous with justice.[31]

It is to Elon's credit that, adopting a historical perspective on the question, he recognizes the diversity of opinion within the tradition and therefore does not try to reconcile conflicting views. But even if his reconstruction of the historical development of the term *lifnim mishurat hadin* is correct (and there may be in the talmudic sources more evidence than Elon concedes for the view that the term denotes a legally binding norm), he leaves one fundamental question unanswered. His discussion concerns only the historical problem of how these different views arose in different historical periods. But we also wish to solve a theoretical issue. That is, granting that the historical development that Elon describes actually took place, we still want to know what these facts can tell us about the interaction of ethics and law in Judaism. The question to be answered is not only how the relationship between *lifnim mishurat hadin* and law changed over time but also why it was so unclear to begin with and why it remained a matter of dispute for so many centuries. It is precisely the problematic relationship of these moral acts to the law that must be interpreted. What then does the evidence we have examined tell us about the character of Jewish law, of Jewish ethics, and of the relationship between them?

In order to answer this question, it seems to me that we must consider briefly the special character of the halakha itself. In doing so we confront a fundamental ambiguity about the very nature and scope of halakha, and it is in relationship to this ambiguity, I suggest, that we must understand the controversy concerning the status of *lifnim mishurat hadin*. That is, by exploring two divergent views of the purpose and scope of halakha we will begin to see the true significance of *lifnim mishurat hadin* and understand the very discrepancies that have confounded previous attempts to interpret its moral force.

Interpreting *Lifnim Mishurat Hadin:* A Fresh Perspective

The halakha's unique character derives from the fact that it fulfills both a religious and a social function.[32] On the one hand, in both origin and development it is understood within Jewish tradition as the definitive expression of divine revelation. As such its purpose is to spell out the conditions for living in accord with the divine will, thereby bringing Israel into harmony with God and bringing the world closer to redemption. In this sense, halakha ultimately embodies a holy way of life and so is meant to serve a transcendent, religious purpose. On the other hand, the halakha in large part and for most of Jewish history has regulated the daily life of Jewish communities. Like every other functioning legal system, then, it has faced a variety of social and jurisprudential issues, among them, the problems of legislating both conduct and attitude, emending prior rulings, enforcing its injunctions, and so on. In this sense, halakha is subject to a whole range of social forces, even as it attempts to regulate and channel those forces. This dual character of the halakha, as civil authority and as religious system, is reflected most strikingly in the role of the rabbi, who is at once both judge and religious leader, legal authority and exemplar of traditional piety.

This dual character of halakha inevitably gives rise to conflicting attitudes toward moral virtues. For insofar as rabbis were civil legal authorities, their task did not include promoting exceptional piety. They mandated only that behavior which they saw as necessary for maintaining a just society. For the purpose of protecting individual rights and enforcing basic social responsibilities, it was not necessary to mandate special acts of selflessness or generosity. Moreover, as a practical matter, rabbis were understandably hesitant to legislate pious behavior that the average person could not be expected to emulate.[33] Thus, for both theoretical and practical reasons, rabbis refrained from giving legal sanction to acts of special generosity that, in any case, were not required to ensure a basically just society. From this standpoint, those who are more generous or selfless than the law requires may be praised for their righteousness and piety but will not be made the standard for the community at large.[34] In short, such actions will be viewed as supererogatory, not as legal duties.

To the extent, however, that halakha is a system of religious instruction its perspective on the attainment of virtue will be entirely different. For as the goal of halakha is to bring the Jew closer to God, the cultivation of certain godlike qualities will be central to its purpose. Of particular importance are those qualities of compassion and mercy that Scripture defines as essential attributes of God and so as the hallmarks of the righteous person. Viewed from this perspective, the halakha represents what we might call an "open-ended" moral system. Within this system, one's moral obligations are potentially limitless, for ultimately one is required to seek moral perfection through a process of imitatio dei. But within the context of a divinely ordained legal system, all such divine imperatives will naturally take the form of legal obligations. It is not surprising to discover, then, that the tradition tends to make all forms of righteous behavior into fully actionable legal duties, for by increasing the extent of Israel's righteousness, the rabbis were bringing the community closer to divine salvation.

Within this context, we can make sense of the very ambiguity that the sources reveal about the status of actions performed *lifnim mishurat hadin*. The extent to which it is obligatory depends entirely upon the way in which one understands the scope and function of Jewish law. When one conceives the purpose of the law in largely this-worldly terms, and consequently attends to the law's social function, the virtue of doing "more than the law requires" can never be incorporated into the law itself. Such compassion and righteousness is of course desirable, but it is both beyond the capacity of the average Jew, and, from a strictly jurisprudential standpoint, unnecessary for the law to accomplish its goal. But when one conceives of the law as a path toward religious salvation, acting *lifnim mishurat hadin* will have an entirely different significance. Righteous action being a divine imperative, it is always at least potentially a legal duty as well. For how can the law fail to require the very sort of righteous behavior that God expects and on which the redemption of Israel depends? From this perspective the law itself demands a higher level of piety and selflessness than that which is needed to maintain a minimally just and lawful society.[35]

This ambivalent attitude toward piety in general, which, as we have seen, applies to *lifnim mishurat hadin* in particular, is evident in a passage from the Mishnah, tractate Avot ("Ethics of the Fathers"), which defines four types of individuals.

> There are four types of moral character among men:
> [First,] One who says, "What is mine is mine and what is yours is yours"—this is the average character.
> But some say this is the character of the Sodomites. . . .[36]

The attitude in question is indeed either ordinary and acceptable or reprehensible, depending upon one's perspective. Keeping what is rightfully one's own and giving to others what rightfully belongs to them is the mark of the law-abiding ("average") individual. From a strictly legal standpoint there can be nothing objectionable in such behavior. But while this attitude promotes the interests of a just and orderly society, it does nothing to help fashion a society in the image of God. The very qualities of selflessness and compassion that distinguish righteous individuals—setting aside their own interests for the sake of others, doing more than is required or expected of them—these qualities could define the accepted standard of moral conduct. And, from this perspective, those who insist upon exercising their rights, yielding to others only when legally required to do so, have shirked their responsibility to God, if not to their neighbor.[37]

It seems then that the status of *lifnim mishurat hadin* is problematic precisely because it is defined in relation to halakha, whose scope itself is variable. Curiously, Lichtenstein recognized this when he pointed out that halakha can be defined either narrowly or broadly, though he failed to see the implications of his own observation. One cannot conclude, as he does, with the statement, "Does the tradition recognize an ethic independent of Halakha? You define your terms and take your choice." For this very terminological confusion at the most fundamental level renders the entire question as Lichtenstein frames it incoherent.

But the problem is by no means Lichtenstein's alone. For his approach to the problem of *lifnim mishurat hadin* follows a typical pattern whereby scholars accept one view on the scope of the halakha (adopting either the more restrictive or the more inclusive sense of that word) and one view on the status of *lifnim mishurat hadin* and then proceed to discuss the relationship between the two. The problem with this approach, of course, is that the very same procedure will lead to quite different answers. Any answer reached in this way is as valid as any other, for each is based on a selective reading both of the sources and of the nature of halakha. In fact, those who discuss the relationship between *lifnim mishurat hadin* and law in this way are actually taking sides in the ongoing debate, rather than analyzing the factors that have led each side in the controversy to reach its respective conclusions.

By contrast, I maintain that the controversy over the status of *lifnim mishurat hadin* cannot be resolved arbitrarily either through semantic juggling or by a selective reading of the sources that harmonizes all contradictory evidence in order to support a single position. Indeed, the controversy as it has been framed cannot be resolved at all, for it fails to take account of radically different assumptions about the scope of Jewish law and so about the relative importance of virtue in achieving the purposes of the law. That there could be legitimate differences within the tradition about such fundamental matters should come as no surprise to critical scholars of rabbinic literature. Those who approach the issue from a specific religious viewpoint, by contrast, may find this conclusion unsettling. For it seems that many of those who explore the relationship of Jewish law and ethics, and so too the problem of *lifnim mishurat hadin,* have a hidden agenda that informs their choice of sources as well as their interpretation of them. Orthodox writers, anxious to maintain the moral authority and comprehensiveness of the halakha, have naturally been inclined to see *lifnim mishurat hadin* as fundamentally "of a piece" with halakha. In so doing, they neutralize the threat that this category appears to pose by the very suggestion that there could be some moral standard that is "extra-halachic." Liberals, on the other hand, are concerned to show that there are extra-halachic moral standards by means of which halakha itself (or at least certain specific laws) can be critiqued. This naturally leads to the view that *lifnim mishurat hadin* represents a moral category, distinct from the law and, in some way, having priority over it. As we have seen, both views can be supported with traditional texts. It seems therefore that any objective and balanced assessment of the issue must take account of both tendencies within the tradition, without arbitrarily giving precedence to one or the other, and must explain rather than resolve the controversy that surrounds the term and its meaning.

In closing, let me sketch briefly what I see as the broader implications of these conclusions for discussions of the relationship between ethics and law in Judaism. For this investigation of *lifnim mishurat hadin* illustrates certain more general difficulties encountered in the field of Jewish ethics. In particular, previous treatments of *lifnim mishurat hadin* have proved problematic in that they have relied to a greater or lesser extent on two methodological assumptions, each of which must be called into question.

The first of these is that the traditional Jewish sources that treat matters of ethical import can readily be analyzed using categories drawn from contemporary philosophical ethics. But the attempt to understand a term like *lifnim mishurat hadin* in terms of categories such as legal duty, moral duty, and supererogation has not succeeded. The very character of halakha as both legal system and divine revelation, I have argued, blurs the distinction between law and ethics.[38] Ethical obligations, like all divine imperatives within the tradition, will be understood as part and parcel of the halakha, that divinely revealed law that governs the ongoing life of Israel.[39] Moreover, the close relationship in Judaism between ethics and piety, between doing the right thing and doing the holy or godlike thing, tends to blur our distinction between moral obligation and supererogation. For within this framework even the greatest acts of selflessness, those that we would view as the paradigm of supererogation, may be regarded as duties, as expressions of the command "to be holy." It follows that any attempt to impose these categories on the rabbinic material will invariably confuse rather than clarify the views contained therein.[40] Indeed, Boaz Cohen among others has observed that the rabbis themselves would not have distinguished sharply between moral considerations and legal ones, but the logical implications of this striking fact for the analysis of traditional Jewish ethics have rarely been drawn.[41]

A second, equally problematic assumption in these discussions has been that the tradition speaks with one voice on matters of law and ethics. This assumption finds its most notable expression in the very form of the question that most often sets the context for these discussions, namely, "what is the relationship between law and ethics in Judaism," or "does Judaism recognize an ethic independent of halacha." Given the prevailing view that there is some one normative, Jewish position concerning the relationship between law and ethics, the task at hand becomes to discern that view from among the sources, often by dismissing or harmonizing those texts that represent conflicting viewpoints. Seldom do we find in these discussions a recognition that the tradition itself may encompass diverse and equally legitimate understandings of halakha and its relationship to ethical norms. The forgoing analysis, however, has led us to doubt whether there could ever be a single, consistent answer to questions of such broad scope.

Finally, to the extent that treatments of *lifnim mishurat hadin* are typical, there has been a tendency within discussions of Jewish ethics to overlook the distinction between normative and descriptive ethics. That is, it is one thing to stand within a tradition and, drawing on its perspectives, to make normative judgments about what is right and wrong, obligatory and optional. It is quite another to describe those perspectives, to analyze their foundations and their implications, without advocating any one perspective within the tradition as more authoritative than any other. Often what passes for descriptive ethics turns out on further examination to be an exercise in "doing ethics," and in cases where the tradition itself presents a range of positions on an issue, blurring the difference between the two can result in serious misinterpretations of the sources.

I began by noting the centrality of the concept *lifnim mishurat hadin* to discussions of law and ethics in Judaism. Let me conclude by suggesting that while the category *lifnim mishurat hadin* may not help us to resolve questions about law and ethics within the tradition, it will compel us to reformulate them in important ways. For, as we have seen, the effort to identify this moral category with an "ethic independent of halakha" overlooks the fact that ethics and halakha are themselves problematic categories subject to the same range of interpretation that we have encountered in our analysis of this term. So our questions about law and ethics in Judaism must be formulated in full recognition of the fact that neither of these is a fixed category. Nor can we assume that the relationship between them has remained constant in different historical periods or even in the views of different authorities of the same period. So too the categories that we employ to interpret key concepts in Jewish ethics must not distort the very material they are intended to clarify. The methodological lesson to be learned from our examination of *lifnim mishurat hadin*, then, is that the assumptions underlying our questions about Jewish ethics may have to be reexamined, and the questions themselves modified, to reflect the ambiguities inherent in the data. For when we try to resolve these ambiguities, as in the case of *lifnim mishurat hadin*, by adopting perspectives and employing categories that the rabbis themselves would not have understood, we risk misinterpreting the data. Worse yet, we may be led to offer solutions that are not satisfactory to problems that we ourselves have created.

Chapter 2

Ethics as Law, Law as Religion

Reflections on the Problem of Law and Ethics in Judaism

In the last chapter, I examined the specific problems associated with the term *lifnim mishurat hadin*, which appears to bridge the domains of both law and ethics. Here I wish to extend this historical and conceptual analysis to other similar terms and, in so doing, to shed some light on the relationship between law and ethics in Judaism.

For some years now, scholars have been engaged in a lively debate concerning the relationship between law and ethics in Judaism.[1] Numerous talmudic texts that appear to suggest that rabbinic authorities of the past indeed recognized a distinction between law and ethics have occupied a central place in these debates. Much of this discussion accordingly turns on (1) how to understand certain key terms and the texts in which they appear, and (2) how to construe the difference between "law" and "ethics." Different answers to the question, "What is the relationship between law and ethics in Judaism," then, rest on the ways in which scholars have addressed prior questions of both hermeneutics and conceptual definition.

I contend that both the hermeneutical and conceptual dimensions of this issue have been muddled by those engaged in this debate. As a result, one finds that scholars invariably cite the same body of texts, but draw from them radically different conclusions about the relationship between law and ethics. Each claims simply to report what the tradition says on these matters, but none seems willing or able to explain why others, drawing on the very same evidence, have reached different positions. In order to clarify this confusing and, as yet, intractable problem, it will be necessary first to review briefly the sorts of evidence that play a central role in the debate about law and ethics,

45

then to clarify the nature of the question itself, and finally to explain why the question cannot be answered, at least in the terms in which it has been framed by those currently engaged in the debate.

The Evidence

The rabbinic sources that bear on the problem of law and ethics fall into two categories. First, there are texts that identify a type of moral behavior that is "extra-legal," that is, morally commendable, but (apparently) not legally required. Second, there are texts that suggest that in certain instances the formulation of the law itself was influenced by moral considerations, instances in which a rabbi interprets or applies a law in a particular way because this yields a more morally acceptable result. While it is impossible here to examine all the sources pertinent to this debate, it will suffice to look at representative texts and to sketch the spectrum of interpretation surrounding them.

One term often cited as evidence of an "extra-legal" morality in Judaism is *ruah hachamim noha heimenu*, "the spirit of the sages is pleased with him." Consider the following passage from Mishnah Shebiit 10:9.

> [As regards] one who repays a debt during the Sabbatical year [even though he has no legal obligation to do so; see Deuteronomy 15:1–2]—the sages are pleased with him. . . .
>
> All chattels are acquired through drawing [them into one's possession. That is, only when the buyer draws the item that he purchases toward him is the transaction formally concluded.] But [as regards] anyone who stands by his word [and does not withdraw from a sales agreement before the buyer has drawn the item toward him, even though either party to the transaction has the legal right to do so]—the sages are pleased with him.

The point would seem to be that certain actions may be legally permitted, yet morally objectionable. The law may not require conformity to these standards of behavior, but the sages highly commend it. We do not know the exact force of the phrase, "the sages are pleased with him," whether this indicates simply moral approval, or whether some social pressure was applied to encourage such commendable actions. It should be noted that there are cases of the reverse, that is, actions that are legally permitted, but if performed, "the sages are not pleased."[2]

Another instance of the same sort is *kofin al midat sdom*, "we coerce a person not to act in the manner of the Sodomites."[3] This term presupposes the notion that the Sodomites' moral failing was their extreme selfishness, their refusal to do favors for others, even when this would cost them nothing (see Mishnah Avot 5:11). Hence, the rabbinic dictum that, in such cases, we should force people to perform such acts of generosity, even if they are not legally required to do so. By way of example, consider the following case from the Talmud (Baba Batra 12b):

> A certain man bought a field adjacent to the estate of his father-in-law. When they came to divide the latter's estate, he said: "Give me my share [actually, my wife's share] next to my own field." Rabbah said: "This is a case where a man can be compelled not to act after the manner of Sodom."

Since the two beneficiaries of this estate must divide the field equally, there is no reason why the one man should not be permitted to take the portion of his father-in-law's field that is contiguous with his own. This would be a great convenience to him and entails no loss to the other beneficiary. The point, then, would seem to be that, even in the absence of a specific legal require-ment to act in a certain way, some rabbis were prepared to enforce what they regarded as morally appropriate behavior. It should be noted that in every in-stance in the Talmud where one rabbi invokes this principle, *kofin al midat s'dom*, another disputes the appropriateness of compelling such behavior.

In still other cases, the rabbis refer to *middat ḥasidut*, "the trait or quality of piety." This seems to denote an especially high moral standard that is char-acteristic of, or expected of, certain individuals. The following talmudic dis-cussion (Ḥullin 130b) is illustrative.

> If a householder was travelling from place to place and needs to take gleanings, the forgotten sheaf, the corners of the field, or the poorman's tithe [all of these being agricultural gifts that, according to Scripture, must be left for the poor], he may take them. But when he returns to his house he must make restitution [by paying the value of the food he had eaten to the first poor man who claims it.]—so Rabbi Eliezer. Rabbi Ḥisda said, "They taught this only as a rule of conduct for the pious." [Since he was in fact temporarily poor at the time, he was entitled to consume this food and has no obligation to make restitution to the poor for it.]

We have here a dispute between rabbis Eliezer and Ḥisda. The former would insist upon restitution to the poor. The latter, however, regards this not as obligatory, but rather as an act characteristic of those truly righteous people who are more generous than the law requires them to be. At least in Ḥisda's view, then, there is a distinction between what the law requires and what the most righteous element in society will do.

But perhaps the most often cited example of a so-called "extra-legal" morality in Judaism is that of *lifnim mishurat hadin*.[4] As explained in chapter 1, this term, meaning "beyond the line of the law," refers to instances in which an individual waives a legal right in order to benefit the other party. Examples include choosing to forgo one's legal rights in a sales contract or refusing to avail oneself of a special exemption to which one is legally entitled. In cases of *lifnim mishurat hadin*, then, one does more than the law requires (or, what amounts to the same thing, presses one's rights less strictly than the law permits). Against this background consider the following quotation (Baba Metsia 30b):

> "That they shall do"—that means *lifnim mishurat hadin*. [Commenting on this explication of Exodus 18:20] Rabbi Yoḥanan said, "Jerusalem was destroyed only because they gave judgments therein in accordance with Biblical law (*din Torah*)." [How can this be?] Were they then to have judged in accordance with untrained arbitrators? [Surely not. So what can be the meaning of Rabbi Yoḥanan's statement?] Rather say this: [Jerusalem was destroyed] because they based their judgments on Biblical law [alone], and did not act *lifnim mishurat hadin*.

Failure to measure up to this high standard of behavior is cited as grounds for the most catastrophic sort of punishment that God brought upon the people of Israel. This strongly suggests that actions designated *lifnim mishurat hadin*, even if "extra-legal" in some sense, are nonetheless part of what God expects of Israel.

In addition to these sources we find texts that suggest that moral considerations sometimes entered into the development of the law itself. In other words, at times the sages appear to construe legal duty in a particular way precisely because this accords with their independent moral judgments. A number of cases of this sort are frequently cited by contemporary Jewish scholars.

Every seventh year, in addition to allowing the land to remain fallow, all debts were to be forgiven, in accordance with Deuteronomy 15:1–2: "At the end of every seven years you shall make a release. . . . Every creditor shall release that which he has lent to his neighbor." This rule had the consequence (not surprisingly) of making it very difficult to borrow money in the years immediately preceding the year of release. According to the Mishnah, the sage Hillel addressed this problem by creating a legal fiction, known as a *pros-*

bul, which authorized a court to collect an outstanding debt on the creditor's behalf during or after the Sabbatical year. This technically did not violate the Scriptural rule that specifies only that the *creditor* cannot collect the debt after the seventh year. By establishing this legal fiction, it is often suggested, Hillel merely interpreted the law very narrowly so that one could observe the law (after all, one can never abrogate a divinely ordained Scriptural rule) while at the same time fulfilling one's apparent moral duty.

In other cases, it is often claimed, the rabbis would deliberately misinterpret a biblical verse or rule if they found it morally objectionable. Perhaps the classic example of this is the rabbinic understanding of Exodus 21:24, "an eye for an eye and a tooth for a tooth." The sages interpret this to mean that one must pay monetary compensation to the victim equal to the value of an eye or a tooth, not that one engages in physical retribution.[5] The plain meaning of the biblical rule presumably came to be regarded as barbaric in light of the moral standards of a later age. As a result, the application of the law had to be changed to accord with accepted principles of ethical conduct.

In yet another sort of case it is argued that the rabbis, when faced with a conflict between a biblical law and their moral principles, would limit the application of the law so severely that, in effect, it became inoperative. Examples here would include the way in which biblical laws sanctioning capital punishment were reinterpreted by later rabbinic authorities. The rabbis introduced extraordinarily stringent conditions that had to be met before a person could be convicted of a capital offense. Since these conditions could never be met, no one could be convicted of a capital offense and the death sentence could not be carried out. Again, it seems that the rabbis were morally opposed to capital punishment and then interpreted the law accordingly.[6]

The Parameters of the Debate

Most contemporary scholars argue that these sources (and others like them) establish definitively that Judaism does indeed recognize a distinction between law and ethics. Moreover, they claim that the rabbinic sources demonstrate that traditional sages employed this distinction quite consciously, though they may not have been explicit about what they were doing. Elliot Dorff's assessment of this "extra-legal" ethic is typical of one commonly held position. He writes,

> Here we see a clear recognition of moral obligation beyond the scope of responsibility as set by the law and two means, short of actual coercion, to prompt people to act in accordance with those

moral obligations, i.e., the opprobrium of being formally cursed in court, and the lesser, but important, stimulus of informing one who breaks his promise that he is a source of shame to the Jewish community.[7]

Robert Gordis articulates a similar position with respect to the cases in which ethical considerations appear to have influenced the development of the law itself,

> Here we can see the genius of Rabbinic Judaism at work. In one case, the law is modified to meet the demands of justice as the Sages understood it. In the other, the law is completely set aside because the Rabbis could not reconcile it with their ethical stance and their fundamental faith that the Torah was designed to teach men to practice justice and mercy. In both instances, and in many others in the Mishnah and the Talmud, this ethical dynamism is clearly evident.[8]

Examining the same evidence, David Weiss Halivni has reached a rather different conclusion. He maintains that the rabbis did not, indeed could not, acknowledge a conflict of any sort between law and ethics. In his words,

> The notion that the Rabbis of the Talmud were aware of a possible conflict between morality and religious law, and consciously resolved in favor of morality, cannot be defended historically. Historically, they gave other reasons for their interpretation.

And in reference to the rabbis' treatment of capital punishment, he writes,

> By retaining capital punishment in principle, and by not overtly saying that capital punishment is offensive to morality, the Rabbis obliquely tell us that their opposition to capital punishment was not based on moral grounds. . . . How could it be morally offensive if the Bible sanctions it? They objected to capital punishment because of lack of confidence in human justice.[9]

Halivni concedes that, on a subconscious level, moral considerations were almost certainly at work in these cases. Yet, he insists, the traditional authorities could never have acknowledged such a distinction, much less employed it explicitly, insofar as this would imply that the received law, and the divine authority behind it, were morally flawed.[10] The rabbis were not deceiving themselves; they simply operated within a framework of assumptions that precluded them from recognizing and articulating the sorts of distinctions between law and ethics that we employ. They were unable to do so because the distinctions that we employ were meaningless in the context of their views about the divine nature of Torah, which encompasses without distinction both law and ethics.[11]

Shubert Spero and Aharon Lichtenstein have adopted positions somewhere between those of Dorff/Gordis and Halivni. Both acknowledge that Judaism recognizes a distinction of sorts between strictly legal duties and other kinds of morally appropriate behavior. The question is how to characterize the distinction and whether, indeed, it conforms in any sense to the sorts of distinctions we have in mind when we differentiate law and ethics. In Lichtenstein's words, ". . . traditional halakhic Judaism demands of the Jew both adherence to Halakha and commitment to an ethical moment that, though different from Halakha, is nevertheless of a piece with it and in its own way fully imperative."[12] The difference, as Lichtenstein sees it, between halakha proper and this other ethical moment is that the latter is contextual or situational. Because no legal system can ever prescribe the appropriate response to every imaginable fact pattern, the need arises to apply the values and principles implicit within the system to situations where no established law exists. But, following Nachmanides, Lichtenstein finds this ethical demand within the Torah itself, as it says, "And you shall do the right and the good" (Deut. 6:18). So the Torah contains both specific demands, which are the realm of halakha proper, as well as more open-ended demands, which must be sought out and applied contextually.

For Spero, the difference between halakha and these other ethical demands turns on the conflict between strict justice and benevolence. The legal system, by its nature, is concerned with enforcing justice and equity. Yet, the tradition also acknowledges that these values do not exhaust the whole of the moral life. Acts of selflessness and lovingkindness that do not fall within the domain of administrative justice are nonetheless morally, indeed divinely, mandated. These additional ethical demands arise not, as Lichtenstein would have it, because legal systems are imperfect, but because they are, quite appropriately, limited in purpose. They are in the business of ensuring social justice, not compelling benevolence.[13]

Reframing the Issues

The inconclusive nature of this debate points toward two distinct methodological problems, neither of which has been adequately addressed by those concerned to sort out the relationship between law and ethics in Judaism. First, the sources out of which answers to this question have been constructed are themselves ambiguous. Second, the key terms in the question, "law" and "ethics," have not been subjected to rigorous conceptual analysis, and so, the question itself remains unclear.

Anyone who examines the texts just cited cannot help noticing that the evidence does not speak with a single voice. Some voices within the tradition openly contradict others. To take just one example, let us return to that category of *lifnim mishurat hadin*, "going beyond the line of the law." According to some medieval authorities these acts were morally praiseworthy, but not legally required. Others, however, regarded such actions as backed by the full coercive authority of the law.[14] Likewise, some endorse the principle of compelling people "with respect to a trait of Sodom," while others do not. Again, what Eliezer sees as legally required, Ḥisda regards as an act of special piety. Those who write about this material, of course, note the existence of these controversies among traditional authorities. But they fail to see that the very existence of such controversies within the tradition invalidates the whole question as they have framed it. To ask, "what is *the* relationship between law and ethics in Judaism," is to assume that there is only one relationship and, so to speak, one Judaism. It is to assume that the tradition is not rich and subtle enough to permit more than one legitimate answer to such a question. But the evidence itself belies this assumption. These texts do not answer our questions about the relationship between law and ethics in Judaism. Rather they are themselves a reflection of the problem, a problem to which traditional authorities responded in divergent ways.

In short, this entire discussion of the relationship between law and ethics in Judaism has been conducted in a completely ahistorical framework. As a result, when the evidence points in more than one direction, contemporary scholars have felt the need to resolve the tensions. After all, if it is assumed at the outset that there is only one correct answer to the question, then all the opposing views within the tradition must be shown to converge at some point into an internally consistent position.[15]

But even if we were to take a more historically critical perspective on this material, other difficulties would remain. The fact is that, as regards distinctions between law and ethics, the sources are simply ambiguous. The problem is not just that different texts say contradictory things. Many sources do not say any one thing very clearly. This explains why the same sources can be cited by contemporary scholars in support of such different conclusions about the relationship between law and ethics.

So, for example, it may be clear that certain actions—designated as "pleasing to the sages," or as "a trait of the pious," or as "going beyond the line of the law"—are morally praiseworthy. But do these represent moral duties incumbent upon all, or only upon those who strive to be exemplary; are they imperatives in force everywhere and at all times, or only in special circumscribed instances. The sources simply do not speak directly to these questions. As a result, it is difficult, if not impossible, to determine what sorts of distinctions were, in fact, at work in these cases.

This brings us to the second main problem with the debate as it has been framed, namely, the lack of clarity about what sort of distinction we are looking for in the first place. Historically, a great many definitions of "law" and "ethics" have been proposed and defended by philosophers and social scientists of all sorts. For the question about law and ethics in Judaism to have any clear meaning, one must first adopt some view of the nature of law and ethics in general. A brief overview of some of the classic options in this respect will suffice to indicate the nature of the problem.

In the first place, it is acknowledged by all concerned that law and ethics are closely related. Both are prescriptive or normative in nature.[16] Both involve attempts to regulate human behavior and, to some extent, attitudes. Implicit in both law and morality is the appeal to some authority taken to be the source of the norms in question. (We may leave aside for the moment the exact nature of that authority, whether divine or human, the state, the church, the individual's conscience, or whatever.) Likewise, law and morality share what some have called a "claim of superiority."[17] That is, in cases of conflict, legal and moral norms, by their very nature, have priority over other sorts of (nonlegal and nonmoral) norms. For example, legal and moral rules take precedence over other cultural rules, such as those concerning proper ways to dress, eat, and so on. Given these broad areas of overlap between law and morality, how can they be distinguished from one another?

In general, several types of differences have been proposed. First, it is often noted that law is enforceable while morality generally is not. One can be forced (by judicial order and, if necessary, by the coercive force of the sovereign authority) to comply with a legal duty. This is not true of moral duties (unless, of course, they also happen to be legal duties).[18] This difference is related to another often cited distinction between law and morality. The function of law is relatively limited to preserving social order and promoting social cohesiveness.[19] The scope and purpose of morality, by contrast, is wider and encompasses potentially every sort of interpersonal interaction. For example, one may have a moral duty to take one's child to the park if one has promised to do so, but most societies will not treat this as a legal duty insofar as keeping such a promise (or breaking it) has few if any social ramifications. Thus, law is strictly social, while morality may govern personal as well as social behavior. Law and morality may also be distinguished from one another in that the former is relatively circumscribed, while the latter is relatively open-ended. That is, the set of laws operative in any given society is finite and capable of being formulated in some determinate way. Indeed, any effective mechanism for enforcement presupposes that this is so. Moral rules, on the other hand, are less susceptible to specific, definitive formulation, because they are less closely linked to social enforcement and because they encompass broader spheres of life.

At present, we need not enter into the debates about the relative merits of any of these ways of distinguishing law from ethics. We need only note that, unless and until Jewish scholars specify which definitions of law and ethics they have chosen to employ, the question they ask is inherently ambiguous. To ask how Jewish tradition understands the relationship between law and ethics is to ask whether any of the distinctions just noted or others like them play any role in the thinking of Jewish authorities over the centuries. Indeed, at this juncture it is possible to reformulate in clearer terms the issue at the heart of this debate. Specifically, (1) is there evidence that traditional Jewish religious authorities recognized any distinction whatsoever between what we identify as law and as ethics; and (2) if they did, did they identify the similarities and differences between them (either implicitly or explicitly) in any of the ways that we do. When the question is posed in this form, it becomes clear that each of the interpretations of the relationship between law and ethics sketched earlier is both partially true and partially false. It also becomes apparent that Judaism by its very nature does not permit a clear, unambiguous answer to the question.

Law and Ethics in the Context of Judaism as a Religious System

The source of the confusion about law and ethics in Judaism lies at the very heart of Judaism as a religious system. To understand the nature of Jewish ethics and its relationship to law, we must begin with a clearer conception of the religious character of the whole tradition. It is in the context of a particular religious worldview, a distinctive understanding of the relationship between God and the world, that all Jewish ethical reflection takes place. The essence of this relationship, as it has been understood from biblical times on, is the covenant that God established with Israel. This covenant was created through God's revelation of Torah to Israel. Through this gift of Torah, Israel became a "holy nation," set apart from others by its divine mandate to live in accordance with God's will as revealed in Torah. And that revelation took the form of law, first the biblical law dictated directly by God, then (so the rabbis tell us) through the proper interpretation and development of that law, which is an expression of God's ongoing revelation to Israel. These facts about traditional Jewish theology are well known and uncontroversial. Yet, their import for the problem of law and ethics in Judaism has not been sufficiently appreciated.

This covenant between God and Israel establishes a communal way of life dedicated to *kedushah*, "holiness." By giving them the law, God makes Israel holy; by observing God's law, Israel affirms and realizes this holiness. All of the demands embodied in these commandments—whether they concern the sacrificial cult or agricultural gifts to the poor, whether they relate to the Sabbath and festivals or to the administration of justice and civil damages—define the content of a life of holiness lived in accordance with God's revealed will. As concerns this life of holiness, there are no distinctions between ritual and ethical imperatives. More to the point of this essay, there are no distinctions between moral offenses that destroy the fabric of society (such as murder or theft) and those that undermine personal relationships (such as cursing parents or hating a neighbor in one's heart).[20] Moral failings in both spheres constitute offenses against God, for the whole of Israel's life is to be permeated with holiness, consecrated to God, an expression of God's will. At this level, then, the sorts of distinctions that we make between social ethics and personal ethics or, as some would have it, between law and ethics, are meaningless.

Similarly, this covenant establishes a framework within which Israel strives to be godlike. As many theologians and biblical scholars have noted, the central underlying commandment is that of *imitatio dei*, the imitation of God.[21] Just as God embodies moral perfection, Israel must strive to do likewise. As the rabbis interpreted the biblical injunction "You shall walk in His ways" (Deut. 28:9):

> What are His ways? Just as it is God's way to be merciful and forgiving to sinners . . . so do you be merciful one to another. Just as God is gracious and gives gifts gratis both to those who know Him and to those who know Him not, so do you give gifts freely one to another. Just as God is longsuffering to sinners, so be you longsuffering one to another.[22]

The covenant and the commandments that it embodies provide Israel with the means of achieving this end. But if the goal of this holy way of life is the quest for moral perfection, then God demands far more than mere compliance with the provisions of biblical law narrowly interpreted. Every act of generosity, of forgiveness, of compassion, in short, every virtuous act is part and parcel of the holy life that God commands Israel to live. Israel is bound both by the letter of the law and by its spirit, or as others would put it, both by a divine law and by a divine ethic, which at one and the same time is embodied in that law and transcends it.

Finally, the provisions of biblical law, being divine in origin, are also backed by divine sanctions. Scripture is replete with God's promises to reward the righteous and punish those who stray from obedience to the law. To be sure, some of the civil and criminal statutes found in the Pentateuch include human sanctions, such as capital punishment, the payment of specific damages, and so forth. Others are not backed by specific sanctions. But from God's perspective, the distinction hardly matters. Israel knows that ultimately it is accountable for its behavior before God. Whether or not humans are authorized to take action against those who violate God's laws, God certainly is. So, once again, the line between moral norms that are humanly enforceable and those that are not, or between law and ethics in this sense, marks a distinction without a difference.

Each of the distinctions noted earlier that we tend to make between law and ethics, then, is undermined at the most fundamental level by the religious worldview of Judaism. At every point, that worldview blurs the lines (1) between the social and the private spheres, (2) between the written law and the unwritten moral imperative, and (3) between moral imperatives backed by human sanctions and those that are not. It should be noted too, that in this very fundamental respect, the religious worldview of Judaism has remained essentially unchanged from biblical times to the present, at least for those Jews today who continue to live their lives within the context of halakha.

It would appear then that we have reached the answer to our question. "What is the relationship between law and ethics in Judaism?" It seems that there is no distinction, they are one and the same, both are part of one seamless body of divine instruction, which as a whole constitutes God's revelation to Israel.

But this is not the whole story. Indeed, we know this from the sources examined earlier. For even if it is not possible to pin down with certainty what the sources meant when they referred to actions as "pleasing to the sages," or as "going beyond the line of the law," they certainly were trying to mark some category of actions as distinctive. By the same token, while divine sanctions stand behind all the commandments of the Torah, it remains true that some also carry human sanctions and some do not. The fact is that within the realm of ethical action distinctions are made both in biblical and in rabbinic texts. The lines between law and ethics are *blurred* by notions of holiness, covenant, and imitatio dei, but never entirely *obliterated.* To understand why this is so, we must consider the dual nature of Jewish law, as explained in chapter one.

The halakha's unique character derives from the fact that it fulfills a social as well as a religious function.[23] Halakha in large part and for most of Jewish history has regulated the daily life of Jewish communities. Like every other functioning legal system, then, it has faced a variety of social and jurisprudential issues, among them, the problems of legislating both conduct and attitude, emending prior rulings, enforcing its injunctions, and so on. In this sense, halakha is subject to a whole range of social forces, even as it attempts to regulate and channel those forces.

Nonetheless, halakha never loses its character as a system of religious instruction. And insofar as halakha attempts to bring the Jew closer to God, the cultivation of certain godlike qualities will be central to its purpose. Of particular importance are those qualities of compassion and mercy that Scripture defines as the essential attributes of God and so as the hallmarks of the righteous person. Viewed from this perspective, halakha represents what we might call an "open-ended" moral system. Within this system, as we noted earlier, Israel's moral obligations are potentially limitless, for ultimately they are required to seek moral perfection through a process of imitatio dei. It is not surprising to discover, then, that the tradition tends to blur any distinction between righteous behavior and fully actionable legal duties. But it is no less surprising that they could not do away with these distinctions altogether.

The same point can be made with respect to the rabbi, who serves both a jurisprudential and a religious role. Insofar as rabbis were lawyers and judges, their task did not include promoting exceptional piety. They mandated only that behavior that they saw as necessary for maintaining a just society. For the purpose of protecting individual rights and enforcing basic social responsibilities, it was not necessary to mandate special acts of selflessness or generosity. Moreover, as a practical matter, rabbis were understandably hesitant to legislate pious behavior that the average person could not be expected to emulate.[24] Thus, for both theoretical and practical reasons, rabbis refrained from giving legal sanction to acts of special generosity, which, in any case, were not required to ensure a basically just society. From this stand-point, those who are more generous or selfless than the law requires may be praised for their righteousness and piety but will not be made the standard for the community at large.

In short, the religious character of Judaism necessarily blurs the lines separating law and ethics. Each way of delineating law and ethics examined earlier is challenged by the most fundamental theological presuppositions upon which the whole tradition is based. Yet, the social reality within which this body of divine law functions tends to reintroduce and reinforce the dif-ferences between law and ethics. So, when we attempt to generalize about the tradition as a whole, we discover that the distinctions between law and ethics are never hard and fast, but they are also never obliterated. There are forces at work breaking them down and others, equally persistent and powerful, that serve to build them up again.

We are now in a position to understand the truth of the assertions that both Spero and Lichtenstein make. They want to acknowledge that there are different spheres of ethics, different sorts of ethical imperatives in Judaism. Some are more akin to our conception of law, some are closer to what we could consider a nonlegal ethic. And they are right to assert that, notwith-standing these differences, all ethics are in a certain sense "of a piece," all en-compassed within God's revelation to Israel. What they fail to appreciate is just how fluid the boundaries between these categories really are. For the very same actions that at one period in history are clearly "extra-legal," at another may become fully part of the legal system. What for one rabbi is merely vir-tuous, for another is fully compulsory and legally binding.

But the boundary between law and ethics is blurred for yet another rea-son. Apart from the tensions that exist as a result of the special character of halakha, there is an ambiguity within the religious worldview of Judaism it-self concerning the nature of the covenant between God and Israel. And, like the tensions discussed earlier, it too is rooted in the very foundations of Ju-daism. Perhaps the best way to get a handle on this ambiguity is to look closely for a moment at one biblical passage that, like so many others, de-scribes the covenantal relationship between God and Israel. Deuteronomy 26:16–19 reads:

> This day the Lord your God commands you to do these statutes and ordinances; you shall therefore be careful to do them with all your heart and with all your soul. You have declared this day con-cerning the Lord that he is your God, and that you will walk in his

ways, and keep his statutes and his commandments and his ordinances, and will obey his voice; and the Lord has declared this day
concerning you that you are a people for his own possession, as he
has promised you, and that you are to keep all his commandments,
that he will set you high above all nations that he has made, in
praise and in fame and in honor, and that you shall be a people
holy to the Lord your God, as he has spoken.

What does this passage tell us about the covenant? First, that God has a
unique relationship with Israel and that this relationship defines Israel's distinctiveness among the nations of the world. That relationship is based on
Israel's willingness to obey God faithfully, to dedicate its communal life to
God. Moreover, that relationship is mutual. If Israel does its part, God will
reward the people; they will be praised and honored above all others. So the
covenant defines a relationship between God and Israel. But the covenant
is also defined by the specific laws that God has given Israel and that they
are to obey. It is, in effect, a legal contract, albeit one of a very unusual sort.
It defines legal rights and responsibilities between the two parties to the
agreement.

Covenant, then, refers both to a relationship and to the laws that define
the terms of that relationship. One might say that the goal or purpose of the
covenant is to create a unique relationship, while its content is the body of
law that to a large extent fills the Torah. But precisely here is the root of the
ambiguity. On the one hand, the covenant, like all relationships, is open-
ended and flexible. On the other, it is fixed in black and white, unchanging
and formal. Insofar as the covenant is a legal contract, its demands are finite
and self-contained. It is complete in itself. But insofar as the covenant is a relationship, like all human relationships it must be dynamic; the demands that
it makes cannot be fixed in advance or set in stone once and for all time.
When we read about "keeping God's commandments, statutes and ordinances," we are in the realm of covenant as contract. When we read about
"walking in God's ways" and "being a people holy to the Lord," we are in the
realm of covenant as relationship.

The difference between these two notions of covenant comes into sharp
relief when we turn back to the sources examined earlier about the way in
which ethics operates within the legal system, influencing the way rabbis interpret and apply Jewish law. There are two ways of understanding what is going
on in these cases. Dorff regards them as clear evidence that the rabbis recognized the difference between law and ethics, indeed, consciously struggled

whenever they felt the tension between the two. Though Dorff does not put it in these terms, he ascribes to the rabbis a view of covenant primarily as an ever-changing relationship. Given this conception of covenant, the relationship is primary and the legal content is secondary. Because he attributes to the rabbis this perspective on covenant, he reads the sources as evidence of a tension between the demands of the law and the demands of this divine relationship. For, on this view, the established law will sometimes clash with what one perceives that God expects. And when this happens, the demands of the relationship as they are perceived at the moment will take precedence over the received legal tradition. Seymour Siegel articulates this position at the very outset of one of his many articles on Jewish ethics, "It is my thesis that according to our interpretation of Judaism, the ethical values of our tradition should have the power to judge the particulars of Jewish law. If any law in our tradition does not fulfill our ethical values, then the law should be abolished or revised. This point of view can be supported historically and theologically."[25] From this theological perspective, it is inevitable that there be conflicts between the received legal rules and what our covenantal relationship with God demands of us, between Jewish law and Jewish ethics. And it is equally inevitable that, when these conflicts occur, they be resolved in favor of ethics.

The other theology of covenant is represented by Halivni and, by now, its implications for our understanding of the relationship between Jewish law and ethics are predictable. If the covenant *is* the law, if fulfilling the covenant means nothing more and nothing less than fulfilling the dictates of the law, then there can be no conflict between law and ethics. For, after all, this law is divine and therefore, by definition, perfect. As Psalm 19:8–10 states, "The law of the Lord is perfect, restoring the soul; the testimony of the Lord is sure, making wise the simple, the precepts of the Lord are right, rejoicing the heart; the commandment of the Lord is clear, enlightening the eyes; the fear of the Lord is pure, enduring forever; the judgments of the Lord are true, they are righteous altogether." From this theological perspective, if any established law ever appears less than perfect, the only conceivable conclusion is that we have not understood it properly. Any apparent conflict between law and ethics is just that—apparent—for God cannot have meant for us to apply a revealed law in a way that is blatantly unjust or unethical. Again, without articulating this view in theological terms, Halivni has attributed to the rabbis a concept of covenant that leads inexorably to the view that law and ethics are one and the same.

Both views of covenant, with their corresponding implications for law and ethics, are equally well rooted in Judaism. So, we dare not ask, whose interpretation of the sources is correct, or which theology of covenant best accounts for the evidence. The answer is that both are correct. There is no way to choose between them and, more to the point, no need to do so.[26] Once it is acknowledged that both theologies of covenant are legitimate options within the tradition, and that they lead to different conclusions about the relationship between law and ethics, then it becomes clear that every solution that contemporary scholars have offered is correct. And it is equally clear that every solution, offered as the whole truth, is incorrect.

To conclude, then, the problem of the relationship between law and ethics in Judaism is genuinely irresolvable in the terms in which it has been formulated. It is not a problem that can be defined away by postulating firm distinctions where none exist. Neither can it be swept under the rug, as though the problem were entirely illusory, a product of our collective misunderstanding. The problem is rooted in the very foundations of Judaism, which is simultaneously a system of religious truth and a functioning legal system. And the situation is further complicated by the fact that the tradition embraces more than one theory of covenant. Thus, the whole enterprise of lawmaking and norm setting can be understood from within the system in two quite different ways. Given these facts—that the law is both divine instruction and functioning legal system, that covenant can be defined both by its specific content and by the relationship that it creates—the paradox is in place. And that paradox is that Judaism both does and does not acknowledge a distinction between law and ethics as we tend to use those terms. Indeed, on one level it must recognize such a distinction and yet just as surely it must refuse to recognize it. Once we have discovered the paradoxical nature of the situation, and once we have recognized that it is inherent in the tradition, we have said as much as there is to say about the relationship between law and ethics in Judaism.

I wish to conclude this analytical discussion with a metaphor that expresses somewhat poetically much of the foregoing argument. The relationship between law and ethics in Judaism is rather like that between the sea and the shoreline. The boundary between them is constantly shifting, and necessarily so. The forces of the sea eat away at the shore, washing away the sand. But the land is equally powerful; it holds back the sea and sets limits to its movement. The one force is dynamic and fluid, the other is stable and solid. From one perspective, we might think of them as opposing forces, working against one another, deadlocked in a fight in which neither can totally prevail. But from another perspective, the ebb and flow between them is a model of complementarity. Neither could exist without the other. There is no question but that there is an absolute difference between the land and the sea—any child can see that. But just as surely there is no way to fix, even at a single moment in time, the precise point where one ends and the other begins. And, viewed from the perspective of a religious believer, these two are really one. They are not two forces working against, or even with, one another. To the religious believer, both are part of a single world, both are expressions of God's creative power, and finally, both have their assigned roles to play in a cosmic order that God has ordained. So it is with the relationship between law and ethics in Judaism.

Chapter 3

Covenant and Contract

A Framework for the Analysis of Jewish Ethics

As I argued in the preceding chapter, covenant plays a central role in Judaism and particularly in the way this religion treats the rather fluid boundary between law and ethics. I want now to explore more fully the category of covenant as it shapes Jewish ethics. The ways in which covenant is conceptualized within the tradition, I believe, have far-reaching implications, not only for an understanding of law but also for questions of autonomy and for the very purpose of Jewish ethical behavior.

The Centrality of Covenant

Israel's theology was 'historically-conditioned theology,' which means covenant-centered theology. God was thought to be a covenant-making, covenant-restoring, and covenant-fulfilling God; Israel a people of the covenant and a covenant-breaking people.

—Ramsey, "Elements of a Biblical Political Theory"

The fact that covenant played a central role in the religious life of ancient Israel has long been recognized by historians, theologians, and other careful readers of the biblical text. Walther Eichrodt's monumental *Theology of the Old Testament* remains perhaps the best known and most extensive treatment of covenant themes in the Hebrew Bible. But in recent years biblical scholars and theologians as diverse as Jon Levenson, James Muilenberg, Eugene Borowitz, Rosemary Ruether, and David Hartman have increasingly devoted their attention to the concept of covenant, both to its biblical roots and to its persistence as a central category of religious life for Jews and Christians into the modern era.[1]

Yet, the implications of covenant for Jewish ethics have not received the attention they merit. To be sure, it is universally acknowledged that Jews, traditionally speaking, have understood their religious obligations within the context of the covenantal relationship between God and Israel.[2] And some have noted that, as a consequence of this, Jewish ethics is addressed to members of a covenanted community, rather than to autonomous individuals.[3] Some have also explored the tensions within the covenant idea between particularism and universalism, while others have distinguished between the conditional and unconditional dimensions of the covenantal relationship.[4] Still, there has been no systematic effort to correlate the category of covenant in all its richness and subtlety with diverse streams within Jewish ethics.

My goal here is to take some preliminary steps in this direction. I will first explicate the category of covenant in Jewish tradition in relation to the concept of contract in the Anglo-American legal tradition, and then sketch its implications for Jewish ethics. Before doing so, I should say a word about analyzing the concept of covenant in terms of a legal category like contract. At first glance, it might appear problematic to analyze religious categories in terms of secular ones. Indeed, in chapter 1 I argued that this sometimes generates "pseudo-problems," issues that arise precisely because religious data often do not fit neatly into western philosophic categories. Yet, in this instance, American legal concepts may be apposite to the task. In the first place, numerous studies have traced the influence of Puritan ideas about covenant and religious community upon the development of early American legal thinking.[5] In the works of Locke and Hobbes, for instance, the social contract was modeled on the notion of a covenanted community, both in ancient Israel and in the contemporary reformed churches that were influenced by Calvinist thought. Given that our most fundamental legal and social institutions were modeled, however indirectly, on biblical covenants, it makes sense to explore further the relationships between the two. Moreover, as Harold Berman has argued, many aspects of our own western legal tradition have their roots in religious law. In particular, Berman traces the foundations of contract law back through canon law to certain biblical norms about taking oaths.[6] To the extent that such a historical connection exists, there is good reason to suppose that an analysis of biblical models of covenant in terms of contract theory may shed some light on the nature of covenantal theology and ethics.

This exploration of covenant theology and ethics investigates two basic questions: first, what sort of relationship is this covenant between God and

Israel, and second, in the context of this covenant, how does Israel understand the nature and significance of its moral life? The biblical text offers more than one model of the covenant between God and Israel,[7] and these diverse understandings of covenant, I suggest, underlie certain classic disputes within traditional Jewish ethics. So, while covenant has provided an enduring theological context within which Jews traditionally have addressed ethical questions, it also has opened the door to numerous (and incompatible) understandings of the relationship between God and Israel, each with quite distinct implications for Jewish ethics.

Before proceeding to analyze Israel's covenantal relationship with God, it is important to be clear about the nature of what we are analyzing. I take it that for ancient Israelites (and for their Jewish and Christian successors, as well) "covenant" functions as a metaphor for the relationship between the community and God. After all, in many respects this divine-human relationship is strikingly unlike any purely inter-human relationship. For one thing, since the divine party to the relationship is not knowable in the way another human is, God's qualities can be apprehended only indirectly. Moreover, the radically unequal power of the divine and human partners to this relationship distinguishes it from any ordinary relationship between individuals or groups of individuals. In particular, God, while a partner to the relationship, also retains the power to enforce its terms, to police and judge Israel's performance of its role within the relationship. Finally, this covenantal relationship is understood to bind God and future generations of Israelites, including those not yet born at the time the covenant was established. God, being eternal, has the ability to enter into a relationship that transcends the temporal limits of individual human lives, or even of whole generations. In this way, too, the relationship between God and Israel is incomparable to any other sort of relationship.

Notwithstanding these obvious differences, it is precisely the biblical writers' (rather audacious) assumption that this relationship is much like a interpersonal human relationship. For the most part, God is conceived in largely anthropomorphic terms, and the relationship that "He" has with "His people," like an interpersonal bond, involves complex emotional ties and mutual responsibilities. So, too, it undergoes the ebb and flow characteristic of all human relationships. Like bonds between people, this covenant between God and Israel does not arise in a vacuum, but rather within the context of a historical relationship between God and this particular group of people beginning with its founder, Abraham. By the same token, the covenant, once established, shapes the subsequent historical relationship between the two parties, providing a certain stability and predictability to their interactions.

To analyze the covenant between God and Israel, then, is to ask about what sort of relationship this is. More precisely, it is to ask what sort of human relationship most closely approximates it and, concomitantly, how Israel understands the nature of its own religious-moral duties in the context of that sort of relationship. In Jewish tradition, as I hope to show, a variety of metaphors are employed to explicate the meaning of the covenant between God and Israel. Our task, as interpreters of this tradition, is to explore the ways in which each is suggestive and compelling, to indicate its limitations, and to sketch its implications for a theory of Jewish ethics.

Covenant and Contract: A Typology of Relationships

> The whole conception of the relationship between God and man is legal. God enters into a covenant with man whereby He contracts that in consideration of man performing certain stipulated duties He will bestow upon him certain rewards. The God of the Old Testament is essentially a lawgiver and a judge, and it is this aspect of the Deity that is constantly emphasized.
>
> —Macmillan, *Law and Other Things*

Macmillan's view, that the covenant relationship is essentially contractual, is hardly a novel one. After all, characterizations of Old Testament religion as legalistic and of the Old Testament God as a stern judge are at least as old as the New Testament. In order to test the adequacy of this view, it is necessary first to explore briefly the nature of contractual relationships, at least as we understand them in the Anglo-American legal tradition.

While it is notoriously difficult to define precisely the nature of a contract, all agree that it is a legally enforceable promise or set of promises.[8] The elements of a contract that distinguish it from a nonenforceable promise are (1) mutual assent (offer and acceptance) and (2) some detriment on the part of the promisee (consideration) that that individual undertook in response to the promisor's offer and that the promisor sought to induce through the promise. Thus a contract is a bargain entered into freely by both parties, (at least) one of whom makes a promise in exchange for the other's doing or giving up something. Of course, contracts can be bilateral, such that both parties make promises to one another. But, in any case, a contract exists only when there is a bargained-for exchange.

Understood in this way, there are several features of contractual relationships that deserve to be highlighted. First, individuals entering into a contract act in a free, uncoerced manner. The creation of a contract, then, always implies that the parties could have elected to contract with others, or not at all. Second, contracts give rise to legal duties and corresponding rights that would not otherwise exist.[9] The purpose of entering into a contract is to create a legal relationship that generally will be enforceable by some legal sovereign.[10] Finally, this legal relationship is self-contained. It does not depend for its validity on there being any extra-contractual relationship between the parties at all. Of course, it often happens that parties to a contract (e.g., friends, spouses, etc.) have significant personal ties to one another, but the contractual relationship per se does not require or presuppose this. In this sense, a contract in itself creates a legal, as distinct from a personal, relationship.

With this understanding of contract in hand, we turn now to examine the nature of Israel's covenant with God. As we do so, it is important to delineate three distinct dimensions of that relationship and to consider them separately: (1) its *origin*, that is, how the covenant comes into being; (2) its *scope*, that is, the terms of the covenant; and (3) its *duration*, that is, whether the covenant is conditional or unconditional, revocable or irrevocable.

In looking more closely at these dimensions of covenant we will discover that, in each instance, the relationship may conform more or less closely to a legal contract. After exploring these aspects of covenant and the various ways in which each has been construed in Jewish tradition, I will take up the implications of this typology for Jewish ethics.

Origins

Jewish tradition provides at least two different accounts of the origins of the covenant between God and Israel. The legalistic or contractual model of God's relationship with Israel can be seen most clearly in Exodus 19:5–6.

> "Now therefore, if you will obey my voice truly and keep my covenant, then you shall be my own treasure from among all peoples, for all the earth is mine, and you shall be to me a kingdom of priests and a holy nation. These are the words which you shall speak to the children of Israel." And Moses came and called for the elders of the people, and laid before them all these words which the Lord had commanded him, and all the people answered together, and said, "All that the Lord has spoken we will do."

This passage surely depicts what we would identify as the formation of a contractual relationship. We find an exchange of promises that has been bargained for—God promises to bestow upon Israel certain benefits in consideration for Israel's promise to conduct itself in divinely sanctioned ways. God's offer is clearly made with the purpose of soliciting a response that, in turn, is given with the purpose of accepting that offer. We therefore have precisely the sort of bargain that, in our terms, establishes a legal contract. Both parties to the contract enter the relationship freely and of their own accord.[11] The terms of the covenant presumably are those enumerated in the Decalogue, which appears in the very next chapter of Exodus and which Mendenhall long ago identified as following the accepted form of ancient near eastern treaties.[12]

But other sources describe the origins of the covenant quite differently. Consider the following passage from Deuteronomy 4:35–40.

> It has been clearly demonstrated to you that the Lord alone is God; there is none beside Him. From the heavens He let you hear His voice to discipline you; on earth He let you see His great fire; and from amidst that fire you heard His words. And because He loved your fathers, He chose their offspring after them; He Himself, in His great might, let you out of Egypt, to drive from your path nations greater and more populous than you, to take you into their land and give it to you as a heritage, as is still the case. . . . So, observe His laws and commandments, which I enjoin upon you this day, that it may go well with you and your children after you, and that you may long remain in the land that the Lord your God is giving you for all time.

On this view, the covenantal relationship is not strictly a contractual one. It fails to be a contract precisely because here there is no bargain.[13] God's mighty deeds on Israel's behalf constitute a gift given before the terms of the covenant were offered and accepted. It is therefore, at best, a kind of past consideration that cannot be invoked in the formation of a later contract. Rather, the Israelites are morally indebted to God for redeeming them from slavery. Doing God's will, then, is a way, perhaps the only adequate way, for the Israelites to demonstrate their gratitude. This passage depicts the covenant relationship and the moral duties that it entails as arising in the context of a preexisting relationship, established through God's acts of benevolence and Israel's experience of deliverance.

This same point of view is reflected in the *Mekhilta*, an early rabbinic compilation of Scriptural exegeses (or *midrash*) on the book of Exodus.

> Why were the Ten Commandments not given at the beginning of the Torah? This may be compared to a person who came to a land and said to the inhabitants, "I will rule over you." The inhabitants replied, "What have you done for us that you should rule over us?" Upon which the stranger built for them a wall, brought in water, led them in battle, and then said again, "I will rule over you." They replied, "Yes, yes." So, too, the Almighty liberated Israel from Egypt, split for them the sea, caused manna to fall, and brought forth water. Then He said to them, "I will rule over you." They answered, "Yes, yes." (*Mekhilta* to Exod. ch. 5)[14]

These texts indicate that Israel's covenant with God is grounded in the gifts that God earlier bestowed and the corresponding benefits that Israel received. Whether God performed these acts on Israel's behalf in order to create a sense of obligation on their part matters little. The point is that Israel has an intimate relationship with God before the covenant between them is established. Thus, Israel's covenantal obligations arise in the context of a preexisting personal and moral relationship with God.

Scope

Turning to the second dimension of covenant, its "scope," we must examine the terms of the covenantal relationship itself. Specifically, we want to know how broadly or narrowly these terms are to be construed. In the most general sense, of course, the terms of the covenant are contained in the Torah. The text of the Torah (lit., "instruction") is God's revelation to Israel. The words of Torah, therefore, contain the terms of this covenant—what God expects of Israel and what Israel may expect, in turn, of God. But the question remains: is the text of Torah exhaustive or only suggestive? Does it specify Israel's covenantal duties fully or only minimally? Here again traditional Jewish sources suggest that covenant may signify either a relationship that is strictly contractual or one that is more holistic and interpersonal.

We find the terms of the covenant presented in a legalistic way in many passages throughout the Pentateuch. The language of Deuteronomy 4:44–45 is typical: "This is the Torah which Moses set before the children of Israel; these are the testimonies, and the statutes and the judgments which Moses spoke to the children of Israel after they came forth out of Egypt." Similarly, Deuteronomy chapter 28, which contains a lengthy list of blessings for those who "observe faithfully all God's commandments" together with a list of curses for those who do not, concludes with the words: "These are the terms of the covenant which the Lord commanded Moses to conclude with the Is-raelites in the land of Moab, in addition to the covenant which He had made with them at Horeb." (vs. 69) On this view, the Torah constitutes a written contract.[15] The terms of God's relationship with Israel are circumscribed, en-compassed fully by the detailed laws found in Scripture.[16]

By contrast, the following passage from Deuteronomy 10:12–13 repre-sents a more holistic view of covenant.

> And now, O Israel, what does the Lord your God demand of you? Only this: to revere the Lord your God, to walk only in His paths, to love Him, and to serve the Lord your God with all your heart and soul, keeping the Lord's commandments and laws, which I en-join upon you today, for your good.

On this view, observing the laws enumerated in the text is only part of what God demands. For one thing, those who scrupulously observe the law might nonetheless lack true reverence or love of God. The covenant demands not only that Israelites conform to a set regimen but that inwardly they possess the proper attitude toward God. Moreover, loving and serving God whole-heartedly might take any number of forms. The specific laws that God en-joins, while indispensable, might be suggestive rather than exhaustive; a bare minimum rather than a thorough compendium. From this perspective, it seems, the covenantal relationship is too fluid to be captured in the terms of a legal contract.[17]

On occasion, we find these two positions articulated side by side in the same Scriptural passage. Consider, for instance, Deuteronomy 26:17–19.

> You have declared this day concerning the Lord that he is your God, and that you will walk in his ways, and keep his statutes and his commandments and his ordinances, and will obey his voice; and the Lord has declared this day concerning you that you are a people for his own possession, as he has promised you, and that you are to keep all his commandments, that he will set you high above all nations that he has made, in praise and in fame and in honor, and that you shall be a people holy to the Lord your God, as he has spoken.

On the one hand, the contractual, reciprocal character of the relationship is clearly reflected here. The emphasis is on the specific duties, spelled out in "statutes, commandments and ordinances," that Israel promises to perform and on the specific benefits, "praise, fame and honor," that God promises to bestow in return. On the other hand, this relationship is, at least partly, open-ended, a matter not so much of observing specific rules as of "obeying God's voice."

Insofar as this covenant between God and Israel is a legal contract, its demands are finite and reducible to writing. The text of Torah spells out the terms of the relationship, and what is not stated explicitly can be inferred from its words. But insofar as the covenant is a holistic relationship it is, like all human relationships, dynamic. The demands that it makes cannot be fixed in advance or set in stone once and for all time. Israel's duties, from this perspective, are potentially infinite; they arise not from the text of Torah, or even from the interpretations of that text, but from living in relationship with God.[18] When we read about "keeping God's commandments, statutes and ordinances," we are in the realm of covenant as contract. When we read about "walking in God's ways" and "being a people holy to the Lord," we are in the realm of covenant as interpersonal relationship. These two views of covenant appear to coexist within the tradition, albeit in tension with one another.

Duration

The third dimension of covenant, its duration, concerns whether this relationship between God and Israel is eternal or revocable. Quite obviously, Israel frequently violates God's law; indeed, the whole Hebrew Bible suggests that the law may have been violated more consistently than it was observed. And it is equally clear that, under the terms of the covenant itself, Israel's transgressions will be met with divine sanctions, whether in the form of natural disasters or of conquering foreign armies. But the question remains: Is it possible that Israel's transgressions could provoke God, not only to punish Israel under the terms of the covenant, but to revoke the covenant altogether? Could the covenantal bond be terminated entirely, or is it irrevocable?

In fact, the possibility of terminating the covenant is first encountered in the biblical narrative immediately following its formation, in response to Israel's worship of the Golden Calf. At that time, God threatens to destroy the people entirely, to found a new nation from Moses' descendants and to form a covenant with them. (Exod. 32–33) Only Moses' intervention on

Israel's behalf saves them and their covenantal relationship with God. This same possibility emerges again in the first two chapters of Hosea when the prophet is told to take a harlot for a wife and have children. One of these is named "Lo-ammi, [lit. "not my people"] for you are not My people and I will not be your God." (Hos. 1:9) This represents a precise reversal of the covenantal formula, "I will be your God, and you shall be My people." (Lev. 26:12) The notion that God is prepared to sever the covenantal relationship altogether could hardly be expressed more succinctly.

Insofar as God retains the right to revoke the covenant with Israel, whether or not God actually exercises that right, it could be said that the covenant more closely approximates a contractual relationship. After all, contractual relationships are, by definition, conditional and so, if the conditions are not met (to any significant degree) they may legitimately be terminated. This legalistic model of covenant is perhaps reinforced by those biblical passages that describe Israel's transgressions as "breaches of contract" with God. The prophets in particular employed legal imagery to describe God's relationship to Israel. We see this in Isaiah 3:14–15, "The Lord will bring this charge against the elders and officers of His people. . . ." and again in Hosea 4:1, "Hear the word of the Lord, O people of Israel! For the Lord has a case against the inhabitants of his land. . . ." In response to this breach on Israel's part, God's only recourse is to suspend performance of God's own covenantal duties for a period of time.[19] Before doing so, however, God invariably gives Israel adequate time to cure its breach, as befits the contractual nature of their relationship, through repentance and/or properly obedient behavior.[20] In fact, it must be noted that nowhere in the Hebrew Bible or in subsequent rabbinic literature do we find the assertion that God has in fact exercised the option of terminating the covenant in response to Israel's sinfulness.[21] Nonetheless, the enduring possibility that this could happen is entirely consistent with a contractual view of the covenantal relationship.

But Scripture also presents the opposing view—that God's covenant is eternal and so, while it may be violated, it can never be terminated. This perspective is presented most powerfully in the words of God's covenant with Abraham, "I will maintain my covenant between me and you, and your offspring to come, as an *everlasting covenant* throughout the ages, to be God to you and to your offspring to come." (Gen. 17:7, emphasis added) The covenant guarantees that God's love for Israel is eternal; nothing Israel does, however grievous, can sever that bond.[22] God may be displeased with Israel and chastise the people severely, but the bond between them is unbreakable. This is expressed with particular poignancy in Isaiah 54:7–10.

For a little while I forsook you, but with vast love I will bring you back. In slight anger, for a moment, I hid my face from you; but with kindness everlasting I will take you back in love said the Lord your Redeemer. . . . For the mountains may move and the hills be shaken, but my loyalty shall never move from you, nor my covenant of friendship be shaken said the Lord, who takes you back in love.

Israel's violations of the covenant have angered God, who has meted out the appropriate punishment and yet, according to Isaiah, the covenant itself remains intact.

This perspective is reinforced by all those passages that utilize the metaphor of the parent-child relationship to describe the covenant, such as Jeremiah 31:36–37.

If these laws should ever be annulled by me, declares the Lord, only then would the offspring of Israel cease to be a nation before me for all time. Thus said the Lord, "If the heavens above could be measured, and the foundations of the earth below could be fathomed, only then would I reject all the offspring of Israel for all that they have done," declares the Lord.

And on the verse earlier in the same chapter (Jer. 31:3), which refers to God's "eternal love" for Israel, the rabbis comment: "It does not say, 'with abounding love,' but 'with eternal love.' For you might think the love with which God loves Israel was for three years or two years or a hundred years. But it was a love for everlasting and to all eternity."[23]

Covenant Theologies and Jewish Ethics

Myth is less likely to dictate specific moral directives than it is to inscribe the general—and normative—contours for moral life. It can point to the nature and locus of the good, to the cosmic context of moral behavior, to the nature of moral agency, and to the significance of moral community. At the same time, the myth may indicate the threats to the moral life as well as the consequences of immoral conduct.

—Knight, "Cosmogony and Order"

To this point I have suggested first, that the concept of covenant is complex, consisting of several dimensions that I have called origin, scope, and duration; second, that there are several views of covenant within Jewish tradition; and finally, that these views can be analyzed in terms of the extent to which they conform to a contractual or legal model. I want now to sketch some of the implications of these possibilities for issues in Jewish ethics. In accordance with Douglas Knight's observation just quoted, I will focus on the general contours or orientation of Israel's ethical life, rather than on any specific rules or principles. What follows is merely suggestive and by no means exhausts the ways in which diverse covenant theologies can and do shape Jewish ethical thinking.[24]

Origins

The way in which we imagine the origins of covenant has far-reaching implications for Jewish ethics. Recall that there were two models for the origins of the covenant: one in which God and Israel freely choose to enter into a contractual relationship, and another in which Israel agrees to the covenant as an act of gratitude for God's benevolence. At stake here is the extent to which Jewish ethics is autonomous. If we think of the covenant as contractual, then Israel has knowingly accepted the obligations and privileges pertaining to this relationship. And their duty arises autonomously, at least in the sense that the basis of the people's moral duties rests in an act of its own free will. Of course, this model of covenant accords nicely with the tradition of liberal theory in politics and ethics and so has broad contemporary appeal. It underlies implicitly the popular contemporary reinterpretation of Israel's chosenness (always a somewhat troublesome doctrine for ecumenically-minded modern Jews) as Israel's being a "choosing" people, electing to follow God's law of its own volition. This perspective on covenant has been particularly attractive to those modern Jewish thinkers, such as Hermann Cohen and Emil Fackenheim, who have attempted to assimilate Jewish ethics into a Kantian framework. Fackenheim acknowledges that this is not full autonomy, for moral duty arises in the context of a choice that God imposes by offering the covenant to Israel. Yet, Israel's response to this offer is genuinely free, not imposed upon it.[25]

		If, on the other hand, we conceive of the covenant as arising out of Israel's gratitude for God's prior acts of salvation and protection, then covenant is grounded in a kind of preexisting moral duty.[26] The moral duty to express gratitude to one's benefactor would appear to be the basis of all legal duties arising under the covenant. As Shubert Spero, a contemporary Jewish ethicist, has put it, "Logically speaking, it is not the case that I do what is right because this is obedience to God but rather I obey God because it is right to do so."[27] On this view, Israel possesses a limited moral freedom; it is the freedom to choose whether or not to fulfill their moral duty. Israel, however, does not have the freedom *not* to enter into the moral situation. That choice has been taken out of the people's hands, as it were, by God's actions on its behalf in the past.

Scope

Diverse views of the covenant's scope lead to different conclusions about the relationship between law and ethics in Judaism. The question for Jewish ethicists has often been phrased in terms of the role, if any, that independent ethical judgments play in the development of Jewish law. Some contemporary Jewish ethicists, like Robert Gordis[28] and Elliot Dorff,[29] have argued that the rabbis consciously interpreted (indeed, even misconstrued) received biblical laws so as to bring them in line with their own moral norms. Indeed, it is claimed that the genius of rabbinic Judaism lay precisely in its ability to modify existing laws to meet the demands of justice as they understood it. Other scholars, like David Weiss Halivni,[30] have suggested that nothing of the sort ever happened. Indeed, it could not have happened because the rabbis were committed to the view that there could be no valid moral judgments outside the sphere of the law. To suggest otherwise, according to Halivni, is to claim that divine laws as they stand could be immoral, and this is clearly impossible.

Yet, as I indicated in chapter 2, how one understands the relationship of ethics and law within the tradition depends in part on which model of covenant one attributes to the sages of the past. Some, like Gordis and Dorff, ascribe to the rabbis the view that covenant is a holistic, ever-changing relationship. On this view of covenant, the relationship is primary and the legal content is secondary. Because they attribute to the rabbis this perspective on covenant, they read the sources as evidence of a tension between the demands of the law and the demands of the covenantal relationship. For, on this view, the established law will sometimes clash with what one perceives that God expects. From this theological perspective, it is inevitable that there be conflicts between the received legal rules and what our covenantal relationship with God demands of us, between Jewish law and Jewish ethics. And it is equally inevitable that, when these conflicts occur, they be resolved in favor of ethics.

The contractual view of covenant, adopted by Halivni, leads to precisely the opposite conclusion. As he reads the tradition, the covenant *is* the law, and so fulfilling the covenant means nothing more and nothing less than

fulfilling the terms of the written contract. Thus, there can be no conflict between law and ethics, for, after all, this law is divine and so, by definition,
perfect. From this theological perspective, if any established law ever appears
less than perfect, the only conceivable conclusion is that we have not understood it properly. Any apparent conflict between law and ethics is just that—
apparent, not real—for God cannot have meant for us to apply a revealed law
in a way that is blatantly unjust or unethical. In Judaism, law and ethics are
one and the same.

But the extent to which the scope of covenant is understood legally will
also affect Jewish ethical reasoning. Those who affirm a more contractual
model of covenant will be inclined to adopt a formalist approach to constructing moral arguments. If the covenant is a legal document, it must be
interpreted accordingly. Legal reasoning emphasizes the creation and application of rules and principles, the search for precedents, and the use of analogies. It strives for consistency, predictability, and logical coherence. It will also
give rise to legal codes containing systematic expositions of the law applicable within each sphere of life. As Elliot Dorff has written, "The Covenant
model, however, provides the basis for Jewish legal development, for God not
only commands but enters into a legal relationship through the Covenant.
Therefore such legal techniques as interpretation, usage, and recourse to
course of dealings became appropriate legal techniques to give meaning to the
parties' original relationship."[31] Of course, Jewish authorities over the centuries have produced a voluminous and complex legal literature precisely because they have understood the covenant and its terms as fundamentally
legal, that is, as a contract.

But the contrasting model of the covenant has also played a role in
Jewish ethics.[32] Those who have understood the scope of the covenant in
non-contractual, more holistic terms have adopted a less formalistic and systematic approach to moral reasoning. They have placed less emphasis on interpreting the words of the text (whether biblical or rabbinic) than on
intuiting and appropriating the spirit of divine instruction. Their ethical reflections have proceeded not case by case, or principle by principle, but rather
in a more homiletical vein. They focus less on defining a uniform system of
ethical behavior than on exploring the inner motivations and intentionality
that is expressed through moral acts and that, for them, is the essence of the
moral life. Through the use of stories and the examples of pious individuals,
these ethicists have sought to inspire a kind of moral life that cannot be defined by adherence to rules alone. Because they understand the covenantal relationship between God and Israel in more interpersonal terms, their style of

moral reasoning is fluid and suggestive, rather than concrete and definitive. This sort of pietistic moral literature was especially popular in the medieval period, the best known example being Bachya ibn Pakuda's *Duties of the Heart*. But it was revitalized in the *musar* movement and in hasidic circles. It continues to exert an influence on modern Jewish thinkers like Martin Buber and, more recently, Eugene Borowitz, who writes of his own brand of liberal Jewish ethics that it consists less "in obedient observance than in authentically living in Covenant."[33]

Duration

Finally, we come to the third dimension of covenant, its duration. One's understanding of covenant as either revokable or irrevokable will have profound implications for the way one understands the significance of Israel's moral life and especially its connection to eschatology. If the covenant with Israel is, even theoretically, subject to termination, then it can be said that Israel, through its deeds, has the power to undo what God has done. While God may have initiated the covenant, once established it can be revoked by either party. Each transgression of the moral law, on this view, pushes Israel closer to the brink and, conversely, each righteous deed brings Israel closer to the ultimate messianic redemption. Israel, then, is in control of its own destiny. Its moral behavior has literally cosmic reverberations. On this view, Israel's ultimate fate in history, and in a sense God's fate in this world, depends upon its deeds alone. This position receives its classic articulation in the rabbinic comment on Isaiah 43:12 " 'You are my witnesses, says the Lord, and I am God.' That is, when you are my witnesses, I am God, and when you are not my witnesses, I am, as it were, not God."[34] (Midrash Psalms on 123:1)

On the other hand, if the covenant is irrevocable, then Israel's responsibility is much diminished and so too is the power of its ethical deeds. Just as Israel could not initiate the covenant, so too it is powerless to dissolve it. God's hand in history cannot be forced. So, while the people can still expect to be blessed by God for their obedience and punished for their transgressions, this drama is played out in the context of a script whose conclusion is never in doubt. This position is closely related to the well-known rabbinic statement that "Israel, even though it sins, remains Israel."[35] Somewhat ironically, given this model of covenant, Israel's place in history is more secure, but only because it depends less on its own deeds.[36]

The very same dichotomy can be expressed in terms of whether Israel's holiness as a nation is inherent and permanent or acquired and conditional.

On the first view, Israel's very status as God's chosen people hangs in the balance, as it were, for the people live with the awareness that they could one day be rejected and another people chosen in their place. Israel's holiness as a people is conditional; it is not bestowed as a gift, but rather must be continually reaffirmed and realized through Israel's own obedience to God's law. The contrasting view represents Israel's status as God's chosen people as fixed and secure. On this view, Israel's holiness is given once and for all time with the revelation on Mt. Sinai.[37] The people are holy by virtue of their unique history; their sole task is to live out the meaning of that mandate. The former position is oriented toward the future, which is uncertain, the latter is oriented toward the past, which is sure. The language of the blessing traditionally recited before performing a biblical commandment reflects this ambiguity: "Blessed are you, Lord our God, who has sanctified us through your commandments and commanded us to . . ." In one sense, Israel has been sanctified already through the giving of the commandments. But in another sense the point is that receiving the law only made Israel potentially holy. They must forever make this holiness actual and effective through the performance of those commandments each and every time they act in accordance with God's will.[38]

Conclusions

These reflections on the nature of covenant and its shaping of Jewish ethics lead in a number of directions. Minimally they suggest that secular legal concepts can provide valuable tools for the analysis of ethics in the Jewish tradition. Even a rudimentary appreciation of principles of contract law can help us refine our understanding of models of covenant and see what the implications of these differing models would be.

More important, the typology of covenant models developed here should challenge certain prevalent assumptions about the meaning of that term in the western religious tradition. It is still widely assumed that the Jewish model of covenant is largely legalistic, especially by comparison to the Christian model. Indeed, this dichotomy has emerged again recently in the work of a Jewish ethicist, Michael Goldberg, who juxtaposes the Jewish covenant, marked by obligations and mutual partnership, with the Christian covenant, characterized by unbounded grace.[39] But clearly covenant bears a range of meanings in Jewish tradition (and, no doubt, in Christian tradition as well) that are far richer and more subtle than Goldberg and others have tended to assume.

And, having recognized the diversity of possibilities inherent in the covenant idea, we would do well to reconsider the suggestions made recently by those in both law and religion to appropriate covenant into our own legal system. Robin Lovin, for example, has proposed that a covenantal model of justice could serve as a valuable corrective to the prevailing secular models of political legitimacy in our society. He writes, "A covenantal paradigm of legitimacy, far better than the contractualist or realist alternatives that have dominated our thinking, promises to link the structure of our politics to the structures of freedom and accountability that give meaning to all human relationships."[40] But it is important that we be clear about which model of covenant we are utilizing here. As we have seen, there are, within Jewish tradition at least, some models of covenant that are quite legalistic and so might reinforce rather than correct the shortcomings of a social contract theory of political legitimacy. By the same token, some models of covenant lead in directions that we would find deeply troubling and almost certainly incompatible with deeply rooted convictions about moral autonomy. Covenant is not one thing, but several. Only when this fact is fully appreciated can we fruitfully consider how we might appropriate covenant into our political and legal thinking, and in what ways it might be useful to do so.

To scholars of biblical theology and/or Jewish ethics, I would suggest that the term covenant requires greater conceptual clarification than it has generally received. David Hartman, for example, has diligently investigated the diverse meanings of covenant, but he too has tended to conflate what are in fact distinct sets of dichotomies. He moves too quickly from conditional versus unconditional covenants to a discussion of formalistic versus dynamic forces within the tradition.[41] But, as I have tried to show, there are several dimensions of covenant each of which can be understood in a more or less contractual way, and each of which functions to some extent independently. Though I have not attempted to sort out the possible permutations, it is at least theoretically possible that one could adopt, for example, a contractual view of the origins of covenant, but a more holistic view of its scope, and so forth. This being the case, when discussing the nature of diverse covenants one must carefully attend both to the distinct levels on which it functions and to the diverse forms it can take.

Above all, this study has served to highlight the power and persistence of covenant as the dominant metaphor for Israel's relationship to God, both in Scripture and in the subsequent rabbinic tradition that builds upon that foundation. The fact that covenant has proved an enduring vehicle for symbolizing Israel's religious life testifies to its ability to express the inexpressible, namely, the mystery of God's election of this people as well as the enormous and bewildering implications of this for its corporate, institutional, and moral life. From its origins as a political concept rooted in ancient Near Eastern treaty formation, covenant comes to embody a unique and multifaceted relationship between Israel and its God. That God—depicted sometimes as sovereign ruler, other times as lover, still other times as parent—continues to be bound by a covenantal relationship to Israel. Covenant proved capable of generating a conceptual framework stable enough to endure the vissisitudes of Israel's history but also elastic enough to support a remarkable range of ethical and political philosophies. Each of the meanings inherent in the notion of covenant has its appeal and its limitations. But even if some appear more prevalent than others, all are firmly rooted in Jewish tradition. Each understanding of the covenant remains a perennial option, providing a rich resource for ethical reflection, as Israel continues its struggle to discern the infinite within the finite, to locate the eternal in the ebb and flow of history, to bring the divine within the realm of the human.

Part Two

Ethics and Theology

Chapter 4

The Quality of Mercy

On the Duty to Forgive in the Judaic Tradition

The quality of mercy is not strain'd
It droppeth as the gentle rain from heaven
Upon the place beneath. It is twice blest:
It blesseth him that gives and him that takes.
Tis mightiest in the mightiest, it becomes
The throned monarch better than his crown.
His sceptre shows the force of temporal power,
The attribute to awe and majesty,
Wherein doth sit the dread and fear of kings;
But mercy is above this sceptred sway,
It is enthroned in the hearts of kings,
It is an attribute to God himself;
And earthly power doth then show likest God's
When mercy seasons justice.
　　　　The Merchant of Venice (IV, i, 184–97)

T he role of religious beliefs in shaping the moral life has been the subject
　of reflection by philosophers and theologians, as well as by poets and
playwrights. And, though they have seldom approached Shakespeare's elo-
quence, many ethicists have adopted a view, like that presented here, which
posits both a conflict and a necessary relationship between divine attributes
and moral norms. In this case, the domain of civil authority, "the force of
temporal power," is contrasted sharply with divine compassion, "the quality
of mercy." But while human justice and divine mercy represent quite distinct moral standards, they are not to be viewed as irreconcilable. In fact, it
is the very point of Portia's famous speech to Shylock that human standards
of justice must at times be supplemented and corrected by an element of

divine compassion. Even the most just laws by human standards sometimes sanction immoral behavior (such as Shylock's) unless we attempt to act in conformity with God's example, to "season (human) justice with (divine) mercy."

The suggestion that divine goodness plays a necessary role in the moral life invites one to explore a question of central importance for scholars of religious ethics, namely, the ways in which religious beliefs, especially beliefs about God's attributes, affect our moral judgments. It is my purpose here to explore this very general issue in religious ethics through a detailed examination of whether and under what circumstances Judaism recognizes a duty to forgive others for the offenses they commit against us.[1]

I begin my analysis of the issue with a general model of forgiveness. The model presented here highlights certain moral issues surrounding forgiveness, which preclude its being regarded as a general moral duty. This is followed by a description and analysis of the classical Jewish sources that bear on the issue of forgiveness. Here I spell out, insofar as the sources permit, the nature of the duty to forgive within Jewish tradition as well as the limitations upon this duty as established by rabbinic authorities over the centuries. The concluding section of the essay explores the religious underpinnings of the Jewish approach to forgiveness. By exposing the religious worldview that lies at the foundation of the duty to forgive in Judaism we will discover both the extent to which Jewish authorities reject the model of forgiveness presented at the outset and the ways in which religious beliefs can shape ethical reponsibilities. This examination of Jewish views on forgiveness, then, will illustrate some of the ways in which religious beliefs can generate a moral duty where, in the absence of these or similar beliefs, none would exist.

A Philosophical Model of Forgiveness

I begin this analysis of Judaic perspectives on forgiveness by turning to the work of Paul Lauritzen. His account of the ways in which and the purposes for which one person forgives another will establish the context for this analysis of forgiveness.

In Lauritzen's view, forgiveness encompasses a set of behaviors and attitudes that he characterizes in the following schematic way:

1. A injures B thus creating a moral debt between A and B and a breach in the relationship between A and B.

2. This debt is characterized, on the one hand, by A's obligation to B to apologize, make restitution, and so on and, on the other hand, by B's justified retributive response of resentment.
3. A discharges his obligations to B and seeks forgiveness from B.
4. B relinquishes his right to resentment (thus cancelling the debt) and readjusts his attitudes toward A in line with a relationship of moral equality (thus repairing the breach in the relationship between himself and A).[2]

This model focuses our attention on several crucial features of situations in which issues of forgiveness commonly arise. In the first place, forgiveness is essentially a restorative process, an attempt to repair a breach in the relationship between two parties. Such a gap may be created when one individual unjustifiably harms another, thus disturbing the preexisting relationship between them. Where they initially had been in a situation of "moral equality," the offense has created an inequity. The attempts to seek and to grant forgiveness arise from a desire to restore this relationship to its original footing, by transcending or moving beyond the act that caused offense. It follows that the process of forgiveness entails, at very least, a change of attitude, a relinquishing of resentment, and, in some cases, no doubt, additional positive steps toward repairing what has been damaged. The difficulty of forgiving another, as well as the requisite steps toward reconciliation will vary, of course, depending upon the nature of the relationship in question, the gravity of the offense, and the desire of the parties (especially the offended party) to restore that relationship. Finally, on Lauritzen's model, forgiveness entails relinquishing a "right" of sorts. That is, the person injured is entitled to feel resentful toward the offender and, ultimately to break off a relationship with that person entirely. To forgive, then, is to relinquish this justified resentment, or right of retribution, for the sake of closing the moral gap that the offense has created. It thus involves, as Lauritzen describes it, a willingness to see the offender as if that person were not guilty, or, at least, to refrain from allowing one's moral condemnation to stand in the way of reconciliation with the guilty individual.

On the basis of this paradigm, it is easy to see why Lauritzen concludes that forgiveness can never be a moral imperative. Put simply, it can never be one's moral obligation to preserve or restore a relationship that the other party has previously violated. This is most obviously the case when the offense involved has been severe or when its effects are irreversible. In such cases there can be no question that the offended party is justified in breaking off the relationship entirely, since, in effect, the relationship has already been undermined.

That there can be no categorical moral duty to forgive is likewise especially apparent when the offender has made no effort to redress the wrong committed. Under such circumstances, granting forgiveness could be tantamount to an outright condoning of the offense, which could lead the offender to repeat such actions in the future. Indeed, in such cases one could argue that it is precisely one's duty not to forgive in order to avoid reinforcing the offender's objectionable behavior. But might there not be a duty to forgive in the case of a relatively minor offense (for example, an insult or insensitive gesture) provided that the offender has made a sincere effort to atone for the wrong? Even in this case, Lauritzen concludes, it is best not to think of forgiveness as a duty, for even a minor offense may lead one to break off a relationship with the offender. The individual hurt may simply feel that anyone who could commit such an offense is just not the sort of person with whom one wishes to be associated. In short, the offended individual always retains the right to end a relationship with the offender, for the latter's good intentions after the fact may not provide a compelling reason for the victim to look beyond an offense already committed.

It seems apparent that there can be no duty, on moral grounds, to forgive another person for any offense that he or she has committed. Moreover, as Lauritzen's model implicitly suggests, this position seems to be grounded in the very way that we usually conceive of interpersonal relationships. Whenever two autonomous individuals choose to enter into a relationship with one another there is an implicit or explicit understanding that they will treat one another with a certain degree of integrity. Once one person violates the terms of this relationship, the other is free to do likewise, since, in effect, the first person's behavior has already undermined the foundation upon which the relationship was based. In this respect, granting forgiveness may be compared to the cancellation of a kind of "moral debt." Just as it can never be a creditor's duty to cancel a monetary debt that a debtor has freely incurred, so it can never be one's duty to forgive, for, as we have seen, this entails dismissing the debt created by the offender's action.

Yet, Lauritzen suggests in the final section of his essay that adopting certain religious views of the world could radically transform the foregoing assessment of forgiveness. This is because certain beliefs about God, especially about God's relationship to human beings, could provide the grounds for regarding forgiveness as a duty. My purpose in the remainder of this essay to explore the Judaic view of forgiveness,[3] which I believe illustrates this last point precisely. That is, in reviewing those classical Judaic sources that bear on the issue of forgiveness, I draw attention to the religious attitudes that implicitly or explicitly shape their perspective on forgiveness. Turning then directly to the questions before us, to what extent does classical Jewish teaching recognize a duty to forgive and what is the religious worldview that informs its perspective on forgiveness?

Judaic Sources on Forgiveness

The primary rabbinic source concerning forgiveness appears in the Mishnah in the context of a discourse on damages and compensation.

A. Even though a person gives [monetary compensation] to one [whom he has shamed] he is not forgiven until he asks [explicitly for forgiveness] from him [whom he has shamed],

B. as it is written, [Genesis 20:7] '. . . he is a prophet and he will intercede on your behalf, and you shall live.'

C. And whence do we derive the principle that he who is called upon to forgive should not be hardhearted?

D. It is written [Genesis 20:17], 'Then Abraham interceded with God, and God healed Abimelech. . . .'[4]

A number of points about the character of forgiveness in rabbinic tradition emerge from this passage. First, the sages of the Mishnah clearly recognize that injury to another person entails two separate offenses. In addition to the material harm, which one rectifies through monetary compensation, there is also a more intangible injury, which can be remedied only through seeking forgiveness. This is significant in that it implies an awareness of what Lauritzen has called the "moral gap" created when one individual harms another. Furthermore, this Mishnaic passage suggests that, as Lauritzen put it, the purpose of forgiveness is essentially restorative. Just as one restores a situation of material equity through the payment of damages, one must likewise restore that state of moral equilibrium that has been disturbed by the offense in question. Such reconciliation can be accomplished only by seeking forgiveness directly from the individual harmed. Moreover, we may infer from the biblical prooftexts provided at B and D that the duty to seek and grant forgiveness is not limited to cases of material injury. Indeed, in the biblical episode referred to (Gen. 20:1–18) Abimelech has only offended Abraham, not injured him,[5] and yet the rabbis say that this is just the sort of situation in which forgiveness is required.

In all, then, the Mishnah appears to confirm Lauritzen's characterization of the basic elements of forgiveness.

Implicit in this discussion of forgiveness is a further assumption of fundamental importance. The rabbis uniformly assume that the primary responsibility for repairing a "moral gap" lies with the person who created it. In the proper course of things, that is, seeking forgiveness precedes the granting of it. This is clear from the very careful way in which the Mishnah states its principle—first, at A-B, the offender has a duty to seek forgiveness (even after compensating the victim), then, at C-D, the one "who is called upon to forgive" must not be hardhearted, and so must grant forgiveness. The Mishnah, then, never proposes that one has a duty to forgive unilaterally, irrespective of the offender's stance, but only as a response to an appropriate gesture of repentance on the part of the offender.[6]

The interrelationship of these two duties—that of seeking forgiveness and that of granting it—is expressed with characteristic clarity and precision by Maimonides:

> Even if one only injured the other in words [and not in deeds], he must pacify him and approach him until he forgives him.
>
> If his fellow does not wish to forgive him, the other person brings a line of three of his friends who [in turn] approach the offended person and request from him [that he grant forgiveness].
>
> If he is not accepting of them, he brings a second [cadre of friends] and then a third. If he still does not wish [to grant forgiveness], one leaves him and goes his own way, and the person who would not forgive is himself the sinner.
>
> One who sins against his fellow and the latter dies before he requested forgiveness, [the sinner] should assemble ten people [the minimum number that can constitute a community for purposes of public worship] and stand them at the grave [of the deceased] and proclaim in their presence, "I have sinned against the Lord, God of Israel, and against this individual in that I did such-and-such to him."[7]

Maimonides emphasizes what the Mishnah passage only implied, that the offender bears primary responsibility for initiating the process of forgiveness. Moreover, Maimonides suggests that this duty is not cancelled either by the victim's reticence to grant forgiveness or even by that person's death. The offender can fulfill his or her moral obligation to the other person only through sincere and persistent attempts to effect a reconciliation. The offended individual, on the other hand, has a corresponding duty to forgive anyone who sincerely requests it and the failure to do so constitutes an offense no less than the action of the initial offender.

This duty to forgive is not surprising when considered in the context of other classical rabbinic sayings about the proper attitude to maintain toward one's fellow. The sages of the Mishnah often warn against being overly judgmental or easily angered. Maxims such as, "Do not judge your fellow until you have stood in his place," and "Let the honor of your fellow be as dear to you as your own and do not be easily angered,"[8] reflect a general concern with empathy that correlates with the duty to forgive. In addition, the granting of forgiveness may be viewed as an extension of humility, another moral virtue often praised by the rabbis. "If thou hast done thy fellow a slight wrong, let it be a serious matter in thine eyes; but if thou has done thy fellow much good, let it be a trifle in thine eyes. And if thy fellow hath done thee a slight favor, let it be a great thing in thine eyes; if thy fellow hath done thee a great evil, let it be a little thing in thine eyes."[9] This duty is quite consistent then with the insistence on humility, minimizing the offenses of others, and restraining one's anger found throughout rabbinic literature. As I noted earlier, these are precisely the attitudes entailed by the act of forgiveness.

Having now described in some detail the traditional Jewish view that there is a duty to forgive, let us turn our attention to the issues that Lauritzen's analysis of forgiveness has raised. How might the Judaic view of forgiveness take into account the objections to this duty that he discusses? As I noted earlier, Lauritzen has argued that we can have no duty to forgive for two distinct reasons. First, because forgiveness may be tantamount to condoning the wrongful behavior of the offender and second, because there are crimes so great that we commonly (and properly) regard them as unforgivable. Any tradition that maintains that there is a duty to forgive, then, should be able to defend itself against these objections. How then do the classical Jewish sources deal with these moral objections to the duty to forgive?

The rabbis directly address the objection that forgiveness runs the risk of collapsing into a condoning of the offense. Maimonides' formulation of the law again provides the clearest expression of the traditional position on this issue.

> When a man sins against another, the injured party should not hate the offender and keep silent, as it is said concerning the wicked, "And Absalom spoke to Amnon neither good nor evil, for

Absalom hated Amnon" (II Sam. 13:22). But it is his duty to inform the offender and say to him "Why did you do this to me? Why did you sin against me in this matter?"

And thus it is said, "You shall surely rebuke your neighbor" (Lev. 19:17). If the offender repents and pleads for forgiveness, he should be forgiven. The forgiver should not be obdurate, as it is said, "And Abraham prayed unto God (for Abimelech)" (Gen. 20:17).

If one observes that a person committed a sin or walks in a way that is not good, it is a duty to bring the erring man back to the right path and point out to him that he is wronging himself by his evil courses. . . . And so one is bound to continue the admonitions until the sinner assaults the admonisher and says to him "I refuse to listen." Whoever is in a position to prevent wrongdoing and does not do so is responsible for the iniquity of all the wrongdoers whom he might have restrained.[10]

Forgiveness, rather than undermining or ignoring the culpability of the offender, is designed to make it explicit. This is the point of the claim, reiterated here, that the duty to forgive is predicated upon the repentance of the offender. As the text says, "If the offender repents and pleads for forgiveness, he should be forgiven." By contrast, where there has been no repentance, there is no recognized duty to forgive.

Indeed, in some sources the rabbis press this point further, proposing that prior to repentance one even has an obligation to hate the sinner.[11] Maimonides indicates that forgiveness is closely related to another duty (one especially incumbent upon the injured party), namely, to chastise the wrongdoer if that person is unaware of the wrong committed. This, of course, serves several purposes. First, it encourages the person involved to repent and thus to improve his or her moral character. In addition, it may also save others from being subjected to similar offenses in the future. But rebuking the wrongdoer also plays an important role in the process of forgiveness. It highlights the point that the act of forgiveness that follows this rebuke is not designed to minimize the offense or to make believe that it did not occur. Quite the opposite is the case. It is precisely because the offense and its effects are very significant to the parties involved that forgiveness is called for. Thus, somewhat paradoxically, forgiveness is meant to call attention to the morally objectionable nature of the offense at the same time that it facilitates a bridging of the gap that this offense has created.

The rabbis then meet the objection that forgiveness entails condoning offensive behavior in two ways. First, they are careful to limit the duty to forgive to those cases in which the offender has acknowledged the wrong committed and, in addition, has sought the forgiveness of the individual harmed. Moreover, the rabbis locate forgiveness in the context of other responsibilities, especially that of rebuking sinners and thereby facilitating their repentance.

The question remains whether the classical Jewish sources recognize a class of sins so heinous as to be "unforgiveable," and, if so, what distinguishes forgiveable from unforgiveable offenses. The answer to this question is more complex for, as I shall explain in a moment, the classical sources themselves do not address the issue directly. That is to say, the problem of "unforgiveable sins" arises only in the context of discussions about offenses committed against God. One must then answer the question indirectly by drawing inferences from discussions of God's willingness to forgive the sins of individuals to the question at hand, whether one has a duty to forgive any sin whatsoever or only certain sorts of offenses.

The general thrust of the tradition on the question of divine forgiveness is clear. Within the Scriptural sources, God is most often represented as a loving and compassionate deity, willing to forgive all of Israel's sins. In the priestly writings this belief is formalized in the establishment of a Day of Atonement, on which the priests perform a rite to atone for the sins of the entire community (Lev. 16:29–34). The existence of this institution testifies to the priestly writer's belief that God provides for cleansing the people from sin and so restoring the proper relationship between himself and the community. Moreover, the biblical narrative is replete with stories of divine forgiveness, insofar as the people repeatedly violate the terms of their covenant with God. Invariably, God rebukes the people and generally punishes them for their misconduct, but ultimately God forgives them and calls them again to uphold His laws and to be His people. This is nowhere more evident than in the prophetic literature, which contains some of the Bible's most eloquent affirmations of divine forgiveness.

> How can I give you up, Ephraim,
> how surrender you, Israel . . .
> My heart is changed within me,
> my remorse kindles already.
> I will not let loose my fury,
> I will not turn round and destroy Ephraim;

for I am God and not a man,
the Holy One in your midst (Hosea 11:8–9)
Return, faithless Israel, says the Lord. I will not look on you in
anger, for I am merciful, says the Lord. (Jeremiah 3:12)
In overflowing wrath for a moment I hid my face from you, but
with everlasting love I will have compassion on you, says the
Lord, your Redeemer. (Isa. 54:8)

The ancient rabbis adopted and extended this view of divine forgiveness. In
their view, the assurance of God's compassion and ultimate forgiveness extended not only to the people as a whole, as the prophets had claimed, but to
each individual sinner. (This view, of course, makes its way into the prophetic
writings as well; see Ezek. 18:27–31.) Thus, throughout rabbinic literature
one finds repeated admonitions to the effect that any sinner who repents will
be met with divine forgiveness.

> Let not a man after he has sinned say, "There is no restoration
> for me," but let him trust in the Lord and repent, and God will receive him.[12]
>
> If your sins are as high as heaven, even unto the seventh
> heaven and even to the throne of glory, and you repent, I will receive you.[13]
>
> See how wonderful a thing is repentance! God says, "If you
> return to me, I will return to you," (Mal. 3:7). For however many
> sins a man may have committed, if he returns to God all are forgiven; He accounts it to him as though he had not sinned (Ezek.
> 18:22). But if he does not return, God warns him once, twice,
> thrice. Then, if the man returns not, God exacts punishment.[14]

In short, the predominant view among the rabbis is that divine forgiveness is intimately linked to the sinner's repentance. If the latter acknowledges
the wrongdoing and seeks reconciliation with God, divine forgiveness knows
no bounds.

This view of divine forgiveness logically implies that the duty of one individual to forgive another is likewise unlimited. Surely an individual offended can hardly be permitted to maintain a stricter standard than God in
matters of forgiveness. Insofar as God is prepared to forgive any repentant
sinner, no matter what the nature of the sin, so too we may rightly expect
that the individuals concerned must do likewise. A number of rabbinic
sources express this very point through a comparison of divine and human

forgiveness. Commenting on the verse, "Thou shalt walk in His ways . . . ," (Deut. 28:9) the rabbis note:

> What are His ways? Just as it is God's way to be merciful and forgiving to sinners, and to receive them in their repentance, so do you be merciful one to another. Just as God is gracious, and gives gifts gratis both to those who know Him and to those who know Him not, so do you give gifts [freely] one to another. Just as God is longsuffering to sinners, so be you longsuffering one to another.[15]

Elsewhere the rabbis recognize that, given the human inclination to be obstinate, forgiveness is often more easily obtained from God than from one's fellow.[16] Such comments, however, do not imply that individuals are less obligated to forgive than is God, only that they are less apt to do so. Despite the fact, therefore, that none of the classical rabbinic sources state categorically that one must forgive absolutely all sins, it appears that the individual's duty to forgive is regarded as unlimited, insofar as it is modeled upon divine forgiveness.

It should be noted, however, that certain rabbinic sources do acknowledge a class of sins for which forgiveness from God is not possible. These sources could be read as evidence that, at least in the view of some rabbinic authorities, God's forgiveness is actually not as unlimited as the foregoing discussion would suggest. On closer examination, however, it can be shown that the sins in question are not too great to be forgiven, but rather indicate that the sinner cannot (or most probably will not) engage in true repentance. And, as we recall, only the repentant sinner can count on God's forgiveness. It is in this light that the following source should be understood.

> Five shall obtain no forgiveness: (1) one who is forever repenting, (2) one who sins repeatedly, (3) one who sins in a righteous generation, (4) one who sins with the intention to repent, and (5) one who has on his hands [the sin of] profaning the Name [of God].[17]

In the first four cases, the problem is clear. One who sins repeatedly (1–2), despite the good example of others (3), or with the (obviously insincere) intention to repent (4) is the sort of person who will find true repentance very difficult, if not impossible. And, lacking the inclination or ability to repent, such a person cannot count upon divine forgiveness. The problem in the final case is somewhat different. Profaning God's name consists of committing any sin that brings Israel and/or God's law into disrepute, thereby, by implication tarnishing God's reputation on earth. A sin of this sort, such as committing idolatry in public or treating non-Jews unfairly, has grave ramifications. Since the damage is intangible and extends in a sense to all Jews everywhere, the offender can never seek forgiveness from all those harmed. For this reason, the sinner can never repent fully and the sin thus cannot be forgiven. It is important to note, however, that the problem in all of the cases mentioned here is not that God's forgiveness is limited, but that the individual's ability to repent may be limited.[18] Forgiveness is impossible, then, only where the sinner will not or cannot repent. God's willingness to forgive, while conditional upon the sinner's repentance, is unlimited with respect to the severity of the sin.[19]

In conclusion, then, the tradition views forgiveness as comprised of two interrelated duties—the duty of the offender to seek forgiveness is primary and unconditional, while the duty to grant it is conditional upon the offender's having fulfilled his or her prior duty. Thus, one has a duty to forgive only if the offender has sincerely repented and sought reconciliation. Where the individual involved is reticent to acknowledge the harm done, one has a further obligation to rebuke the sinner in order to prompt that person to repentance. On the other hand, one does not have a duty to forgive the person who will not or cannot repent, for this entails overlooking or minimizing their sinful behavior. Apart from this condition, however, the duty to forgive is unlimited with respect to the offense commited. Since any sinner who truly repents will be received by God no matter what the offense, it appears that the individual's duty to forgive is similarly unlimited.[20]

The Theological Foundation of the Duty to Forgive

Having thus described the duty to forgive as it is expounded in the classical Jewish sources, let us turn now to the task of interpretation. For while the texts examined here have been quite clear in defining this duty, they have indicated very little about the rationale behind it. Our ability to understand the tradition's view of forgiveness, however, depends upon our ability to explain why a Jew is obligated to forgive. Before examining some of the sources that would appear to provide the answer, it will be helpful to reflect for a moment on the question. As the initial analysis in this chapter suggested, forgiveness represents a decision to overlook an offense or to forgo the resentment it engenders for the sake of reconciling oneself with the offender. A duty to forgive, then, is essentially a duty to maintain a relationship with those who have offended or hurt us. It follows that the question at hand can be reformulated, and its focus sharpened, as follows: on what grounds does the tradition hold a Jew responsible for preserving his or her relationship with others no matter what treatment one has received from them? Formulated in this way, the question points us in the direction of an answer, for it suggests that the grounds of this duty will be found in a certain view of the nature of human relationships and so, of the duties to which they give rise. While I do not mean to suggest that the sources speak with a single voice on matters of this sort, certain beliefs about moral responsibility are so central to the tradition that they provide the underpinings of all specific moral duties, including the obligation to forgive. Let me spell out briefly some of these beliefs and suggest their connection to the question of forgiveness.

The commandment to follow in God's ways by imitating the divine attributes is central to the Judaic ethical tradition.[21] Those who have traced the concept of imitatio dei through traditional Jewish sources note that its classic Scriptural expression is the central commandment of the Holiness Code, "You shall be holy, for I the Lord your God am holy" (Lev. 19:2). This verse is taken to mean that Israel is to replicate in its life as a community the qualities that it attributes to God. The implications of this view are especially significant for Israel's understanding of the moral life. In a number of places, the biblical writers specifically refer to Israel's ethical duties—to care for the stranger, to love justice, and so on—as reflections of God's own actions.[22] In the same vein, the rabbis linked the obligations to clothe the naked, attend the sick, comfort mourners, and bury the dead to God's benevolent actions towards Israel.[23] But, as just noted, the doctrine of imitatio dei has especially profound implications with respect to questions of forgiveness, as the following passage suggests:

> The Lord, the Lord, a god compasionate and gracious, long-suffering, ever constant and true, maintaining constancy to thousands, forgiving iniquity, rebellion, and sin and not sweeping the guilty clean away. . . . (Exod. 34: 6–7)

This verse, which figures prominently in traditional Jewish liturgy, appears in the context of God's self-revelation to Moses. Given the belief that God's most essential trait is compassion and willingness to forgive, the duty to forgive becomes thoroughly understandable. To the extent that Israel is to pattern its own moral life on God's example, the obligation to forgive must become one of its central moral duties. By forgiving those who hurt them, Jews draw themselves closer to God and make God's own compassion the operative force in their relations with others.

Moreover, certain rabbinic passages suggest a further connection between human and divine forgiveness, that so long as Israel is merciful it will merit

God's mercy.[24] This represents the corollary of the foregoing view, for if God desires Israel to emulate divine compassion, then God can be expected to reward Israel for doing so. To be forgiving, then, is both to emulate God and to secure the blessings of God's own approval and compassion. In all, the view that God is infinitely forgiving conjoined with the belief that one is obligated to imitate God's ways provides one clear sanction for the duty to forgive.

But the doctrine of imitatio dei is not the only, or perhaps even the most far-reaching, traditional Jewish belief that generates a duty to forgive. Central to the entire tradition of biblical and rabbinic law is the conviction that God has entered into a special covenant with Israel. The terms of this covenant, set forth in the laws of the Torah, establish the duties that Israelites have toward one another, as well as toward God. This belief that both Israel's existence as a people and the laws that define the character of its society come directly from God has profound implications for its understanding of moral duties in general and of forgiveness in particular. Given Israel's covenant with God, moral duties to others are also absolute duties to God. It follows that duties such as assisting the poor or respecting the elderly in no way depend upon receiving like treatment in return. Precisely because these represent absolute duties to God, the personal feelings that one may have about a particular poor or elderly person, including feelings of animosity, cannot relieve one of the duties owed that person. This point emerges clearly when we examine the Scriptural rules that govern helping one's enemy and loving one's neighbor.

> If you meet your enemy's ox or his ass going astray, you shall surely bring it back to him again. If you see the ass of him that hates you lying under its burden, and would forbear to unload it, you shall surely unload it with him. (Exod. 23:4–5)
>
> You shall not hate your brother in your heart; you shall surely rebuke your neighbor, and not bear sin because of him. You shall not take vengeance, nor bear a grudge against the children of your people, but you shall love your neighbor as yourself: I am the Lord. (Lev. 19:17–18)

The rationale behind these injunctions against hating other Israelites, and by extension against acting on such hatred through callousness or revenge, is implicit in the very nature of Israel's covenant. Since, as I have said, one's obligation to treat others compassionately is a duty toward God, it makes no difference whatever if that person happens to be an enemy or a friend, whether that person has treated you fairly in the past or is likely to do so in the future. The implications of such a view for the question of forgiveness are easily discernable. No offense, whatever sort of moral gap it creates, can be adequate grounds for dissolving a relationship with the offender, for in itself this would be a violation of one's duty to God.

This perspective on human relationships with its consequences for forgiveness could not contrast more sharply with that offered by Lauritzen earlier. There, as we noted, social responsibilities were understood on a quasi-contractual model. If one party breaches the terms of the implied contract, by offending the other, the latter has the right to respond retributively, by dissolving the relationship entirely. From this perspective, a duty to forgive would unjustifiably restrict peoples' moral autonomy by binding them in relationships that could never be severed. Perhaps it is Kant's legacy to western moral thought that we tend to view individuals as autonomous beings and moral imperatives as deriving from this autonomous nature. In any event, such a view, which supports a social contract model of moral responsibility, is implicit in the philosophical paradigm that Lauritzen's essay presents. But, as we have seen from this analysis of the sources, precisely because the Jew's relationship to other members of the community is not voluntary or contractual, such concerns with the agents' moral autonomy are out of place.[25] The duty to forgive, then, rests upon a covenantal view of the Jew's relationship to others and on the sense of absolute duty that such a relationship entails.[26]

Moreover, viewed from the perspective of this covenantal relationship the duty to seek forgiveness, like the duty to grant it, is seen as an obligation to God. The strongest evidence for this is contained in another passage from the Mishnah that discusses the character of the Day of Atonement. "For transgressions that are between man and God the Day of Atonement effects atonement, but for transgressions that are between a man and his fellow the Day of Atonement effects atonement only if he has appeased his fellow."[27] Implicit in this passage is the view that a sin against another individual entails a sin against God as well. In this context we can understand the point Maimonides makes about the duty to seek forgiveness even if the offended individual has died and so is unable to grant it. As we recall, the offender must assemble the community (a quorum of ten) at the individual's grave and say, "I have sinned against the Lord and this individual." Precisely because an interpersonal offense entails a sin against God the offender is not relieved of his responsibility to seek forgiveness even when the offended individual dies. But by making the offended individual's forgiveness a prerequisite for God's, the sages of the Mishnah are making a more profound point. Seeking forgiveness from the offended person is simultaneously taking a step toward reconciliation with God. Indeed, one cannot achieve such a reconciliation without first fulfilling one's duty toward that person. Thus, the restoration of a proper relationship with God is not only the consequence but also the goal of seeking forgiveness.

We may conclude, therefore, that the Jewish view of forgiveness implicitly rejects the view embedded in much of western moral philosophy that persons are autonomous beings whose relationships with one another are based in general on a contractual model. Within Judaism one is not an autonomous moral agent, but a member of a covenanted community. This covenant, established through a historic act of divine revelation, determines the Jew's most profound moral obligations not as an individual human being, but as a member of a holy community with a special relationship to its God. Among these obligations is the duty to imitate divine perfection, especially God's love and compassion for humankind. From this vantage point, the passage from *The Merchant of Venice* with which this chapter opens takes on an ironic dimension. For it is Shylock, the Jew, who is chastised for his harsh legalism and his insistence on exacting his due under the law. He shuns that attitude of compassion that alone could lend his actions divine sanction. But, as we have seen, the tradition that Shylock is intended to represent could never condone such an attitude. Indeed, Judaism maintains that human morality must be infused with qualities of divine benevolence in ways that Shakespeare, judging from his portrayal of Shylock, did not comprehend. In the case of forgiveness, at least, the Judaic tradition clearly holds that the demands of human justice and the quality of divine mercy are entirely compatible and even integrally related.

Let us return finally to the original question that Lauritzen raised, namely, how does religious belief affect the way we perceive our ethical duties. On the basis of this examination of forgiveness, we may conclude that within the Judaic tradition religious belief helps to shape moral judgments in at least two distinct ways. First, it provides a conception of the deity that serves as the model for human perfection. Thus, the belief in a God who is compasionate and forgiving will have direct consequences for one's obligations toward others. This is especially apparent in the case of the duty to forgive, since within the Jewish tradition, forgiveness is regarded as one of God's most essential attributes. Moreover, the religious worldview of classical Judaism encompasses a myth about God's covenant with Israel that shapes the very way in which Jews view themselves and their relationships to one another. Within the context of these beliefs, moral duties toward others will be viewed as reflections of a more fundamental duty, to live in accordance with God's will. This means that one's obligation to act responsibly toward another cannot be altered by any personal offense that that individual may have committed. Thus, one has a duty to forgive, for one is obligated to preserve a relationship even with a person who has violated the terms of that bond.

The sources that we have examined, then, suggest that religion provides a certain vision of our relationship to God and of the purpose of our lives in terms of which our moral actions take on additional significance. In particular, a religious worldview may instruct us to view our relations with one another as having supernatural implications and these ramifications will be felt particularly in one's relationship with the divine being. This will tend to foster the belief that there is a great deal more at stake in preserving these relationships than the empirical evidence alone would suggest. This is the religious orientation that, within the Judaic tradition at least, provides the grounds for viewing forgiveness as both a moral duty to one's fellow and a religious duty to God.

Chapter 5

Jewish Theology and Bioethics

As I indicated in the preceding chapter, Jewish religious thought gives rise
to specific moral obligations that in a strictly philosophical context
might not exist. It follows that to understand any moral duty, such as that of
forgiveness, we must attend to the theological presuppositions that inform a
religious way of life. Here I turn my attention to issues of broad general concern in the area of bioethics and sketch the ways in which certain Jewish theological views shape moral obligations in this sphere of life.

I begin by explaining some of the classical theological underpinnings
that account, in large part, for the distinctive cast of Jewish bioethics. Traditional views about God's revelation of Torah to the Jewish people, the content
of that revelation and the unique relationship that it established between God
and Israel together create a distinctive context for classical Jewish ethics. I
then explore elements of a Jewish theology of creation that yield specific
moral principles and rules in biomedical ethics. Finally, I take up one of the
main challenges facing all religious ethicists today, namely, what contribution, if any, they can make to the discussion of bioethical issues in a secular,
pluralistic society. I suggest that Jewish ethics, in common with other systems
of religious ethics, can contribute to the larger societal discussion surrounding the ethics of biomedical technology. Moreover, I believe that it can do so
without compromising its distinctively religious character.

The Character of Traditional Jewish Ethics

It will be helpful to begin by considering briefly some of the ways in which
theology can shape a system of ethics. Once we have examined the general
case, we will be able to appreciate more fully the distinctive features of Jewish theological ethics. I construe "theology" here broadly to include religious

101

reflections of all sorts on the nature of divinity, of humanity, and/or of the relationship between them. These reflections may be systematic or fragmentary, included in a scriptural text or not, expressed in the language of philosophy or narrative or law or some other form.[1] In all its forms, theological reflection shapes ethical discourse first and foremost by providing an orientation toward human life and the natural world, including a sense of the meaning and telos of human existence. Theology tells us how the world is in reality and how it is meant to be.

For those committed to such a religious worldview, certain modes of moral reflection and patterns of behavior will seem "natural," simply an extension of the way one conceives reality. Clifford Geertz has expressed this relationship between a religious "worldview" and "ethos" succinctly.

> The powerfully coercive 'ought' is felt to grow out of a comprehensive factual 'is,' and in such a way religion grounds the most specific requirements of human action in the most general context of human existence. . . . Sacred symbols thus relate an ontology and a cosmology to an aesthetics and a morality: their peculiar power comes from their presumed ability to identify fact with value at the most fundamental level.[2]

It follows that to understand the moral views of a religious community we must look to its most basic assumptions about the nature of things—its ontology and cosmology, that is, its "theology."

When we attempt to analyze Judaism in this way, we encounter serious difficulties. Most obviously, a religious tradition that has flourished within many diverse cultural contexts over a period of some 3,000 years has developed more than one theology and corresponding system of ethics. Any attempt to generalize about "Jewish theology and ethics" will necessarily gloss over important historical variations.[3] Nonetheless, arguably, there exists a core of religious beliefs so fundamental that they are simply assumed by all traditional Jewish theologians across the centuries. In particular, universally accepted views about the nature of Torah as God's revelation have determined the basic method utilized by traditional thinkers (and, as we shall see, by many contemporary ones as well).

For the writers of the Hebrew Bible, God's definitive revelation occurred at Mt. Sinai, when the Torah was given to the Jewish people. Torah itself means "instruction" and, while Scripture instructs in many ways, Jewish tradition has always assumed that God's will is most fully revealed through Scripture's "statutes and ordinances" But, for the rabbis of the first century

C.E. and beyond, God's will was not fully contained within the words of Scripture. The biblical rules required amplification and elaboration as they were applied to changing circumstances. Moreover, the rabbis felt themselves invested with the authority, itself rooted in Scripture, to promulgate new laws as the need arose. Thus, Jewish law, or *halakha*, came to include not only Scriptural injunctions, but the entire body of rabbinic literature from ancient times to the present. From the standpoint of the tradition, this vast corpus of legal, interpretive, and homiletical literature was understood as part of God's ongoing revelation. For rabbinic Judaism, as Gershom Scholem put it, "revelation comprises within it everything that will ever be legitimately offered to interpret its [Scripture's] meaning."[4]

The methodology of Jewish ethics flows directly from this theology of revelation. The Jewish ethicist discovers within God's revelation norms that can guide us in the present. The traditional rabbi, much like judges in a common law system, finds the proper precedents within this biblical and rabbinic literature and then applies them to the case at hand. To be sure, Jewish values sometimes are gleaned from nonlegal sources as well, including historical narratives, the virtuous examples of biblical and rabbinic figures, homilies, sermons, and the like. In addition, philosophical modes of reasoning sometimes influence Jewish ethicists. But classical Jewish ethicists never construct their arguments in purely philosophical terms. They do not determine the correct course of action either by reference to some fixed notion of human nature or by an analysis of which means can be expected to maximize certain ends. Nor would they posit a few principles (as, for example, some Christian ethicists posit *agape*) as the foundation of the moral life. For Jewish ethics, what God wants of us can be determined only by careful analysis of a certain body of religious-legal texts. Thus, when asked to articulate a Jewish ethical position, a rabbi will draw almost exclusively on the legal discussions in the Talmud and related literature.

This legalistic quality of Jewish ethics is apparent in contemporary Jewish discussions of euthanasia, as I demonstrate at greater length in chapter 8. When asked whether it is permissible to disconnect a comatose patient from a respirator or other life-support equipment, rabbis will search for legal precedents. And, given the belief that this legal tradition is an expression of God's will, and that God surely has provided guidance for all our moral questions, precedents *will* be found. In this instance, a certain thirteenth-century German pietistic text figures prominently in the discussion. It states that if a person is in "the throes of death" (Hebrew, *goses*) and the only obstacle preventing this person's dying is the noise of a nearby woodchopper, we make the woodchopper stop so that the individual can die. Using simple analogical, judicial reasoning some modern Jewish ethicists argue that respirators, like the noise of the woodchopper, are simply impediments to death and so can be removed. Other authorities reject this analogy, noting that the respirator serves a legitimate therapeutic function, unlike the noise of the woodchopper, which is simply an annoyance. Hence, they reason the rule governing the latter should not be applied to the former. Still others argue that the woodchopper case is not applicable to a respirator because the comatose person can be kept alive indefinitely and so is not technically "in the throes of death."

Other talmudic and medieval legal texts figure in the debate in similar ways. In each rabbi's analysis, legal precedents are cited and analyzed using methods of legal reasoning. These include the effort to discern analogies and disanalogies among cases, to distill principles from a series of precedents, and to apply these resources to the adjudication of novel problems. Of course, the possibilities and limitations of a particular analogy will continually be reexamined by subsequent authorities. On one level, modern ethicists may view such a legalistic approach as archaic, ill-suited to the complexities of modern, biomedical issues. By the same token, however, it must be noted that *halakha* is not as formalistic or rigid as is often supposed. A fuller understanding of halakhic process reveals its remarkably pluralistic and flexible character.

Like all legal systems that rely primarily on the interpretation of precedents, *halakha* has an open-ended quality. Since no two cases are ever precisely alike, the question of whether or not to apply an earlier ruling is almost always an open one. As the famous legal theorist Karl Llewelyn put it, each precedent really has two meanings for subsequent jurists, depending on whether one chooses to apply it broadly or narrowly.[5] In common law systems such as *halakha*, decisions about the application of precedents entail making judgments that the precedents themselves do not dictate. They generally are based on a variety of factors—common sense, promoting broad social goals, and the practical limitations of a functioning legal system. In *halakha* there are few, if any, generally accepted procedural rules to dictate when and how an individual rabbi can exercise discretion in applying precedents.[6] To be sure, at times general jurisprudential principles or procedural norms have been articulated as, for example, that earlier authorities should be given greater weight than later ones, or that no rule should be promulgated if the community cannot reasonably be expected to observe it. But historically these have never been uniformly adopted. It should not be surprising, therefore, that rabbinic debates sometimes appear to continue endlessly, as different authorities select, interpret, and apply precedents that themselves have been variously applied by many earlier generations of authorities.

But *halakha* is unusually flexible, even among common law systems, because historically it has been decentralized. With the possible exception of a brief period in ancient times when, according to tradition, a supreme court (Sanhedrin) had ultimate jurisdiction over Jews in Palestine, there has never been a heirarchy of courts with increasing degrees of authority. Consequently, each rabbi, individually or in consultation with his peers, would render decisions for his own community.[7] This means that similar cases arising in different communities would often be decided differently, depending on the judgments of the local authorities and the prevailing customs in that place. Authorities draw upon a large repertoire of often conflicting opinions all of which can potentially be cited as valid precedents.

Finally, as indicated by my analysis of law and ethics in chapter 2, within *halakha* legal and religious elements have never been clearly and consistently distinguished. On the one hand, *halakha*, like all functioning legal systems, is responsive to a whole range of social pressures and practical constraints. In this sense, its purpose is limited—to ensure a functioning, stable society. Unlike most other legal systems, however, *halakha* has also been understood as the embodiment of God's will. In this sense, its purpose is nothing less than imitatio dei, the imitation of God, and any pious behavior consistent with this goal will tend to be concretized in legal rulings. This tension has important implications for understanding the legal process. Clearly, rabbis with differing philosophies of *halakha* (or even a single rabbi who does not adopt one philosophy consistently) will approach the same case with differing assumptions about the purpose of the law, its scope, and the proper way to interpret and apply precedents.

Given these characteristics of *halakha*—its open-endedness, lack of centralized authority, and peculiar legal/religious character—one can begin to appreciate both its complexity and diversity. Classical Jewish ethics is legalistic, but not mechanical or formalistic. Indeed, within such a system diversity of opinion was not only inevitable, but openly fostered. As the Talmud says concerning the early disputes between the sages Hillel and Shammai, "Both these and those are the words of the living God."[8] Yet, one point was universally affirmed—that the law, in its totality, with all its multiformity, constituted divine revelation. Consequently, it constituted the primary, if not the only, source of ongoing moral guidance for Jews.

The second main methodological feature of classical Jewish ethics is its particularism. Traditional Judaism is deeply nationalistic and, in a sense, ethnocentric. Unlike Christianity, which, virtually from its inception, understood its divine revelation as valid for all human beings, Judaism always understood its revelation as given exclusively to a single nation, the Jews. And unlike philosophical ethics, which concerns the moral life of humans qua humans, Jewish ethics concerns the moral life of a certain people with a unique relationship to God. Jewish ethics is of Jews, by Jews, and for Jews. To be sure, Jews address ethical issues of general human concern, and sometimes reflect on the ethical responsibilities of non-Jews.[9] But these concerns are generally peripheral to their central focus. Given the theological assumption of the entire tradition, that God entered into a unique and exclusive covenant with the Jewish people, this could hardly have been otherwise. Yet, there are sociological, as well as theological, reasons for the particularism of Jewish ethics. Historically, Jews rarely have exercised political power over non-Jews. Insofar as rabbis had authority only over the Jewish community, they had little reason to address themselves to moral issues affecting the wider society, unless some specifically Jewish concern was at stake.

Turning our attention from classical to contemporary Jewish ethics we can see both radical shifts of perspective and points of continuity. Many modern Jews, in the aftermath of Jewish emancipation and under the influence of historical criticism and humanistic values, rejected the traditional view of revelation. Most modern Jewish thinkers have considered Scripture (as well as the whole of the rabbinic tradition) to be, at best, one imperfect expression of God's will. For liberals, all revelations are limited by the historical circumstances in which the divine word is written and transmitted.[10] For them, moral questions can no longer be answered simply by reference to the norms and rulings of previous generations. Moreover, many modern Jewish thinkers, like their Christian counterparts, have been skeptical of religious authority, preferring to vest religious power in the conscience of the individual or the democratic processes of the religious community. By the same token, they have tended to be less chauvinistic about God's revelation to Israel, recognizing that truth is not the exclusive possession of any one religious or cultural group.

This more liberal view of revelation has clear implications for Jewish ethics. In particular, the legal method of classical Jewish ethics has been supplemented (though by no means supplanted) by other approaches. To be sure, there are still many "orthodox" scholars for whom Jewish ethics continues to function solely within the framework of *halakha*. Indeed, the majority of the work on biomedical issues has been produced by orthodox rabbis.[11] The writings of J. David Bleich typify this approach:

> not all bioethical problems are questions of black and white. . . . A person who seeks to find answers within the Jewish tradition can

deal with such questions in only one way. He must examine them through the prism of Halakhah for it is in the corpus of Jewish law as elucidated and transmitted from generation to generation that God has made His will known to man.[12]

But the works of conservative rabbis (such as David Feldman, Elliot Dorff, David Novak) and reform rabbis (such as Solomon Freehof) are marked by a less legalistic understanding of revelation. For these writers, Jewish law is not the only (and for some, not even the best) resource for doing contemporary Jewish ethics. Even when their arguments rely heavily on the interpretation of classical legal sources, they utilize the tools of historical criticism and bring to their exegetical work an appreciation (to varying degrees) for liberal, democratic values. Moreover, because they are more open to the possibility that divine truth can be found outside the Jewish tradition, they tend to develop their positions in dialogue with other philosophical and Christian ethicists.

Interestingly, particularism has remained a striking feature of contemporary Jewish ethics, notwithstanding the shift toward more liberal theological views. Most contemporary authors have written for Jewish audiences in an idiom that is often inaccessible to non-Jews. Little effort has been made to translate their reflections into forms more familiar to those outside the Jewish community. Indeed, it is no easy matter to find philosophical grounds within Jewish tradition itself for the extension of Jewish ethical norms to non-Jews (without relying on the unworkable assumption that non-Jews must accept the authority of Jewish law). Only one scholar to my knowledge has devoted sustained attention to this problem.[13]

Moreover, anyone scanning the contemporary Jewish literature would note that on many important issues in bioethics Jewish authorities have had little to say. These include questions about the distribution of scarce medical resources, the social policies that should govern the availability of organs for transplantation, guidelines for AIDS testing, and the economic ethics of our health care delivery system. In all the books on Jewish medical ethics to appear in recent years, there is virtually no attempt to address any of these social policy issues.[14] Perhaps this is not surprising. After all, the vast resources of the Jewish legal/ethical tradition were never designed to apply to non-Jews.

Some Principles of Jewish Biomedical Ethics

Up to this point I have argued that the methodology of classical Jewish ethics, which is basically legalistic and particularistic, follows directly from central theological beliefs about revelation. Moreover, in modern times, the methods employed by some Jewish ethicists have changed partly in response to changing views of revelation. Let me turn now from matters of method to questions of content. Here, too, I hope to show that theology is of the essence. Admitedly, scholars rarely develop moral positions by reflecting directly on theological categories since, as I have explained, ethical deliberation proceeds primarily through analysis of legal precedents. Still, theological categories provide a useful heuristic device for analyzing the thrust of Jewish medical ethics. In the first place, theological concepts constitute the ideological substructure of much of the law, and, in addition, particular theological views often guide specific interpretations of the legal tradition.[15] In biomedical ethics specifically, the category of creation figures prominently, since the story of creation concerns the origin, value, and purpose of human life.

The creation story in Genesis is often cited, by both Jewish and Christian ethicists, as the source of the view that human life is sacred. Yet, while both Jews and Christians agree that human life is sacred, they have often reached significantly different conclusions about the moral implications of this theological assertion. The question is what "sacredness" means and how it translates into specific norms. I want to suggest that, for Jewish ethicists, the sacredness of human life translates into several distinct but related sets of principles that, in turn, are exemplified in a variety of specific rules. While the following analysis is sketchy, it should suffice to demonstrate some of the ways in which a Jewish theology of creation shapes biomedical ethics.[16]

> God created man in His image, in the image of God He created him, male and female He created them. (Gen. 1:27)

In the Genesis account only human beings are singled out as reflections of God's own image. Human life is holy because it shares something of the essence of divinity. That human life is sacred means, in the first place, that *it possesses intrinsic and infinite value*. Its value is absolute, not susceptible to quantification and not relative to the value of anything extrinsic to it. Thus, Jewish scholars traditionally have rejected any argument evaluating human life in terms of its "quality," for this implies that its value is relative to some other good, such as health or happiness or consciousness. Accordingly, rabbinic authorities have not sanctioned measures that shorten one's life simply because ordinary physical or mental capacities have been compromised. Similarly, they have not supported the abortion of fetuses with known or suspected abnormalities, since a low quality of life in no way diminishes its sacredness.

The sanctity of life generates a second major principle of Jewish ethics, that *the preservation of life is the highest moral imperative.* The rabbis were especially sensitive to those situations in which obedience to the law conflicted with the preservation of life. Since the law, like life itself, comes from God, a moral conflict between them is especially profound. But the tradition resolves all such conflicts in favor of the preservation of life. Thus, to treat a critically ill person one can violate the laws of the Sabbath, prepare non-Kosher food, and so on.[17] Moreover, if there is any doubt whatever as to the condition of the patient, we err on the side of preserving life. By the same token, Jewish law proscribes individuals from engaging in life-threatening activities, unless of course they do so in the interest of saving another life. Thus, experimental procedures with significant (or unknown) risks are never mandatory and often not recommended, except in cases where performing the procedure is necessary for saving a life.

The view that human life is sacred implies a third central principle, that *all lives are equal.* Because Jewish tradition offers no criteria for valuing one life more highly than another, issues of triage are especially problematic. As one handbook of Jewish medical ethics puts it,

> This is the foundation for the practice of triage, and is fundamentally incompatible with Jewish values and Jewish law. Since, in Judaism, all human life is equally sacred, including each moment of an individual's life . . . no selection is justifiable among those with the need for, and the possibility, however slim, of cure.[18]

It seems that only a random or arbitrary system of allocating scarce medical resources (among patients who need the resource equally) is compatible with the sanctity of life, as Jewish scholars have understood it.

The sanctity of human life gives rise to a fourth important tenet of Jewish medical ethics, that *our lives are not really our own.* Human life is not even a gift so much as a loan, which we possess conditionally and ultimately must return to its source. Thus, Jewish ethics allows little room for notions of personal autonomy that figure so prominently in Kantian ethics. The implications of this perspective are especially evident in discussions of abortion. Rabbinic authorities over the centuries have tended to permit abortion in cases where the mother's life or health (including possibly her psychological health) is endangered. In this sense, and only in this sense, the tradition does recognize distinctions between lives—the actual life of the mother clearly takes precedence over the potential life of the fetus. But the notion that a mother could terminate a pregnancy for any reason whatever on the grounds that she has a right to control what happens to her own body is entirely foreign to Jewish tradition. The fetus, though not regarded as fully a "person," is still alive, and insofar as all human life is sacred, it can be terminated only for the most compelling reason, in order to preserve other lives. This same principle emerges in Jewish discussions of suicide. One does not have a right to take one's own life, even under the most debilitating circumstances.

Similarly, we do not control the timing or circumstances of our death. This undergirds the leniency among many traditional authorities with respect to treatment of the dying. When a person is in a moribund state, we are not required to prolong the moment of death. The principle of "sit and do nothing" is consistent with the view that God controls the ultimate disposition of our lives. When death is imminent, it is a sign of humble resignation before God's will to refrain from action.

Finally, as understood by Jewish authorities, *the sacredness of human life inheres in the human being as a whole*, both body and soul. Indeed, the Hebrew term "nefesh," used in Genesis 2:7 ("Then the Lord God formed the man, dust from the earth, and breathed into his nostrils the breath of life, and he became a living being [*nefesh*]") refers to both the physical and spiritual dimensions of a human being. Thus, as one traditional scholar puts it, "Man is created . . . in the image of God; an assult upon the body of the deceased thus constitutes an act of disrespect toward God."[19] As a result, autopsies are permitted in very few circumstances, generally when the results will save another human life. And this must be a specific individual; the possibility that the knowledge gained from desecrating a human body may one day help save some unknown person's life is generally held to be insufficient warrant. Similarly, organ transplantation, either from living donors or from cadavers, is permissible only when the recipient's life is at risk. Otherwise, this constitutes a violation of the sanctity of the human body.[20] Plastic surgery is problematic from a Jewish point of view because it involves unnecessary "wounding" of the body, which belongs to God. Beautification in itself is not generally regarded as sufficient reason for cosmetic surgery, unless the psychological or financial well-being of the patient depends upon it.

The foregoing analysis represents only a general orientation within Jewish medical ethics. It must be emphasized again that very significant differences of opinion exist, both within the classical texts themselves and, by extension, among contemporary interpreters of the tradition. Needless to say, even where there is broad consensus at the level of general principles, there may be substantial disagreement at the level of specific, and often highly complex, cases. By their nature, general principles of this sort function in rather indeterminate ways. Even principles as weighty as the sanctity of human life are bound to conflict at times with other principles, and then the priority assigned to each will depend on the judgment of the individual interpreter.[21] So, for example, some scholars have noted that, even within the tradition, the sanctity of life is not an absolute value, for the law sanctions capital punishment as well as martyrdom. This suggests that there may be times when it is permissible, or even required, to sacrifice a person's life for the sake of some greater good (of the community, or of God). The creative theologian/ethicist will seize upon these tensions within the tradition and seek to draw out their implications for cases involving abortion or euthanasia or other medical issues.[22]

The fact that we cannot specify how a given theological doctrine will be translated into concrete judgments in no way detracts from the point of this exercise—that theology permeates Jewish biomedical ethics. At times, as we have seen, these connections are drawn quite explicitly. At other times, the ethicist may fail to articulate his or her operative theological principles, or even to be fully conscious of them. If Geertz is correct, the move from ontology to ethics may seem so natural that only through subsequent analysis can the link between them be uncovered. This much, in any event, is clear. Jewish attitudes toward human life and death, and especially toward lives that are only potential or seriously compromised or threatened, reflect deeply rooted theological commitments.

Jewish Medical Ethics in a Wider Context

By now it should be apparent that Jewish tradition provides a rich resource for reflection on biomedical issues. But of what use is this tradition to those who address these issues in the public forum? What role, if any, could Jewish bioethics play in contemporary debates on these issues in our society? To many, the prospect of introducing theological arguments into public discussions of biomedical issues seems fraught with difficulties. In the first place, it appears that the secular, pluralistic character of our society is undermined if we begin to address moral issues in theological terms. On the other hand, it is sometimes suggested that theologians can play a role in public debate only if they translate their claims into a kind of neutral, secular discourse. Yet, even if this is possible, doing so appears to compromise the integrity of the religious views themselves. Thus, by bringing theology into our common discussion of moral problems, we threaten either the religious neutrality of our society or the theological commitments of the religious ethicist, or both.

We can, if we choose, avoid this conflict entirely. Following Stanley Hauerwas, we can argue that religious ethicists should not attempt to translate their distinctive value systems into terms accessible to "outsiders." Their goal ought to be the creation of a moral community among believers, not the conversion (or even influencing) of nonbelievers. Hauerwas expresses this position quite clearly in relation to the ethics of caring for mentally retarded persons. Moreover, he claims that our general moral discourse is not adequate to express specifically Christian moral convictions.[23] Yet, many religious ethicists (and I suspect most Jewish ethicists among them) will reject this view, for they feel responsible to contribute to the moral improvement of the larger society.

How can this be done? To answer this, we must first meet the objection that the very religious character of theological ethics disqualifies it from public debate. On this view, the religious roots of a moral position "infect" it, such that urging the adoption of that position is, in effect, a form of proselytizing. But surely this is an oversimplification of the relationship between theology and ethics. At very least, it fails to allow for the fact that some nonreligious persons may be persuaded by moral arguments whose theological premises they do not accept. Lisa Sowle Cahill has made this point forcefully:

> public bioethical discourse (or public policy discourse) is actually a meeting ground of the diverse moral traditions that make up our society. Some of these moral traditions have religious inspiration, but that does not necessarily disqualify them as contributors to the broader discussion. Their contributions will be appropriate and effective to the extent that they can be articulated in terms with a broad if not universal appeal.[24]

It would seem that American constitutional jurisprudence has affirmed a parallel principle with respect to the establishment of religion. In dealing with the constitutionality of Sunday closing laws, the Supreme Court has held that, notwithstanding their religious origins, these statutes are proper if they can be shown to serve a legitimate secular goal.[25] If the historically religious origins of a practice or institution do not preclude its having valid nonreligious functions, the same can surely be said for ethical views with historically religious origins.

Next, we must meet the objection from the other side, that theologians cannot speak in a language accessible and acceptable to a secular society without betraying their own religious convictions. Here it must be admitted that certain sorts of religious arguments cannot by their nature play a role in public discourse. Appeals to specific religious authorities, for example, will convince only those who already accept the legitimacy of that authority. Thus, non-Catholics would remain unconvinced by appeals to the authority of the magisterium. Similarly, no Jewish ethicist could expect that citing halakhic texts would add to the moral force of his or her argument for a non-Jewish audience. Specifically religious authorities cannot play a meaningful role in moral suasian within a pluralistic society.

Nonetheless, certain aspects of religious traditions may legitimately contribute to public moral discourse. Specifically, as Cahill notes, those principles, values, or rules that people find compelling independent of their theological origins will play the most significant role. This is apparent if we reflect for a moment on the principles articulated earlier in connection with the sanctity of life. One need not refer to the biblical account of creation (much less regard it as God's revelation) to be persuaded that human life is infinitely precious. Nor, as secular humanists attest, need one be a theist to regard the preservation of human life, or the essential equality of all human lives, as moral principles of the highest order. Again, no Jewish ethicist would expect that these principles, or the rules that flow from them, would be regarded in the same fashion by non-Jews as they are by Jews. But neither does the theological source of these moral principles preclude them from resonating with the moral intuitions of nonreligious individuals. After all, western civilization as a whole, and perhaps the American experience in particular, has been shaped by beliefs, themes, and values found in the Hebrew Bible (refracted, to be sure, through Christianity). Even secular-minded Americans are likely to find many Jewish concepts at least somewhat familiar and potentially attractive.[26]

Allowing, then, that a theologian's religious convictions do not preclude making a contribution to public debates in bioethics, but also that that contribution will necessarily be limited to values that are intelligible outside of a strictly theological context, I return to the central question. In what ways might a Jewish theology of creation contribute to bioethical discussion within a pluralistic society? I want now to suggest that at every level of moral discourse—about obligations, values, and virtues—Jewish theology could offer distinctive perspectives.[27]

A Jewish ethic would stress certain obligations in connection both with terminating and saving human lives. In the abortion debate, Jewish ethics would stake a middle ground between those who claim that a pregnant woman has the right to destroy her fetus for any reason at all and those who argue that abortion is morally indistinguishable from murdering any other living human being. Jewish ethics recognizes that the fetus is a form of human life and so has some claim upon us. On the other hand, its claim is not as strong as that of the mother whose life and health (including, for some, her mental health) must be protected.

In cases involving the allocation of scarce medical resources, especially organs for transplantation, Jewish ethics would urge us to adopt a position of radical equality among persons. Because all lives are from God, all have prima facie the same right to survive. We should not discriminate on the basis of sex, age, social condition, economic status, or any other factor, nor permit those who publicize their plight to "jump ahead" of others. With respect to questions of euthanasia there is substantial disagreement among Jewish scholars but also a general consensus that we are not universally required to do everything in our power to save the life of the dying. Recognizing God's sovereignty means accepting the fact that "there is a time to be born and a time to die" (Eccles. 3:2).

With respect to values, a Jewish theology of creation would affirm that human life contains a spark of the divine and so is an awesome mystery. It must never be viewed or treated as a possession or commodity. This has implications especially in the area of reproductive technology, where certain procedures tend to reinforce the view that human life can be manipulated to suit our needs. Examples might include surrogate motherhood, which treats conception and pregnancy as a service that can be bought, and the practice of in vitro fertilizing and implanting numerous eggs with the intention of selectively eliminating those that are not needed. From the standpoint of traditional Jewish theology, these activities could only be seen as demeaning human life, as a violation of the ultimate sanctity of humankind.

Finally, a Jewish ethic would tend to emphasize the virtue of humility. Recent advances in medicine have given us the power to cure disease and extend human life in ways unimaginable only a generation ago. On the whole that power has been enormously beneficial, but Jewish theology would urge us to consider the risks of exercising it too readily. As we increasingly control the material conditions affecting life and death, we may lose sight of the modest role that we are called upon to play in the unfolding of life on this planet. As we set out to decode the human genome, for example, Jewish ethics would call on us to remember that our task is to enhance and nurture the life that God gives us, not necessarily to redesign our lives or make us into "more perfect" creatures. To be sure, the lines of permissibility in this area are difficult to draw, and certainly no easier for Jewish theologians than for anyone else. But Jewish ethics would urge us to see ourselves as servants, not masters, of human life and so to approach our task with a deep sense of humility.

The religious ethicist, then, can play a constructive role in shaping public policy by doing what theologians have always done—directing our attention to dimensions of the human situation that may have escaped our notice. By expanding our vision of who we are and what kind of world we live in, they can deepen our appreciation of the moral dilemmas we face and of the options available to us for responding to them. Jewish ethicists who wish to contribute to the larger public debate about bioethics need not jettison their theological convictions. They need only recognize that their views have varying degrees of relevance to various audiences, depending upon the degree to which those audiences find these religious views consonant with their own moral intuitions. Religious ethicists (no matter what their denominational affiliation) should not feel they have compromised their integrity just because their message to "outsiders" is more limited than to members of their own religious communities. In the broader "marketplace of ideas" their view will be only one among many, and frequently in the minority. But this does not diminish the importance of the distinctive contribution they can make, nor the possibility that others who hear them might just be led to see their moral lives differently.

Chapter 6

Nature and Torah, Creation and Revelation

On the Possibility of a Natural Law in Judaism

The preceding chapter demonstrated that Jewish theology shapes both the form and substance of Jewish biomedical ethics. But theological commitments can inform ethical theory as well as practice. That is, the very way in which we conceptualize the nature of Jewish ethics reflects certain theological presuppositions. Here I consider two apparently incompatible views, first that Judaism affirms a universal, rational ethic, a kind of "natural law," and second, that Jewish ethics is particularistic rather than universal, grounded in revelation rather than reason. Both views, I believe, rest on certain theological premises, about nature and Torah, creation and revelation, and the relationships between them.

Natural law theory has a long and complex history in western ethics and jurisprudence.[1] Its origins may be traced to the Stoic dictum "Follow nature." Via Platonic idealism and Aristotelian teleological thinking, it became the centerpiece of Aquinas' moral theory, thereby securing a preeminent place in all subsequent Catholic moral theology.[2] In ancient times, it was closely identified with the *ius gentium*, that body of Roman law that applied to all noncitizens of Rome. During the Enlightenment, it found adherents in legal and moral thinkers such as Grotius, Hobbes, and Locke and had a profound influence on the doctrine of "natural rights" that lies at the heart of American legal and political theory. Among contemporary scholars, natural law theory permeates the work of Josef Fuchs,[3] Germaine Grisez,[4] and John Finnes,[5] and appears in more attenuated forms in the thought of John Rawls, Lon Fuller, and even avowed positivists like H.L.A. Hart.[6]

117

Given the richness and persistence of the natural law tradition, it is hardly surprising that Jewish thinkers for centuries have explored the extent to which natural law plays a role in Jewish jurisprudence. The issue has been complicated by the fact that natural law doctrines have taken so many forms, sometimes being linked to a specific concept of the *telos* of human life, sometimes to a concept of rationality as the basis of moral obligation, at times functioning as a theory of "natural morality," and at other times as a criterion for distinguishing between valid and invalid law. Reading the literature on Jewish natural law, one quickly realizes that participants in the debate are talking past one another—a text that one author invokes as evidence for (or against) Jewish natural law another dismisses as entirely irrelevant. Thus, while scholars like Marvin Fox,[7] Jose Faur,[8] and Leo Strauss[9] have denied the very possibility of natural law in Judaism, Michael Levine,[10] J. David Bleich,[11] Robert Gordis,[12] and David Novak[13] have affirmed that natural law can and does play some role in traditional Jewish thought. Clearly, we will make no progress toward resolving this issue until we achieve some conceptual clarity about the character of natural law and especially the factors that account for its very uncertain place in the history of Judaism.

I begin by offering a definition of natural law that serves as a point of departure for this analysis. Plainly, until we are clear about what sort of position qualifies as a natural law theory, we cannot determine the extent to which Jewish thinkers have endorsed it. Next I uncover the assumptions that have framed the discussion and reexamine some of the texts that have figured centrally in this controversy. Finally, I suggest that how we understand the place of natural law thinking in Judaism depends fundamentally on how we interpret basic theological categories in the tradition—specifically creation, revelation, and the relationship between them. My thesis is that within the history of Jewish theology we can discern two divergent theories of the relationship between creation and revelation and that our assessment of natural law in Judaism depends finally on which of these two theories we adopt.

Natural Law: Issues of Definition

In the broadest sense, natural law can be understood as referring to "any moral philosophy or legal theory that posits 'objective' grounds for practical reason, or moral grounds for jurisprudence."[14] This very general definition highlights a certain ambiguity regarding natural law that must be addressed at the outset. Natural law sometimes serves as a theory of morality, sometimes as a theory of law. Indeed, it has often been suggested that natural law's greatest contribution to western thought is its insistence that law is (or ought to be) founded on morality. Thus, natural law theorists have suggested that the validity of law as an institution, or of particular sets of laws, depends upon their conformity to prior standards of morality. Laws that fail this test are not "bad laws" or "immoral laws," but actually not laws at all.[15] By the same token, natural law theorists have generally held that morality is grounded in "nature," meaning that there is a natural order and an innate human nature that determine certain basic moral truths. The term "natural law," then, denotes both a theory of law and a theory of ethics.[16]

The complexity of natural law doctrine is evident in the following frequently cited passage from Cicero:

> True law is right reason in agreement with Nature; it is of universal application, unchanging and everlasting. . . . It is a sin to try to alter this law, nor is it allowable to attempt to repeal any part of it, and it is impossible to abolish it entirely. We cannot be freed from its obligations by Senate or People, and we need not look outside ourselves for an expounder or interpreter of it. And there will not be different laws at Rome and at Athens, or different laws now and in the future, but one eternal and unchangeable law will be valid for all nations and for all times, and there will be one master and one ruler, that is, God, over us all, for He is the author of this law, its promulgator, and its enforcing judge.[17]

Cicero's view of an eternal and unchangeable law, created by God and consonant with nature represents one important formulation of the concept of natural law. But it is important to identify and analyze the distinct elements within Cicero's view, for they do not always appear linked in this configuration.

In this regard, the definition of natural law offered by Leo Strauss provides a useful starting point. "By natural law is meant a law which determines what is right and wrong and which has power or is valid by nature, inherently, hence everywhere and always."[18] This definition highlights the first and most obvious criterion of natural law, that it must be "natural," something that is independent of human decision and prior to all human lawmaking or norm-setting. Natural law is discovered, not invented. It is "built in" to the fabric of the world and, in particular, to the very nature of human beings. Natural law, thus, stands in opposition to the entire tradition of western moral thought from Hume onward that insists upon a radical disjuncture between "is" and "ought," that from the way things are we can draw no conclusions about how they ought to be.[19] Natural law theorists, by contrast, believe that the "nature of things" does provide a source from which the basic principles of morality can be derived. And, as Strauss rightly notes, from the notion that this moral order is inherent in human nature, it immediately follows that it is universally valid. Natural law, then, is believed to transcend the values and laws of particular cultures and countries, of all historical periods and places.[20]

A related but separate criterion of natural law is stated succinctly by Joseph Boyle. Natural law refers "to a set of universal prescriptions whose prescriptive force is a function of the rationality that all human beings share in virtue of their common humanity."[21] This definition focuses our attention on how natural law is discovered, namely, through reason. It is through our rational faculty that we recognize order in the world. Unlike other animals, we are able to discern both the physical and the moral laws of nature because we have been endowed with the gift of reason. And because reason is the common possession of all humankind, it assures universal access to the natural law (in theory, if not in actual practice).[22]

It is important to note here that these two criteria represent related, but logically separate, dimensions of natural law. There is a *substantive*, in a sense metaphysical, aspect of natural law, embodied in the claim that there exists a set of moral norms the *content* of which is dictated by *nature*. And there is an *epistemological* aspect of natural law, embodied in the claim that human *reason*, which is universal, enables us to discern its principles.

It should be apparent, on the one hand, that these two criteria of natural law are closely related. Natural law is unchanging and universal, first because it is dictated by the natural order (which is understood as unchanging) and second because it is known through reason (which is understood as capable of grasping the necessary truths of nature). In a sense, the universality of natural law is twofold: it is both *applicable to* and (in principle) *knowable by* all people.

On the other hand, it should also be apparent that the substantive and epistemological aspects of natural law theory are logically separate. One could hold, for example, that reason provides access to a set of moral norms that are universally applicable but that do not derive from human nature or the order of the natural world. Kant is perhaps the most obvious example of a philosopher who held that reason dictates a set of universal moral principles, but who regarded these as postulates of practical reason, not dictated by human nature.[23]

In addition, it should be noted that natural law in the sense discussed here is rooted in an anthropology or theory of humankind. In its classical Thomist form, natural law presupposed that human beings have an innate nature and an unchanging *telos*, or purpose. If the goals of human life are inherent and invariable, it follows that that which promotes the realization of those goals is naturally "good," and must be pursued, while that which impedes the realization of those goals is naturally "evil" and should be avoided. Post-Enlightenment natural law theorists (at least outside the Roman Catholic tradition) have generally jettisoned the teleological assumptions behind the classical theory because they can identify no self-evident *telos* or set of goals that all human beings are meant to pursue at all times and in all places. In its place, they emphasize the other aspect of natural law, that it can be derived wholly through reason.[24] Still in all, natural law theorists remain committed to the basic claim that some facets of human nature are universal and have moral implications for human life.

Finally, it should be recognized that natural law, at best, provides a set of general moral principles, not a full-fledged system of moral rules.[25] Explications of natural law invariably include prohibitions against murder, appropriation or destruction of another's property, and other norms necessary to a stable society. Even so, natural law theorists have generally acknowledged that the detailed rules necessary for governing social life are not dictated directly by natural law, but ought merely to be consistent with it. Natural law, then, is not a surrogate for "positive," humanly enacted law, but rather a set of a priori, universal moral principles that both ground and transcend all human moral and legal action.

Natural Law in Judaism: Redefining the Question, Reexamining the Texts

Relying upon this general exposition of natural law, we can proceed to ask whether Jewish tradition recognizes the existence of a universal moral law that is natural and/or rational. Before proceeding to a more detailed examination of the sources that bear on the question, we must attend to a few further preliminary matters. The very form of the question, "does Judaism recognize natural law?" appears to require a yes or no answer. The temptation to assume that such an answer is possible, like the widespread assumption that Judaism is an internally consistent system of religious belief and practice, is clearly misguided. Approached from a historical, critical perspective, Judaism is a single name for an array of religious beliefs and practices that have evolved over centuries in numerous intellectual and social contexts and that persist in perennial tension with one another. Yet, many authors, in their desire to reconcile the tensions within the tradition, assume that there could not be multiple and contradictory answers to this question. My point of departure, by contrast, is to recognize those tensions where they exist and to explore the reasons for them.

Notwithstanding this caveat, it must be acknowledged at the outset that nowhere in scriptural or classical rabbinic texts do we find a full-blown theory of natural law of the sort, for example, that Aquinas developed. Indeed, it is often noted that only one Jewish philosopher before modern times, the fifteenth-century Spanish thinker Joseph Albo, uses the term "natural law" at all and even he, it seems, does not accord natural law a place of great importance in Jewish ethics.[26]

The significance of this fact, however, should not be overrated. Rabbinic literature is notoriously nontheoretical and, at times, even overtly hostile to philosophical speculation.[27] We should not be surprised to discover, then, that there is no developed theory of natural law in classical rabbinic literature. Like so many other theoretical questions in ethics—such as the source of moral obligation or the relationship between ethics and law—answers must be constructed out of rabbinic texts that do not directly address such theoretical matters. Both halakhic (legal) and aggadic (nonlegal) sources can be richly suggestive in this regard. The absence of a natural law theory, then, reflects the nature of rabbinic discourse and does not in itself constitute evidence that Judaism rejects natural law thinking.

But there is a more substantive reason to suspect that natural law is foreign to the spirit of classical Judaic thought. It seems axiomatic that the ultimate source of moral and legal authority in Judaism is located in God's commandments as conveyed in Scripture and interpreted by the rabbis. This doctrine of "dual Torah," written and oral, defines the modes through which God communicates the divine will to Israel and thereby the parameters of classical Jewish moral and legal theory. And that theory would seem to require that Jewish moral and legal obligations flow, not from nature, but from the special and "supernatural" relationship between God and Israel. Moreover, these norms are understood by the community as authoritative, not because they are "rational" but because they are divine commands. Thus, the defining characteristics of natural law—being dictated by nature and being authoritative because of its rationality—appear to be at odds with fundamental principles of Jewish theology.

Precisely for these reasons, Marvin Fox has written, "In Judaism there is no natural law doctrine, and, in principle, there cannot be. . . ."[28] By way of explication, he adds, "In ancient Hebrew thought there is only one source of the knowledge of good and evil, the commandments of God as they are revealed to man."[29] In Fox's view, then, God's revelation is *the* source of moral truth and necessarily precludes any other source, whether in nature or in reason. Jose Faur has taken a similar position, arguing that in Judaism the absolute distance between God and humanity precludes there being any common ontological element, such as reason, which grounds the relationship between them. Moreover, he notes, many of the biblical rules usually identified with natural law may have applied only within the covenant community, rather than universally.[30] Thus, for Faur, as for Fox, the covenant between God and Israel is the sole context for Jewish moral teaching.[31]

No one familiar with the structure of classical Jewish theology can dispute the essential plausibility of the Fox-Faur thesis. Yet, we can concede that God's revelation to Israel and the covenant that it establishes are, indeed, the primary locus of moral/legal norms in Judaism without granting the extreme position they adopt. Even Fox acknowledges that there are occasional sources that appear to recognize a universal morality and, while he argues that none actually establishes what he would consider natural law, their existence suggests the possibility of a natural law, however modest, in Judaism. Indeed, as a survey of the literature reveals, there are many more such sources than either Fox or Faur acknowledge in their treatments of natural law in Judaism. Before proceeding to an examination of some of these texts, it will be useful at this point to reformulate the question. If, indeed, there is a kind of natural law tradition in Judaism, how would we recognize it?

Recall that the hallmarks of natural law are that it denotes a body of norms, either in the legal or the moral sphere, that are understood as (1) universal and (2) independent of positive, enacted law. The source of these norms is (to borrow terminology from the Roman Catholic natural law tradition) either in the "order of nature" or in the "order of reason." That is, natural law principles follow from the very structure of reality and especially from the essential, invariant features of human life and, in most natural law theories, are universally accessible through the exercise of human reason. The question of whether Judaism recognizes natural law, then, must be broken down into two separate (though, again, related) questions:

1. Can we find within classical Jewish sources evidence of moral norms that exist independent of the covenant between God and Israel and, if so, are these understood as linked necessarily to a concept of the natural order, (nature, rather than God's word, being authoritative), and/or

2. Can we find within classical Jewish sources evidence of moral norms that are "rational," that is, obligatory for all people

because reason dictates that they be followed, independent of Israel's covenantal responsibilities, (reason, rather than God's word, being authoritative)?

The first possibility, it should be noted, directs our attention to norms that exist outside the covenant, and so are applicable to all human beings qua human beings. The second possibility could also include norms that are communicated to Israel through divine revelation, but that would be obligatory by virtue of their rationality alone or, as one source puts it, "even if God had not commanded them." The existence of either sort of norm within the tradition would constitute evidence for the claim that Judaism embraces some version of natural law.

Natural Morality

Notwithstanding the view of Strauss and others that the biblical tradition is entirely lacking in a concept of "nature,"[32] the notion that there is a natural moral order is hardly foreign to biblical thought. Douglas Knight has noted that the cosmogonic myths in Genesis have powerful moral implications for human life.[33] In the Hebrew tradition, in contradistinction to other ancient Near Eastern cultures, the world is created by a divine being who possesses moral qualities. In Genesis 1, God evaluates the creative work of each day and pronounces it "good." The central theme of the second creation myth, in Genesis 2–3, as well as the dominant motif in other myths concerning the antedeluvian period, is the moral behavior of humanity. When Cain murders his brother Abel, God reprimands Cain with the words, "What have you done? The voice of your brother's blood cries out to me from the ground." (Gen. 4:10) Clearly, without having received any prior moral instruction, the exchange (and Cain's subsequent punishment) assumes that Cain should have known that his behavior was immoral. Later, God sees that "the wickedness of mankind is great in the earth" (Gen. 6:5) and so resolves to destroy the world, but Noah, who is "a just man and perfect in his generations," (Gen. 6:9) is saved. The emphasis on humans' responsibility for their actions, of course, is pervasive throughout the biblical tradition, and prophetic literature in particular focuses on Israel's failure to observe basic standards of moral behavior. But even independent of the Israelites' covenant with God, Knight demonstrates, the biblical authors conceived of God as establishing a moral relationship with humanity and of human beings as creatures capable of moral discernment. The fact the people are granted dominion over the natural world (Gen. 1:28), he notes, is but one more indication of this for, in the ancient Near Eastern context, such dominion presupposed a duty of care and responsibility.

Thus it seems evident that the biblical writers conceived of humanity as possessing the capacity for moral decision and an awareness (however undefined) of right and wrong that predates the covenant with Israel and the revelation of the Torah. The text of Scripture, of course, does not provide an account of how humanity comes to know its moral responsibilities, or even exactly what these are. But just as clearly it assumes that they exist. In this regard Knight notes,

> the order symbolically depicted in the [creation] myth correlates to the people's vision of order in the world, and thus also to the quality of life in this world and to the moral terms for living. Myth is less likely to dictate specific moral directives than it is to inscribe the general—and normative—contours for moral life. It can point to the nature and locus of the good, to the cosmic context of moral behavior, to the nature of moral agency, and to the significance of moral community. At the same time, the myth may indicate the threats to the moral life as well as the consequences of immoral conduct.[34]

Taken as a whole, Knight's analysis of Israelite cosmogony amounts to something less than a full-fledged theory of natural law in the Hebrew Bible, but it surely provides strong evidence that, for Israelite authors, human beings "in a state of nature" are invested with moral qualities and responsibilities. At very least, God holds people accountable for their moral deeds and misdeeds, quite apart from the specific legal duties generated by the covenant between God and Israel.

Possibly the most significant, and controversial, body of data that bears on the question of Jewish natural law concerns the so-called "Noahide laws." In his exhaustive and masterful study of this material, David Novak has demonstrated that the concept of a universal law, applicable to all descendants of Noah, arose in Tannaitic times and continued to be a source of theological and legal interest throughout the centuries.[35] In Tosefta Abodah Zarah 8:2 we find the following passage:

> Seven commandments were the sons of Noah commanded: concerning adjudication, concerning idolatry, concerning blasphemy, concerning sexual immorality, concerning bloodshed, concerning robbery and concerning a limb torn from a living animal.[36]

As Novak demonstrates, those who reflected on Noahide law did so from two perspectives. On the one hand, they regarded these seven commandments as the universal law applicable to all people. In this sense, Noahide law embodied a Jewish theory of non-Jewish ethics. On the other hand, they viewed Noahide law as reflecting the norms obligatory for Jews prior to the Sinaitic revelation. As Novak puts it, ". . . if revelation made the Jews what they now are, what does revelation presuppose."[37] The answer presumably lies in the Noahide law.

A full explication of the history of interpretation of Noahide law is beyond the scope of this analysis.[38] But the very existence of such a category indicates a clear recognition on the part of the rabbis that a moral law exists independent of revelation. The fact that the Noahide law is derived exegetically from Scripture and thus (from the rabbinic perspective) is itself part of divine revelation does not disqualify it as a form of natural law as it was defined earlier. The essential point is that the rabbis regarded this body of rules as pre-Sinaitic and universal insofar as its authority does not depend upon God's revelation to Israel.

This immediately raises a fascinating and perplexing question—how would non-Jews, who do not have access to Scripture and divine revelation, know of their obligations under Noahide law? The best known treatment of this question is offered by Maimonides and is, itself, the basis of substantial controversy.[39] While the details of that scholarly debate need not detain us here, the passage from Maimonides is directly pertinent to the nature of the Noahide law and so deserves to be quoted in full.

> Any man [i.e., non-Jew] who accepts the seven commandments and is meticulous in observing them is thereby one of the righteous of the nations of the world, and he has a portion in the world to come. This is only the case if he accepts them and observes them because God commanded them in the Torah, and taught us through our teacher, Moses, that the children of Noah were commanded to observe them even before the Torah was given. But if he observes them because of his own conclusions based on reason, then he is not a resident-alien and is not one of the righteous of the nations of the world, but he is one of their wise men.[40]

The main point of Maimonides' discussion, for our purpose, is his acknowledgment that the Noahide laws could be observed by non-Jews either because they recognized the divine authority behind them or on the basis of their own reason. The latter possibility accords with one criterion of natural law, that it is accessible to everyone through the use of reason. Indeed, Maimonides seems to assume that this is the usual basis for non-Jewish adherence to the Noahide law, since the person who observes these laws because they are divinely ordained is singled out as "one of the righteous of the nations."[41]

Apart from Maimonides' views regarding those who observe Noahide law, the content of the laws corresponds closely to generally accepted principles of natural law. While the rabbis do not explicitly connect these prohibitions with a theory of human nature, it is hard to resist the conclusion that they regarded them as a kind of minimal natural morality, given to humankind at the time of their creation and linked to the needs or purposes common to all people.

Rational Law

A second criterion of natural law, as we noted earlier, is that it is accessible to all through the use of reason.[42] Within rabbinic literature, two passages in particular are often cited as evidence for the view that certain commandments in the Torah are rational, that is, knowable independent of revelation. In Erubin 100b we find, "If Torah had not been given, we could have learned modesty from the cat, aversion to robbery from the ant, chastity from the dove and sexual mores from the rooster." Fox chooses to interpret this passage in a way that minimizes its relevance to the question of natural law. The text, he argues, assumes only that, after receiving these moral commandments from God, we can recognize such moral behavior in the animal kingdom as well. But that is to interpret the passage as if it read, "Since the Torah was given, we can learn . . . ," which is contrary to the plain meaning of the text. The counterfactual, "If the Torah had not been given . . ." most likely means just what it says—independent of Scripture's explicit commandments, these moral behaviors could be learned from another source. The text suggests that those who have not received the Torah still have access to a natural source of moral guidance, as it were.[43]

A second passage is equally intriguing. Yoma 67b, in commenting on Leviticus 18:5 "You shall keep [my ordinances and] my statutes," reads, "This (statutes) refers to those commands which had they not been written should properly have been written. These include the prohibition of idolatry, adultery, bloodshed, and blasphemy." The counterfactual "had they not been written . . ." emphasizes that the obligatory nature of these moral behaviors is obvious to us even without Scripture's explicit instruction. This point is underscored by the rabbinic view that the distinction between "ordinances" (*ḥukim*) and "statutes" (*mishpatim*), both of which are mentioned in the verse from Leviticus, is precisely the difference between those rules whose rationale is unknown (such as the prohibition against mixing diverse kinds; see Lev. 19:19) and those that are reasonable or whose utility is obvious (such as prohibitions against robbery and murder).[44] Fox again chooses to minimize the connection of this passage with natural law, noting that both sets of commandments are obligatory because they were revealed by God in the Torah. But this is to miss the point. Unlike the ordinances that are obligatory *only* as divine commands, these statutes are obligatory *both* because they are divine imperatives *and* because reason dictates them. The plain meaning of the text is precisely that with respect to these basic moral norms, either source alone—revelation or reason—would be sufficient to establish their obligatoriness.

This notion of a rational law received its most famous exposition in Saadia Gaon's doctrine of rational commandments (*mitzvot sichliyot*). Relying on the distinction just discussed, Saadia distinguishes between rational and ritual commandments. The former include the requirements of gratitude and reverence and the prohibition against aggression toward others. All of these, in Saadia's words, are dictated or required by reason (Heb., *ha-sekhel meḥayyeb*). When Saadia discusses the prohibition against bloodshed in particular, he adduces the following reasoning:

> Wisdom lays down that bloodshed must be prevented among human beings, for if it were allowed people would annihilate each other. That would mean, apart from the pain suffered, a frustration of the purpose which the Wise (God) intended to achieve through them. Homicide cuts them off from the attainment of any purpose He created and employs them for.[45]

This notion, that reason prohibits that which is contrary to the purposes of human social life, represents a clear appeal to the teleological tradition of natural law reasoning.

Yet, not everyone has understood Saadia's doctrine of rational commandments as an instance of natural law thinking. In discussing Saadia's views, Fox writes,

> They are commandments for which we can produce good reasons from our own purely human standpoint. They have an obvious social utility or can, by reflection, be shofn [sic] to serve pur-

poses of which reasonable men generally approve . . . but that utility does not serve as an independent and universal substitute for
divinely revealed commandments. Having received them by revelation, we can now admire God's wisdom in commanding us to
live in this advantageous way.[46]

Fox's view once again is that such laws are merely "reasonable" or useful and
are known as such only after they have been revealed by God.[47]

But Saadia's understanding of rationality is stronger than Fox supposes.
In his discussion of revelation, Saadia notes that reason dictates only general
prohibitions, not specific rules; hence, revelation is needed to "fill in the details" of these general rational laws. For example, reason requires that every
crime be punished, but does not indicate exactly what sort of punishment is
appropriate in every instance. Similarly, reason dictates that adultery should
be forbidden but does not specify the rules governing marriage. Thus, with
respect to the rational laws, revelation adds only details but is not necessary
for the establishment of the basic principle.[48] And this, as we noted earlier, accords with the commonly held view that natural law provides general principles of moral conduct but not a fully developed legal system.

Moreover, even if Fox is correct that the *mitzvot sichliyot* are only "reasonable" and not "binding on account of their rationality," this reasonable-
ness itself presupposes that they have a kind of universal basis. After all, if
they are reasonable, as Fox claims, it is because they clearly serve useful purposes not only for Jews but for all people. The prohibitions against murder,
robbery, adultery, and so on, are universally useful, insofar as all people have
the same basic needs. And Saadia's implicit recognition that such basic needs
exist, that certain laws address them, and that these laws are (in some sense)
"rational," surely qualifies his view as a form of natural law theory.

One further instance of Jewish natural law deserves to be noted. J.
David Bleich adduces one instance in which the Talmud derives a principle
of law as binding on the basis of reason alone, without Scriptural authority.[49]
The principle concerns the proper response if one is forced to choose between
violating God's law and sacrificing one's life in an act of martyrdom. The Talmud (Sanhedrin 74a) concludes that one must violate the law to save one's
life, except in cases of idolatry, sexual licentiousness, and murder. Unlike the
first two cases, which are based on scriptural exegesis, the rule regarding murder is based on *sevarah*, rational deduction. This, argues Bleich, demonstrates
that reason alone can, at times, establish a halakhic rule. This, in his view,
represents an instance, albeit a limited one, of natural law thinking.

Reason as the Basis of the Covenant

To this point, I have discussed texts suggesting that there are either "natural" or "rational" moral norms. But Jewish natural law could also express itself in the form of a moral principle at the foundation of the entire religious-legal system. Novak, for example, has argued that the covenant between God and Israel presupposes natural law principles in two respects. First, the Israelites' acceptance of the covenant must be understood as flowing from their recognition of the "goodness" of God's law. According to Novak, "In order for the people to know that God's commandments are right for them, they obviously have to possess some knowledge of what is right in general. This precondition is simply unavoidable."[50] Second, the covenant as a kind of contract "presupposes the norm that promises are to be kept. . . . Without this presupposition, a contract would have no duration and would be, therefore, meaningless. This natural law precondition seems to be an integral part of the convenantal [sic] theory in Scripture."[51] In short, certain moral norms are not commanded by the Torah, but instead are the basis on which the covenantal relationship is established and so on which the Torah's authority ultimately rests.

Moreover, the idea that there is a source of moral knowledge outside of God's revelation is assumed by other biblical narratives as well. Novak points in particular to the encounter between Abraham and God over the destruction of Sodom and Gomorrah. Abraham challenges God with the rhetorical question, "Shall not the judge of all the earth do justly?" (Gen. 18:25) Abraham's question would make no sense, Novak argues, if he did not have access to moral standards independent of God's direct commands.[52] Similarly, Noah and Job, among many other biblical characters, are referred to as "righteous," but without benefit of access to God's revelation. Such stories, of course, do not provide probative evidence for a doctrine of natural law, but they provide at least circumstantial evidence that biblical authors recognized sources of moral knowledge apart from revelation and this, at least, opens the door to a natural law position.

Novak's view of the covenant stands in stark contrast to that of Jose Faur, who suggests that the covenant is created strictly through mutual agreement between God and Israel without any presuppositions whatsoever. Faur writes,

> If we understand 'morality' as duties that bind man to God, then for Judaism the sole constitutive of morality is the Law of Sinai-Moab. This Law is fundamentally conventional: it owes its validity to an agreement between God and Israel, not to its intrin-

sic truth. It is authoratative [sic] on the basis of an extrinsic factor, a specific historical pact, not on the basis of a universal principle. Thus, Jewish morality is essentially nomistic or legalistic: The Law of Sinai-Moab, and only that Law, determines good and evil. Moral good is observance of the commandments of the Law, moral evil is transgression of these commandments. . . . The pact is the object of morality, the people of Israel its subject: outside the pact there are no duties to God.[53]

The disagreement between Novak and Faur concerns the nature of the covenanting act. For Novak, God and Israel agree to enter a covenant, both parties knowing that this entails making mutual promises and also knowing (a priori, as it were) that, as a matter of moral principle, promises must be kept. For Faur, on the other hand, God and Israel create the covenant de novo. In the act of covenant-making, they establish their obligations to one another, including the penalties they will assume if they breach their covenantal duties. Their covenant, then, presupposes no prior general principle about promise-keeping, as Novak has suggested, but only a commitment to do what they have agreed to do by the terms of this covenant.

J. David Bleich likewise explores the moral underpinings of Israel's covenantal obligations, but in a somewhat different vein. He suggests that Judaism's response to the age-old question "why be moral?" can only be answered by appeal to "an antecedent metaphysical principle, viz., man ought to obey the will of the Deity insofar as he is capable of discerning His will. Since it was created by God, and since it exhibits a ubiquitous rationality, the universe testifies to God's desire that all of creation guide itself by the principles of reason. . . ."[54] While Bleich at this point appears to be endorsing a kind of natural law principle underlying the whole edifice of the law, the conclusion of his argument moves in another direction. This requirement to follow reason, he argues, is an instance of the biblical injunction of imitatio Dei (based either on Lev. 19:2 "You shall be holy for I, the Lord your God, am holy" or on Deut. 28:9 "you shall walk in His ways."). Thus, on Bleich's analysis, the basis for the requirement to follow a dictate of reason lies in a specific divine command. As he says, ". . . if Judaism does attribute even limited legislative authority to the intellect, this, too, is so only because such authority is vested in reason by virtue of a direct divine command."[55]

These explorations by Novak, Faur, and Bleich into the basis for the covenant are the most intriguing, but also the most speculative, aspects of the Jewish natural law debate. A balanced appraisal of these arguments must begin from the recognition that the biblical text is simply silent both on the question of Israel's motivation for entering the covenant and on the theoretical underpinings of covenantal relationships. This fact opens the door for Novak, Faur, and Bleich to speculate on matters that, apparently, were not of great concern to the biblical writers.

Furthermore, none of their analyses succeeds entirely in creating a coherent theory of the covenant since, in fact, the biblical evidence on this score is not all of a piece. Thus, in response to Faur's view that the formation of the covenant at Sinai is a discrete contractual act, it must be remembered that the whole flow of the biblical narrative suggests otherwise. The more natural reading of the event at Sinai would place it in the context of the ongoing encounter between God and Israel beginning with Abraham and Sarah and continuing through the Exodus. By the time Israel is encamped at Sinai, they already have a long history of interacting with God and the covenant with Abraham to rely upon. Novak, on the other hand, reads the biblical narrative as a story of Israel's response to God's benevolence and sees Israel's choice to accept this covenant as deliberate and rational. But it is equally possible to interpret their decision to covenant with God as based, not on moral considerations, but on fear of God's awesome power, which is surely the dominant motif of the Exodus narratives. On the other hand, Bleich's effort to make the authority of reason dependent on revelation, like Fox's effort to minimize the significance of appeals to reason, appears to misread the biblical text. Nothing in the texts Bleich cites suggests that natural law thinking needs to be subsumed under a theory of divine command. In short, all of these speculative arguments clearly bear on the potential place of natural law in Judaism. But, insofar as none of these authors has fully explored alternative readings of the biblical texts they cite or explained why their interpretations are more plausible, their discussions fail to provide probative evidence either for or against the existence of natural law in Judaism.

Still, these speculations about the origin and basis of the covenant do lead in a fruitful direction, one that has received all too little attention in the discussion of Jewish natural law. As I noted at the outset, the primary locus of moral and legal norms in Judaism is the covenant. The question at hand is how natural law might play a role in Jewish ethics and jurisprudence *alongside* revelation. But the answer to that question may depend crucially on just how we understand revelation and the covenant created through the offer and acceptance of God's law. Novak, Faur, and Bleich have strikingly different conceptions of "covenantal obligation," and this is surely a key to understanding why they view the possibility of a natural law in Judaism so differently. It is time, then, to turn to the theological roots of this problem, which lie in our understanding of those categories that shape Jewish concepts of ethics and law.

Nature and Torah, Creation and Revelation

We have seen that natural law theory can entail either a metaphysical claim—that nature dictates certain basic moral norms—or an epistemological claim—that human reason, which is universal, can discern the authority of certain moral norms. Most often, natural law encompasses both claims. In the Jewish context, we have examined a number of biblical and rabbinic texts that suggest (to a greater or lesser degree) a recognition that a universal moral law does exist apart from God's revelation of Torah to Israel. Sometimes this body of norms is related to nature, sometimes to reason.

Given the fact that these elements of natural law thinking do appear in many biblical and rabbinic texts, it is striking that the concept of natural law is so undeveloped in Judaism. Why is classical Jewish jurisprudence seemingly so reticent to give either nature or reason a more prominent role in moral or legal reflection? The answer, I believe, is largely theological.[56]

It has long been recognized that the structure of classical Judaic thought revolves around the categories of creation, revelation and redemption.[57] Each of these marks a distinctive mode of divine power that manifests itself in the world. Creation establishes the order of the universe. God's power here is revealed, not through word, but in the very structure of reality. The orderliness of the natural world is evidence of purpose and design, or, as the Psalmist puts it, "The heavens declare the glory of God, the sky proclaims God's handiwork." (Psalm 19:1). Humankind stands in a special relationship to God, both because people represent the pinnacle of the created order and because they alone have the distinction of being made "in God's image." In one version of the creation story, human beings, after eating of the forbidden fruit, become godlike, "knowing good and evil." (Gen. 3:22) It follows that we can no more avoid the moral condition than we can avoid being the creatures that we are, for God has invested us with moral knowledge.

Thus, creation—both of the world and of humankind in particular—has important normative implications. The world is created as a cosmos, revealing the design and purpose of a benevolent creator, and human beings are created (or very early on become) creatures with moral discernment. Taken together these two aspects of creation manifest themselves in the view, implicit throughout Scripture, that all human beings stand in an irreducibly moral relationship with a God who both created them for moral purposes and judges their moral conduct.

Revelation, on the other hand, establishes an exclusive covenant between God and Israel in the context of which all religious, including moral, obligations are defined. Unquestionably, the centrality of Torah as a religious category throughout the history of Judaism testifies to the enormous significance of God's revelation to Israel as the foundation of all value judgments and the source of all normative behavior. Certainly, the content of that revelation, first in Scripture and by extension through rabbinic legislation, determines the scope and substance of Israel's moral life. Thus, revelation creates both a religious community and a normative way of life.

Creation and revelation, then, represent two aspects of God's relationship with the world or, viewed from human perspective, two means by which God's power in the world is experienced. Both of these dimensions of God's involvement with the world have normative implications. Indeed, it is this similarity between creation and revelation that appears to have been on the mind of the psalmist when he wrote "the heavens declare God's glory," and continued a few verses later, "The Torah of the Lord is perfect, restoring the soul; the testimony of the Lord is sure, making wise the simple." (Psalm 19:2,8) Attention to God's creation leads directly to consideration of God's revelation. Both, after all, testify to the purposeful, ordering activity of the same loving God.

Having examined the moral implications of both creation and revelation, we are in a better position to formulate the critical question with respect to the status of natural law in Judaism. How is the normative order established by creation related to the normative order established through revelation? Or, more specifically, how is the moral order that God has created naturally and for all of humanity related to the moral order that God has established "supernaturally" for Israel alone? I believe that there are fundamentally two possible ways of answering that question, and how one views natural law in Judaism is determined by which of these options one endorses. Let me briefly sketch the two options and spell out their implications with respect to natural law.

Within the history of Judaism, the relationship between creation and revelation has sometimes been viewed as *sequential* and *progressive*. From this perspective, creation is only a prelude to revelation in the history of God's relationship to the world. God's will is only partially revealed to humanity at large, but is fully revealed to Israel at Sinai. It follows that the normative order established through covenant and Torah takes precedence over that established through creation. Any universal moral law, then, is but a precursor to Torah and is necessarily subordinated to it.

This view finds expression in midrashic statements that, in God's mind, "the thought of creating Israel preceded all else" and "the world and the fullness thereof were created only for the sake of Torah."[58] God's purpose in creation can be fulfilled only through revelation. In effect, Rashi expresses this view in his famous commentary on Genesis 1:1. The Torah begins with God's creation of the world, he suggests, so that when Israel comes to possess the Land of Canaan and expel the native inhabitants, they can appeal to the fact that God has created the world and can give it to whomever God chooses. For Rashi, the whole purpose of creation is to justify Israel's place in the world. Such a view, of course, has significant implications for the doctrine of Israel's chosenness. Israel possesses a truth unknown to the rest of the world and to this extent the differences between Jews and non-Jews are more significant than the similarities.[59]

On the other hand, the relationship between creation and revelation may be viewed as *correlative* and *complementary*. From this perspective, creation and revelation are separate but related modes through which God's will is made known to the world. Creation establishes a normative world that retains its own integrity even after the Torah is given. Thus, God's engagement with the world does not involve a simple progression from creation to revelation, or from humanity as a whole to the chosen people, but rather operates differently in different spheres and among different peoples. This point of view has been expressed most cogently by David Novak:

> even though the covenant between God and Israel transcends nature, it still accepts nature as a limit (*peras*) and its own precondition. Jews are human beings who have been elected through the covenant, but they are still human beings within the natural order of things. Nature, constituted as the covenant's general background and horizon, is not overcome.[60]

It follows that Jews have a double relationship to God, first as human beings and second as members of the covenanted community. Those who adopt this view of creation and revelation, then, will necessarily be inclined to stress the similarities as well as the differences between Israel and the rest of humanity.

While this position is not developed explicitly within classical sources, it may be inferred from a number of texts. At the conclusion of the creation story, God says, "Behold, the man has become like one of us, knowing good and evil," (Gen. 3:22) suggesting that moral discernment of a certain sort is universal and derives, not from God's revelation to Israel, but rather, in mythic terms, from the first human's eating fruit from the tree of the knowledge of good and evil. Moreover, God instructs Noah at the conclusion of the flood story, "Whoever sheds man's blood, by man shall his blood be shed, for in the image of God he made man." (Gen. 9:6). Thus, the immorality of murder is traced to the very nature of human beings as divine creatures and so has the status of a universal moral norm, again independent of divine revelation. And, as we have seen, the doctrine of Noahide law represents the rabbinic attempt to articulate this universal moral order.

At this point it is not difficult to see how each of these positions shapes an attitude toward natural law. For those with a sequential view of creation and revelation, both nature and reason—the touchstones of any natural law position—are subordinated to Torah and revelation. The natural order is only the backdrop and prelude to the supernatural order established by God through the revelation of Torah to Israel. Once Torah is given, all prior moral instruction becomes strictly preliminary. To suggest that natural or universal moral principles could retain an integrity of their own (for Jews) entails the virtually heretical suggestions that Torah is not the comprehensive expression of God's will, and that Israel is not the focal point of God's plan for the world. Similarly, reason as a source of truth (moral or otherwise) is superceded by revelation. Indeed, as many religious thinkers over the centuries have noted, revelation itself seems to imply that whatever we can know of God's will on the basis of our own rational capacity is not sufficient. In all, on this view, there can be only one moral truth (Torah), one mode for receiving it (revelation), and one community that is defined by it (Israel).

In this regard, it is interesting to note that Marvin Fox, himself an Orthodox Jew, wrote in a telling comment, "In spite of his minimal recognition of natural law, Albo is still a loyal Jew who can find no place for law without God's revelation."[61] Clearly, from one perspective within the tradition, natural law poses a threat to revelation, for it affirms a source of moral truth besides Torah. Fox believes that to endorse natural law is to minimize the significance of revelation, a belief that he also attributes to Albo. But, clearly the tradition encompasses more than this one perspective.

For those with a correlative and complementary view of creation and revelation, natural law exists both within and alongside of Torah. "Within," for Torah encompasses and affirms universal moral norms, and "alongside," for the values derived from the created order remain operative for non-Jews who are not recipients of God's revelation. From this perspective, the natural order constitutes a source of moral instruction, a "natural torah," as it were, more limited in scope than the Torah revealed at Sinai but significant nonetheless. And reason functions as a vehicle for discovering these universal moral norms, insofar as God has created us with the capacity to understand human nature and the order of existence. Accordingly, there are two parallel sources of moral truth, one universal, determined by nature and discovered by reason, and the other particular, determined by revelation and discovered in the words of Torah.

It is telling in this regard that Novak devotes several pages in one discussion of natural law to developing a theory of truth that avoids the potentially untenable conclusion that the universal moral law and the Jewish moral law are irreconcilable.[62] Any Jewish thinker who regards reason as an independent source of moral guidance will face the challenge of balancing the respective authority of reason and revelation.

It would be wrong to suppose that the two views just discussed exhaust the range of theological possibilities. But they do represent fundamental alternatives and perennial options within the tradition. On the whole, it would seem, Orthodox Jewish thinkers have endorsed the former view, affirming the absoluteness of revelation, and so the indivisibility of truth. Accordingly, the moral implications of the created order have been minimized, together with the power of reason. This may account, at least in part, for the fact that historically Jewish thinkers have regarded the Greek philosophical tradition, with its emphasis on universal truths discoverable through reason, with significant suspicion. By the same token, notwithstanding the affirmation of a Noahide law, Jewish thinkers have been less concerned to articulate the universal moral law than to expound the law operative within the covenant. God's will, on this view, is ultimately a mystery that we understand, if at all, only by the grace of divine revelation. The fact that human reason affirms some of the commandments is a happy coincidence from our standpoint and an irrelevance from God's.

And yet, as we have seen, the alternative view continually reasserts itself. The moral implications of the human condition per se can be minimized, but they cannot be negated entirely. All human beings stand in a moral relationship to God, all have the capacity to discern God's will through the exercise of reason and through the observation of natural processes. If God's concern for humanity has not been channeled entirely through Israel, there must be a universal moral order, however limited. And so the meaning and authority of Torah must be affirmed in a way that allows for an independent source of moral truth, one that operates outside of Torah for non-Jews and alongside Torah for Jews. Jewish philosophy continually reasserts itself as a response to this challenge of reconciling faith and reason or, in the present context, synthesizing the universal implications of creation with the particularist implications of revelation. In the pursuit of that goal, the rationality of some of God's laws will be greeted as opening the door to a kind of pluralism, but inevitably at the expense of limiting Israel's distinctiveness as a moral community.[63]

In conclusion, then, the extent to which Judaism can affirm natural law thinking ultimately rests on the extent to which revelation can accommodate creation. Or, more precisely, on the way one construes the relationship between Torah as the embodiment of God's moral instruction to Israel and nature as the vehicle for God's moral instruction to humanity, inclusive of Israel. I suggest that the conflict over natural law in Judaism is but a reflection of this deeper theological tension within the tradition. And this tension precludes any simple pronouncements that Judaism either is or is not hospitable to natural law thinking. The fact that Israel stands in a unique relationship to God by virtue of divine revelation is balanced by a recognition that all humankind stands in relationship to God by virtue of divine creation. How we construe the relationship between creation and revelation will have significant ramifications, not only for a doctrine of natural law, but for the concept of Israel's chosenness and for the scope of Israel's moral obligations to non-Jews. Contemporary Jewish thinkers, like their predecessors over the centuries, must choose among these alternative theologies of creation and revelation. The status of natural law in Judaism will be but one consequence of that choice.

Chapter 7

Religious Faith, Historical Relativism, and the Prospects for Modern Jewish Ethics

In the last few chapters I have examined the history of the relationship between theology and ethics in Judaism. I have argued that certain questions of both ethical theory (e.g., whether Judaism can accommodate natural law) and applied ethics (e.g., decisions concerning the use of biomedical technology) historically have been linked to certain theological views within Jewish tradition. I want now to consider this relationship, not from the perspective of the historian of Judaism but from the perspective of the theologian. In particular, I want to tackle what I take to be the central problem facing liberal Jewish ethics, that in this age of historical relativism we find it difficult to affirm a God who makes moral pronouncements from the mountaintop (or who speaks through sacred texts). Yet, Jewish ethics presupposes that ethical norms are discovered in the context of a living relationship with God. How can we develop a concept of God that is both consonant with our modern historical consciousness and adequate to ground a sense of Jewish moral obligation?

In the context of traditional Jewish thought, the foundation of all moral judgments is the belief in divine revelation. In the Orthodox view, God's will has been revealed definitively to Israel through the gift of Torah, and this body of revealed truths constitutes the authoritative source of religious norms for the Jewish people for all time. This written revelation, of course, has been supplemented and extended over the centuries through the interpretations of the rabbis, and this "oral Torah" is similarly understood as an expression of God's will and as eternally binding. Within this framework, traditional Jewish ethicists approach questions of modern Jewish ethics as halakhic questions to be decided on the basis of authoritative texts, which alone give us access to an understanding of God's will. So long as revelation and the authority of the textual tradition are understood in traditional ways, there are no new theological questions that modern Jewish ethicists need to ask, only new moral issues that need to be adjudicated.

Since the rise of liberal religious thought in the eighteenth century, however, this traditional view of revelation has been regarded as untenable by most Jewish and Christian thinkers. For them, the modern humanistic study of religion and the historical-critical study of texts have forever altered the framework within which normative questions are addressed. Once the will of God is no longer identified with a canonical body of texts or a fixed group of interpreters, the authority of the tradition itself is called into question and, concomitantly, the status of all normative judgments becomes ambiguous. For the modern liberal Jewish ethicist, then, a fundamental theological question must be faced: how are we to identify within this tradition "what God wants of us morally," hence what we regard as normative for our time?

Liberal Jewish thinkers in the modern period, like their Christian counterparts, have grappled with this question, which is unquestionably one of the defining issues for all modern religious thought in the West. In this chapter, I revisit the problems of revelation and the construction of normative judgments as these arise in the context of modern Jewish ethics. I suggest that some of the theological responses frequently offered by liberal Jewish ethicists to these issues are inadequate. A different understanding of God's presence in history, and with it a new understanding of covenant, must be articulated as the basis for modern, liberal Jewish ethics. I believe that the implications of these theological reinterpretations for Jewish ethics are far-reaching. In the end, we will need to reconceptualize the very nature of Jewish moral obligation and the means by which we today can create authentically Jewish moral norms.

Revelation, Historicism, and the Search for Moral Norms

Perhaps the most cogent statement of the theological problem facing all modern liberal religious thinkers was provided by the Protestant thinker Ernst Troeltsch shortly after the turn of the century. Troeltsch correctly recognized that modern historical consciousness poses the most serious challenge to traditional religious thought and thus devoted much of his career to analyzing the problem of historicism and its effect on theology. The nature of this challenge bears reviewing before we proceed to present and analyze liberal Jewish responses to it.

Modern historical study as it developed during and after the Enlightenment is devoted to the analysis of events from an objective standpoint. As one of the newly emergent social sciences, historical study aimed to discover the causes and effects of events and to formulate explanations that did not rely on the religious beliefs or personal biases of the historian. Even though efforts throughout the eighteenth and nineteenth century to make history a scientific endeavor akin to the natural sciences ultimately failed,[1] the idea that historical inquiry must be based on a dispassionate assessment remains a cornerstone of the discipline of history to this day. In addition, modern historical consciousness regards all human affairs as proper subjects for historical investigation. There can be no separate realm of human action that is immune to historical explanation. In this sense, history is akin to the natural sciences like physics; just as physicists regard all events in the physical world as subject to the laws of physics, so historians regard all events in the human sphere as explainable potentially in terms of historical forces and circumstances. In short, modern historiography is characterized by these beliefs, that no a priori metaphysical assumptions should prejudice the historian's analysis of the historical record and that all events, if they are to be understood, must be contextualized historically.

This historical perspective, when applied to religious traditions such as Judaism and Christianity, challenges the very basis of religious authority and truth. Both traditions, of course, make the same fundamental claim, that God entered human history in a decisive way at a particular point in time. Such revelational events, whether in Torah or in Christ, cannot be analyzed and contextualized historically without undermining the traditional understanding of them. And once the event of revelation, as well as the written record of it in Scripture, are viewed historically, they lose their a priori claim to religious authority and so their normative force. Each claim to religious truth is but one more human response to historical circumstances, which believers attribute to a divine source but which is now contextualized and relativized by means of historical analysis. Thus, if modern religious thinkers wish to continue making normative judgments, they must explain how, within a historical framework, they identify what is "divine" and so "true" and "binding." In Troeltsch's cogent and elegant formulation of the question, "How can we pass beyond the diversity with which history presents us to norms for our faith and for our judgments about life?"[2]

In short, the central issue for modern religious thinkers is historicism. The modern study of history (a) places all purported revelational events into a human, historical context, and so (b) relativizes all claims to absolute truth, or divine imperatives, based on such revelations. Those Orthodox thinkers who reject this historical approach can, of course, continue to regard Scripture as the definitive record of divine revelation. For them, the question is not "what is normative," but only "how shall we apply these divinely ordained norms to the situation we face?" All other Jews, like their Christian counterparts, must search within their tradition, understood as an historically evolving phenomenon, for that which they accept as normative. For Jewish ethicists, this means that, absent a supernatural Archimedian point that provides an absolute standard and basis for authoritative judgment, the foundation for religious/ethical judgments must be constructed anew. In other words, as Troeltsch rightly understood, we must find religious norms within history.

Perhaps the most well developed strategy employed by Jewish and Christian thinkers for overcoming the problem of historicism, at least in the nineteenth and early twentieth centuries, relied on the notion of a religion's "essence." It was argued that, through historical study itself, one could discover the essence of a religious tradition and that this supplied the necessary criterion for what is normative in the present. In this way, one could embrace the historical approach to religion and yet not fall victim to a historical relativism that precluded making all normative judgments. Of course, different thinkers identified the essence of the religious tradition in different ways. Sometimes it referred to those aspects of a religious tradition that remained static over time (in contrast to those that changed) or to the earliest, pristine form of a religion (in contrast to later accretions). Under the influence of Hegelian thought, some assumed that the essence of a tradition unfolded through time in a progressive fashion, later stages of development being by definition more advanced.

Many nineteenth- and twentieth-century liberal Jewish thinkers identified the "essence of Judaism" with its ethics and, moreover, supposed that the universalist, prophetic ethos represented the dominant thrust, or the highest expression, of this ethic. A united humanity under a common God whose moral concern and protection is extended to all alike—this vision was taken to be the essential religious/moral truth at the core of Judaism and its fundamental message to humankind. This view was pervasive among liberal thinkers, "reformers," in the nineteenth century and received its fullest exposition in the work of figures such as Kaufman Kohler. It was expounded in the famous Pittsburgh Platform that he drafted and that was adopted in 1885 at a conference of American Reform rabbis. A much more philosophically sophisticated version of this view was developed by Hermann Cohen in the context of his own effort to rework Kantian philosophy. For Cohen, this universalist "ethical monotheism" was the essence, not only of Judaism, but of all religious truth insofar as religion could be rationally, philosophically constructed. The historical roots of this religion of reason, he believed, lay in the biblical prophetic tradition.[3]

Although the Reform rabbinate has reformulated its understanding of Judaism several times since the late 1800s, and although Cohen's philosophy no longer has many adherents, the notion that Judaism's essence is its universalist ethic continues to exert its influence. Thus, Robert Gordis, a prominent thinker in the Conservative movement, in his recently published *The Dynamics of Judaism*, affirms the "primacy of ethics" within the tradition and regards the prophets as the quintessential expression of Jewish ethical values. Gordis's comments on revelation are especially telling.

> Both in the biblical text and in the rabbinic tradition, Moses' encounter with God on Sinai is the central event in revelation. The Decalogue is the basic product of that encounter; this, the most famous of all codes, underscores the primacy of ethics as the heart of Jewish religion.[4]

Certainly, Gordis is less naive than earlier thinkers in acknowledging that "tradition is never monochromatic—it will contain contradictions and inconsistencies."[5] But, like earlier thinkers, he regards the ethical core of Judaism as unchanging within a tradition that otherwise evolves in response to shifting historical circumstances.

This "essentialist" strategy has considerable appeal among liberal religious thinkers for what may be obvious reasons. It enables them to embrace the historical perspective on their own religious tradition, but to retain the view that some element of that tradition is genuinely "divine" and so timeless. In a sense, one can "have one's cake and eat it too," by allowing that all truths are historically conditioned, save those that are "essential" and so valid or authoritative independent of historical circumstances. In short, anyone who wishes to affirm both historical-critical approaches to religion and also a core of eternal, ahistorical religious truth will be drawn to reconceptualize the tradition in terms of "essential" and "historically conditioned" elements.

But all such efforts to overcome historicism through an essentialist theory run into several problems. In the first place, religious traditions, especially those that have evolved over many centuries, cannot so easily be reduced to a single core idea. Rather, traditions contain within themselves numerous ideas and values that often are in tension with one another. To select a single perspective as "essential" to the exclusion of others is invariably an oversimplification of the historical data. As Troeltsch again astutely pointed out with respect to Christianity, any essence worthy of the name must go so far as to bear opposites and tensions within itself. It must contain within itself an oscillation between several basic ideas. . . . A historical phenomenon as powerful and as infinitely rich in consequences as Christianity draws the contents of its thought from various elements of the preceding development and simply reorganises them around a new spiritual centre. . . .[6]

So the essence of any religious tradition must always be complex, rather than simple. In the case of Judaism, the tradition of universalist ethics must be counterbalanced with the equally prevalent and persistent tradition of parochialism. Both strains are present and to identify the former as the "essence" of Judaism is willfully to ignore historical realities.

Moreover, the essence of a tradition, however it is identified, never appears fully formed at any point. It is never really "there" at any single point in the historical development of the tradition, so much as it is a construct created by historians on the basis of their analysis of the historical data. In this sense, all essences are what Max Weber called "ideal types." Troeltsch appreciated this aspect of the problem as well:

The unified idea of the essence only exists after all in the thought of the historian summarising the material. Reality nowhere displays the essence as the absolutely clear, complete and convincing result of the process. It displays instead great, divided churches, in none of which the essence can be perceived to be realised, and which do not even realise the essence all together.[7]

So, essences are not really within a tradition, but in the mind of the historian as he or she analyzes it.

Liberal religious thought thus faces a monumental challenge. It cannot return to the world of traditional religious belief according to which God's presence in history is a given nor can it affirm an absolute standard of truth and criteria for behavioral norms that lie outside the sphere of historical analysis. On the other hand, it cannot take refuge in a notion of religion's essence as the criterion for what is normative, since, on further analysis, all such essentialist moves either ignore the subtlety and multiplicity present in the tradition, or represent the imposition of the historian's construct upon the historical data, or both. But the problem remains: how to identify a divine source of values within a religious tradition now understood as itself a product of human, historical processes.

God's Presence in History: Reconstructing Jewish Theology

The problem of historicism could be avoided, of course, by simply rejecting any religious basis whatsoever for Jewish moral norms. This would entail divorcing the moral tradition in Judaism from the religious worldview that gave rise to it, viewing it as a resource from which Jews (and non-Jews) today can draw freely as they choose. In effect, this has been precisely the position of those who identify themselves as "humanistic" or "secular" Jews, jettisoning the religious claims of the tradition entirely and embracing only the moral truths that they regard as timeless. In the view of Sherwin Wine, who founded the first Humanistic Jewish congregation,

> The Torah is a book of shared conclusions. The priestly writers often reached ethical conclusions that humanistic Jews have also reached. The priests came to these moral precepts with the reasoning of an authoritarian God. Humanistic Jews come to these rules with a commonsensical testing of their consequences. Rabbinic Jews come to these commandments with the knowledge that the Torah gives them validity. Humanistic Jews approach them with the awareness that human experience makes them worthwhile (even if the Torah never existed).[8]

For many modern thinkers, however, this move is both disingenuous and unsatisfying. It is disingenuous, for it extracts from Jewish ethics the one thing—its religious basis—that makes it distinctively Jewish. Humanistic Jewish ethics is really indistinguishable from the tradition of post-Enlightenment humanism; to call it Jewish is both to mislabel the values one endorses and to insult the richness of Judaism's ethical tradition. More to the point, many thinkers still believe, or wish to believe, that God plays a role in human affairs and that that is particularly so in the moral sphere. From this perspective, extracting religion from Jewish ethics is not only a falsification of the tradition but an impoverishment of the ethical life that we today, like our ancestors long ago, feel called upon to live.

So the liberal Jewish religious thinker cannot avoid the problem of historicism by embracing a secular worldview according to which there is only history, no divine or supernatural dimension to our lives, either as Jews or as human beings. In this respect, Arthur Cohen was correct when he wrote that the central problem of modern Jewish theology was to understand the relationship between history and God or, as he put it, between the "natural" Jew (who lives wholly within the historical realm), and the "supernatural" Jew, (who lives in relationship with God and who feels marked by a divine destiny). In Cohen's words, "Theology is . . . the science of sacred history. It sets itself but one task: to apprehend and interpret the presence of God in time and history."[9] In effect, Leo Baeck made a similar point decades earlier when he wrote that the essential idea of Judaism is "that of the incursion of the Infinite, Eternal, the One and Unconditional into the finite, temporal, manifold and limited, and of the spiritual and moral tension of the human fibre which is its result."[10] To Baeck and Cohen and many contemporary Jewish thinkers, the question is not *whether* God is present in human life, and especially in the historical life of the Jewish community. Rather, the question is how we *conceptualize* God's presence in history, this mysterious interweaving of the divine and the human that is the inescapable subject of all Jewish theology and the necessary foundation for any understanding of Jewish moral/religious obligation in modern times. How can we understand God's presence in history without abandoning either the historical critical perspective—as the Orthodox do—or the possibility of divine presence—as the secularists do?

This question has seemed intractable, in part I think, because we have felt constrained to conceptualize God in personal, anthropomorphic terms. God is conceived as a "being" who is not only described metaphorically as possessing human physical features (e.g., "an outstretched arm," "a face," "hands," etc.) but who possesses a will and, that most quintessentially human quality, speech. Throughout Jewish tradition—in Scripture, in rabbinic literature, in liturgy, and in popular imagination—God is encountered as the powerful, yet benevolent, being who speaks and calls the whole of creation into existence, who speaks again and formulates the laws that define Israel's existence as a "kingdom of priests and a holy people." (Exod. 19:6) The defining moment of revelation, at Sinai, is followed by endless others, through prophets and later, in a more attenuated form, through sages. But throughout, God's "voice" represents the dominant mode through which God's presence in history is apprehended.

But this is precisely the conception of God's presence that today is so problematic. All claims to the effect that God has spoken thus and such either stand outside the natural sweep of history or, if subjected to empirical historical inquiry, immediately lose their claim to divine, normative status. To conceptualize God in anthropomorphic terms is to place ourselves precisely in the path of the historicism's devastating critique, leaving us with either an orthodoxy that is (for liberals) intellectually untenable or a secularism that is religiously vacuous. To steer a middle course between these alternatives is the task of formulating a theological foundation for modern, non-Orthodox Jewish ethics. Fortunately, the tradition itself is not without resources to which we can turn.

While it is unquestionably true that Jewish tradition overwhelmingly conceptualizes God's presence in history in anthropomorphic terms, there is important material within the tradition itself that opens the possibility for an alternative conception. This alternative is seen most clearly in those biblical passages that concern God's name. In the context of ancient Near Eastern thought, the name of an object designated its essence. Hence, to name something was to define its essence, to know its name was to comprehend its defining characteristic. Adam's naming of the various animals in the Garden of Eden (Gen. 2) represents the most striking example of this. Similarly, changes in a biblical figure's name signify changes in his or her essential nature or destiny. In this context, it is not hard to understand the extreme reticence of the biblical writers to reveal God's name, as well as the taboo on invoking God's name in connection with false testimony (Exod. 20:7).

We see this most clearly when we look at Exodus 3:13–15, where Moses receives his commission as God's prophet. He has just discovered God's presence in the form of a bush that is on fire, but not consumed, and God proceeds to direct Moses to bring the Israelites out of Egypt. Moses, knowing that the people will be wary of his claims to speak for a divine being, asks God to identify "himself." The answer he receives represents one of the most perplexing and frequently discussed passages in the Hebrew Bible.

> Moses said to God, "When I come to the Israelites and say to them 'The God of your fathers has sent me to you,' and they ask me, 'What is His name?' what shall I say to them?" and God said to Moses, "Ehyeh-Asher-Ehyeh." He continued, "Thus shall you say to the Israelites, 'Ehyeh sent me to you.' " And God said further to Moses, "Thus shall you speak to the Israelites: 'The Lord, the God of your fathers, the God of Abraham, the God of Isaac and the God of Jacob, has sent me to you: This shall be My name forever, This My appellation for all eternity.' "

God's answer to Moses is intentionally evasive, suggesting that God's essence or nature cannot be fixed. Significantly, the very word that God offers in place of a name is not a noun at all, but a verb. "Ehyeh-Asher-Ehyeh," which the translators of the Jewish Publication Society text judiciously left untranslated, could be rendered as "I am (or will be, or am becoming) that which I am (or will be, or am becoming)."

So Moses is told only that God will be whatever God will be. This God will appear or manifest itself in whatever form or way God chooses. The answer appears to suggest that Moses' question itself is not answerable, at least not in conventional terms. God's presence in the world is not definable, because it is dynamic, changing, emerging over time in ways that are not predictable in advance. This God, whose name is designated by the equally enigmatic YHWH—which exhibits the root letters of the verb "to be"—refuses to be defined in straightforward, intelligible terms. Rather, God is an unspecified presence, an action or activity rather than a person or thing, manifesting itself through time. At the very moment when God commissions a prophet to lead the people from slavery to freedom and to their momentous encounter with divine destiny, God refuses to identify Godself, except as a Presence that will be with the people on their journey, as God was with their ancestors on theirs.

A similarly mysterious exchange occurs earlier in the patriarchial narratives of Genesis, when Jacob, after years of living with his father-in-law Laban, returns to his native land to confront his estranged brother Esau.

> Jacob was left alone. And a man wrestled with him until the break of dawn. When he saw that he had not prevailed against him, he wrenched Jacob's hip at its socket, so that the socket of his hip was strained as he wrestled with him. Then he said, "Let me go, for dawn is breaking." But he answered, "I will not let you go, unless you bless me." Said the other, "What is your name?" He replied, "Jacob." Said he, "Your name shall no longer be Jacob, but Israel, for you have striven with beings divine and human and have prevailed." Jacob asked, "Pray tell me your name." But he said, "You must not ask my name!" And he took leave of him there. So Jacob named the place Peniel, meaning, "I have seen a divine being face to face, yet my life has been preserved." (Gen. 32:25–31)

This, of course, represents a critical juncture in Jacob's life, the point at which he receives his name, which is to be carried by the entire people who are his descendants. Jacob emerges from this encounter, which significantly occurs in the shadowy between-time that is neither night nor day, altered both physically and spiritually.

Of greatest interest for our purpose is that the identity of this assailant is deliberately concealed; Jacob's request to know his identity is declined. And the etiology that the text offers for the name Israel reinforces the ambiguity—is this a man or a divine being with whom Jacob contends? The name he gives to the place attests to his belief that this was a divine being, and yet, if so, he cannot account for his surviving this confrontation. He cannot know for certain how, or even whether, he will encounter this adversary/partner again. He cannot even refer to this being by name or call upon him again at other moments of crisis in his life. He knows only that he has struggled with a divine/human force of some sort, and that his name and destiny have been forever changed as a result.

Here, as in the earlier encounter between God and Moses, we find an alternative to the dominant conception of God's presence in human history. This is not the God of Sinai who pronounces immutable commandments, whose majesty and presence literally overpowers the people, or whose will can be captured in words that transcend mundane historical reality. In that conception, God enters history definitively, at a specified time, and most of all, has an identity that is clear and unambiguous—"I am the Lord your God who brought you out of the land of Egypt, out of the house of slavery." By contrast, this less anthropomorphic God is present in mysterious ways—in a burning bush or in a violent encounter at night. This God either has no name, and so no firm identity, or offers to reveal only that the divine presence "is as it is." Jacob's wrestling with this unidentified divine being suggests that God is encountered not (or not only) in majestic, dramatic heirophanies, but in grappling (physically and spiritually) with mysterious forces that may be human in form but divine in nature.

I want to suggest that these passages offer a metaphor for the divine presence in history apposite to our time. Israel as a people, like its illustrious namesake, is defined by its struggle with God. And yet, like Jacob, we cannot be certain who or what that divine presence is that we discover in shadowy times and in unexpected places. We know only that the encounter itself is real and powerful. In wrestling with this mysterious and unnameable power, we may find the strength to face those obstacles to the fulfillment of our destiny, who may be either political (Pharaoh) or familial (Esau) adversaries. Moreover, we bear the marks of this "God-wrestling" with us as we move through history.[11] Israel as a community can attest to God's presence, in mysterious and undefinable ways, in all times and places. But because God cannot be named, we cannot say in advance just how God's presence will be manifested. In a sense, this is part of the special burden of Israel's mission in the world: to attest to a divine presence that can in the last analysis be defined neither in words nor in images, but whose reality we take to be central to our collective life as a people.

This view of God has much in common with process theology, a movement with its roots in the philosophy of Alfred North Whitehead, which has recently been the subject of renewed interest among those attempting to develop a "postmodern" theology.[12] Among Jewish thinkers, Mordecai Kaplan most closely exemplified this approach to God.[13] Like Kaplan, I suggest that we conceive of God as an impersonal process, whose existence we experience naturally in the course of our lives. Yet, contra Kaplan, whose positivist predilections led him to adopt a thorough-going rationalism, it is possible to affirm the reality of intuitive knowledge and mystical experiences of God. While Whitehead asserted that God is both transcendent and immanent ("dipolar," in Whitehead's peculiar philosophical idiom), the central point for our purpose is that God is revealed to us through God's immanence, by being in the world, not beyond it.[14]

This way of understanding God's presence in history would seem to resolve the problem of historicism as it was presented here. So long as God is conceived as a transcendent being who enters history at a definite moment in time and whose self-revelation is understood as an incursion into the ordinary sweep of history, it contradicts modern, historical consciousness. But there is an alternative. With the help of these suggestive passages, we can imagine God's presence as diffused throughout history, as something we encounter potentially in all places and times, but that at any given point we cannot define with certainty. The whole of our journey through time, as individuals and as a people, is infused with divine significance, though we cannot positively identify this mysterious divine power whose presence we sense, much less know for certain where our God-wrestling will lead us.

But the question remains: how, based on this theology of divine encounter, can we understand the source of Jewish moral obligation? In particular, how does it square with the central theological conviction that the covenant between God and Israel is the context within which Jewish moral obligations arise? Finally, what sort of normative, moral guidance emerges from God's presence in our lives, understood in this way? It is to these questions that we now turn.

Jewish Theology, Covenant, and Ethics

The move from a transcendent and personal to an immanent and nonpersonified God[15] will strike many as a radical break with Jewish tradition. In particular, it seems to preclude any notion of a covenant, a pact freely entered into by God and Israel, in the context of which religious (including moral) obligations traditionally were understood to arise. To be sure, covenant does form the basis of all traditional Jewish concepts of religious obligation,[16] and detaching Jewish obligation from the will of a transcendent God does represent a significant departure from traditional views. But I believe it is possible to reinterpret, and demythologize, the traditional covenant idea so as to retain much of what it has always symbolized, and especially to see it as a source of Jewish religious/moral obligation. In doing so, we can continue to use covenant as a metaphor for our relationship with the divine that serves as the foundation for a modern Jewish ethic.

We do well to begin exploring this relationship between theological reflection and constructing ethical norms by taking up the theological question recently posed by the contemporary Protestant thinker, Gordon Kaufman. He suggests that all theological reflection begins with our experience of human existence (indeed, of all existence) as a mystery. Thus, the primary question that theologians must ask, in his words, is, "In view of the ultimate mystery within which our existence falls, how are we humans to orient ourselves in the world?" For Jews and others who stand within a tradition of theological reflection, we must add a further question, "How do we interpret, appropriate, and extend the answers to this question that have been formulated by earlier generations of our people in ways that are meaningful in our time?"[17] If we can answer these questions, we can formulate a Jewish theological foundation for a modern Jewish ethic.

Following Kaufman's suggestion, we must begin by articulating the sense of "mystery" that informs our most profound existential questions and our search for moral guidance. In this respect, there is much that we can affirm in common with countless generations of human beings who have preceded us. Within the natural realm, we can still stand in awe, as our ancestors did, at the mysteries of birth and death, at the intricate web of life, at the natural beauty around us and the vast expanse of the universe, about which we now know more than any previous generation. And, within the human realm, we can still marvel at the working of the human psyche, the power and creativity of the human spirit, the dynamics of love and hate, and the profound transformations that sometimes occur in the lives of individuals and communities. All this we recognize as manifesting a power greater than our own, which, though it cannot be defined and named, still evokes in us a range of responses: awe and terror, anger, wonder, perplexity, and reverence. Above all, it forces us to confront our own finitude and the profound mysteries that both animate and surround human life.

In response to this awareness of mystery, we can make two basic religious affirmations. First, that life as we experience it has purpose and meaning, although at any given time we may grasp this only incompletely. God is the name we give to those aspects of reality we find purposeful, orderly, and meaningful, as well as to the inner impulse we feel to orient ourselves toward those dimensions of reality. God then can be found both outside and within us, in the world as it is and in our own responses to it. Our second theological affirmation is a specifically Jewish one: we believe it is our purpose as a people to witness to that divine reality and to live out the implications of that commitment as a distinct people. This means that Israel as a people is devoted to bringing about a greater awareness of God and, insofar as we do so, God's presence in the world is increased through our faith and our actions.

These theological affirmations would appear to be far removed from the notion of a covenantal pact between God and Israel as it has been conceived throughout Jewish history. As scholars established long ago, the biblical covenant concept has its roots in Hittite suzerainty treaties through which conquering kings defined their relationship to conquered peoples in a set of promises and obligations.[18] Thus, God, as Israel's ruler, was understood to have made a similar pact with "His people" according to which they would serve God alone and God in turn would protect the people and cause them to prosper. Other conceptions of covenant assume greater parity between the parties to the agreement. In Hosea, and through much of rabbinic literature, the metaphor of marriage is used for the God-Israel relationship. From this perspective, the Torah represents a sort of *ketubbah* (marriage contract), and violations of covenantal responsibilities are portrayed as a form of marital infidelity. While suzerainty and parity models of covenant represent distinct trends within classical Jewish theology,[19] the underlying assumption throughout the biblical sources is that God exists as a separate being who enters into relationship with Israel definitively at a distinct point in its history and whose will is Israel's command.

But does the notion of a covenant necessitate conceiving of God as an all-powerful king whose will defines Israel's religious obligations? The comments of Eugene Borowitz, perhaps the foremost contemporary liberal exponent of covenant theology, are instructive in this regard. Although he himself continues to affirm a transcendent and personal God as a covenantal partner with Israel, Borowitz has acknowledged that the covenant idea does not depend on this view.

> I do not see that thinking in terms of Covenant prohibits after-the-fact explanations of the God with whom one stands in relation, as an impersonal principle, or a process which has certain person-like characteristics (e.g., the conservation of values.)[20]

But how would we imagine such a covenant?

In fact, a demythologized concept of covenant has been formulated by Arthur Green in the context of his immanentist, quasi-mystical contemporary Jewish theology. He writes,

> But God as *chooser* is a highly anthropomorphized notion of Y-H-W-H. Once we see the very depiction of God as a person to be the result of human projection onto the universe, divine choosing will also have to be recognized as projection, as *Israel's way of asserting that it stands as a people in a unique relationship with the Divine. . . .*
>
> If relationship with God is more like breaking down a wall (or seeing through a veil) than it is like building a bridge across a chasm, covenant, too, becomes a commitment to *keeping faith with the deepest Self that is manifest within us.* It is a decision to live in such a way that allows this One to be revealed to others through us. Covenant is our willingness to be a channel, to serve as a conduit of God's presence to those with whom we live.[21]

Once the ancient notion of a covenant between God and Israel is stripped of its mythic aspects, including the notion of a personified God with a will who "chooses" Israel, this is what remains: a belief that through Israel God's presence in the world can be made manifest. The extent to which awareness of God is found in human life depends on the extent to which Israel maintains its commitment to orient its communal life to that spiritual reality. This is what the rabbis meant when, in commenting on Isaiah 43:10 "You are My witnesses, and I am your God" they wrote, "If you are My witnesses, then I will be your God. But if you are not My witnesses, then, as it were, I will not be your God."[22] Indeed, when Israel fails to witness to this divine dimension of human and cosmic life, then, to just that extent, it fails to be present in the world.

Covenantal living, then, does not depend on a mythological view of the relationship between God and Israel. We need not abandon the notion of a bond between Israel and the spiritual force we call God. We need only recognize that covenant is today, as it always has been, a metaphor for a relationship we sense between ourselves and what we regard as ultimate reality. Today, covenant can be understood as a metaphor for a relationship of mutual dependence and interconnectedness between spiritual and human powers.[23]

But the question remains: how do Jewish moral obligations arise in the context of a covenant conceived in this way? I suggest that in the context of a covenantal bond with the divine force within and around us, Jewish ethics will emerge out of a matrix consisting of three elements: communal experience, textual study, and spiritual awareness. Each of these requires some elaboration.

The central questions about life and its meaning have always been asked by Jews primarily on the communal, rather than the individual, level. From earliest times, Jews have seen their destiny as that of a "kingdom of priests and a holy nation," whose corporate life testifies to their faith in a single God. Thus, religious and moral norms were addressed to the people as a whole, and to this day, prayers for atonement are recited in the plural, as a communal confession. In formulating a modern Jewish ethic, then, we must look to Israel's communal experience and its collective sense of responsibility to further the moral task passed down through the generations. Jewish ethics must always be about the collective conscience of the people—what *we* understand to be permitted or required—not the personal conscience of any individual.

But this conscience cannot be generated from scratch by any group of living Jews; it must represent their deepest sense of the moral direction of the Jewish community across time. No Jewish ethic is authentic that does not begin with a commitment to perpetuate and extend an ethical tradition reaching back across centuries. This is why extensive textual study is integral to the process of creating a modern Jewish ethic. Only when we have become thoroughly familiar with the religious-moral wisdom of previous generations can we formulate an ethic that is Jewish—part of a historically-evolving tradition—rather than merely the product of our contemporary collective wisdom. This textual investigation will not be restricted to a process of halakhic interpretation nor will modern liberal Jewish ethicists feel bound by the canons of interpretation that constrained earlier exegetes. They will also be willing to look to the values embedded in nonlegal materials, and will feel free to amplify voices that historically have been in the minority. But their ethic will grow out of serious engagement with traditional moral concepts and rules as articulated in the classical Jewish religious literature.

Finally, no modern Jewish ethic worthy of the name can result from merely studying and explicating texts; constructive religious ethics can never be only an exercise in applying ancient views to modern problems. Rather, it must be consciously formulated as a response to our own collective and historically informed spiritual insights. It must be moral guidance that grows out of our striving to live in God's presence and to orient ourselves in the world so as to reflect those ultimate spiritual concerns. A modern Jewish ethic will direct us to treat ourselves and one another in ways that further the presence of the divine in the world. It will be nourished, not by philosophical categories drawn from other moral traditions, but from our God-wrestling, which is both our own active quest to understand and actualize the divine and our best attempt to learn from the ways in which our ancestors have done so.

It may be helpful at this juncture to provide a slightly more concrete picture of how such a Jewish ethic might take shape. Doing so requires that we imagine a community of Jews who commit themselves to a process of exploring their religious/moral obligations together. They are fully literate in the traditional sources, actively engaged in the life of the Jewish community, spiritual seekers for whom the Jewish and secular components of life are thoroughly integrated. They meet on a regular basis for extended periods of time to worship, study, and share the personal dimensions of their lives. In this context, they attempt to formulate Jewish moral guidelines for specific issues that concern them. Each question is addressed through a combination of textual research, intensive discussion, and significant sharing of personal, spiritual perspectives.

The precise way in which all these elements come together cannot be dictated in advance; it occurs organically as members of the group discuss their own sense of how best to orient their lives toward the divine presence that they experience and how best to integrate this with their best reading of the tradition as it has evolved to this point. For them, developing a Jewish ethic will not be a matter of "discerning God's will," nor will it be restricted to an exercise in textual-halakhic interpretation. Rather, they will see themselves as a Jewish moral-spiritual community, bound together by a common sense of their collective, covenantal responsibility to Jews past and future. Accordingly, they will formulate moral guidelines and nurture moral character development in the context of a holistic Jewish religious life. God will be very much present in their moral-religious deliberations, but understood as a force whose presence they feel in their prayer life and in their own moral questioning, in their own personal lives, as well as in the views of sages from an earlier time.

A modern Jewish ethic as I have envisioned it here, then, will differ from more traditional approaches to Jewish ethics in a number of respects. First and most obviously, Jewish moral obligations will no longer be understood as "what God wills us to do." This, as we have seen, depends on a notion of God as a willing, speaking, acting being that many liberal Jewish thinkers can no longer affirm. Knowing, as we now do, that the universe contains as many as fifty billion galaxies, it is hardly credible to imagine the force active throughout creation in anthropomorphic terms. Divine presence, rather than divine will, provides the religious foundation of this Jewish ethic.

In addition, we will have to recognize that, given the limitations of our religious understanding, our moral discernment will be similarly restricted. The idea that there exist absolute moral norms, valid for all time, that we can discover through some procedure will have to give way to a more realistic, and fragmentary, notion of moral truth. Our faith in God is less certain and our religious experience less constant that it once was. We have what Irving Greenberg has called "moment faiths,"[24] which alternate with moments of skepticism and despair as we attempt to maintain a relationship with God. We cannot then expect that our moral compass will be as reliable or as constant as it is (and has been) for those with a more traditional faith in God.

Accordingly, all moral norms that arise in the context of this covenantal relationship will be provisional, subject to revision in light of our ongoing wrestling with God and our persistent efforts to rework the tradition. It follows, of course, that the content of our covenantal moral obligations cannot be dictated in advance, nor will they be shared by all members of the community. In a certain sense, this has always been true. Over the centuries, rabbinic authorities have often differed profoundly in their understandings of what God expects morally of the Jewish people in the context of their covenant. Nonetheless, they could affirm that even diametrically opposed opinions were both "the words of the living God."[25] Today, given a more tenuous relationship with God, we will have to embrace even more fully the value, indeed the necessity, of pluralism.

Finally, although we will not abandon the idea that normative values can be found in the texts of our tradition, we will need to recognize that they are not found *exclusively* there. The texts are a window into the religious and moral experience of those who preceded us. As such they are indispensable in the formation of any authentic Jewish ethic. Yet, it is not the texts themselves that are authoritative, but the experiences of those who wrote them. And so the primary task of a modern Jewish community in search of an ethic is to recreate the conditions for those spiritual experiences that alone can provide religious-moral orientation in the world. In fact, the study of classical Jewish texts can prompt us to religious awareness, tutor our moral sensibilities, and direct us to those experiences (in nature and/or in relationship with others) that will enhance our sense of life's sacredness. So, the textual tradition is a means, not an end in itself.

To be sure, these conditions for the construction of a modern Jewish ethic are not easily met. At least in North America, outside of Orthodox enclaves, there are today very few Jewish communities that could engage in the sort of spiritual-ethical work outlined here. The level of Jewish literacy is abysmally low and the interest in Jewish spiritual life is only moderately more in evidence. The creation of a compelling, authentically Jewish ethic requires a vibrant, religiously active, highly educated Jewish community, one with both the capacity to understand the forms of past religious expression and the creativity to revitalize those forms and generate new ones.[26] Now as always, the precondition for generating Jewish moral norms is a spiritually vital Jewish community.

In conclusion we must return to the issue with which we began—how does a modern Jewish ethic as it has been described here overcome the challenge of historicism? Given our historical-critical perspective on our religious tradition, how can we determine what is normative? In the context of our historical understanding and of our refashioned covenantal theology as outlined earlier there would seem to be no standards for choosing one moral position over another. In a sense, any moral position that we formulate in response to the tradition and to our own religious experience is as valid, as "authentically Jewish," as any other.

To be sure, we cannot identify within the tradition specific moral norms that are, in themselves, "divinely ordained" and so outside the purview of historical analysis and contextualization. There is no single truth isolated in a particular text or revealed at a particular point in time that provides a supernatural, ahistorical point of reference and standard for determining future norms. In the end, the relativizing power of history cannot be overcome. But it can be embraced. That is, we can acknowledge that religious experience, viewed historically, yields no absolute norms—neither for us, nor for those who preceded us. The time-honored idea that, through revelation, we have access to a realm of truth immune from historical change must be regarded as an illusion that we do well to abandon. In its absence, however, we are not left in a situation of moral chaos. We can, in community with one another, in conversation with religious virtuosi of earlier generations, and in communion with that divine power at work in the world, choose a moral direction. No direction that we choose, no set of moral norms that we affirm in this way, will be absolute. But neither will they be arbitrary or capricious. Although we can no longer live with the assurance that our moral choices accord perfectly with God's will, we need not abandon the notion that our lives have divine significance. As Jews we can make moral choices in the context of our encounter with the mystery we call God and guided by the historical records of our people's centuries-old encounter with that same mystery.

If this way of constructing modern Jewish ethics does not give us clear, unambiguous moral guidelines, we should be neither surprised nor dismayed.

As liberal Jews, our moral vision can only be as certain as our experience of God. And given the tentativeness of the latter, the former must also be indeterminate. To Orthodox believers, this is anathema, a sign of the moral chaos that besets modernity. To us, it is simply an honest reflection of what we can believe in an age of historical consciousness and what we can understand of moral obligation in a time when God no longer proclaims moral imperatives from the mountaintop.

It is fitting to close with a quotation from Max Weber, one of the giants of modern sociology. Like his friend and colleague, Ernst Troeltsch, Weber recognized that modernity represents a major challenge to religious traditions, for it precludes both the simple reaffirmation of older religious truths and the possibility of replacing these with absolute, objective norms drawn from our social scientific worldview.

> We know of no scientifically ascertainable ideals. To be sure, that makes our efforts more arduous than those of the past, since we are expected to create our ideals from within our breast in the very age of subjectivist culture; but we must not and cannot promise a fool's paradise and an easy street, neither in thought nor in action. It is the stigma of our human dignity that the peace of our souls cannot be as great as the peace of one who dreams of such a paradise.[27]

In such an era, the most that we as Jews can do is to live our moral lives in response to that sense of mysterious divine presence that historical study can relativize but cannot erase. And that, in the end, may be sufficient.

Part Three

Methodological Issues
in Contemporary Jewish Ethics

Chapter 8

Woodchoppers and Respirators

The Problem of Interpretation in Contemporary Jewish Ethics

The central problem of constructing a contemporary Jewish ethic has been expressed succinctly by Immanuel Jakobovits, whose work on Jewish medical ethics is widely published and quoted.

> How does *Jewish law* go to work in relating to very modern issues, many of which obviously are the result of spectacular advances in medicine that are of very recent times? How can we apply to contemporary perplexities insights that have their origin in the timeless traditions of our faith and are imbedded in virtually all the layers of our *literature* going back to earliest biblical times? How we can [sic] find principles enshrined in those early *sources* that have relevance and application to the highly complex questions that arise from these dramatic advances in medicine?[1] (emphasis added)

Constructing a contemporary Jewish ethic, as Jakobovits and many others conceive it, involves interpreting traditional Jewish texts and applying their norms to complex, often unprecedented, contemporary issues. Textual interpretation, it seems, provides the foundation for contemporary Jewish ethics.

My purpose here is to explore the ways in which Jewish ethicists derive answers to contemporary moral problems from traditional texts.[2] I do this by examining the modes of interpretation that they employ, the ways in which they read traditional Jewish texts and use them to articulate Jewish views on contemporary moral problems. To illustrate this process and the hermeneutical issues to which it gives rise, I will focus on the contemporary Jewish ethical

161

debate surrounding euthanasia. The issue of euthanasia is particularly well-suited for this purpose in several respects. First, euthanasia has received a good deal of attention in recent years by Jewish ethicists of both traditional and liberal orientations. Thus there is a wealth of literature on the topic.[3] Moreover, the situations in which questions of euthanasia arise in our time are largely unprecedented, owing to recent dramatic advances in medical technology. As a result, the problem of applying traditional sources to contemporary cases in this instance is especially acute. At the same time, I want to emphasize that the interpretive problems raised here are in no way limited to this specific moral issue, or indeed to biomedical ethics generally. To the extent that this process of textual interpretation is central to all contemporary Jewish ethical discourse, so too are the methodological problems that accompany it.

I will proceed by exposing, then challenging, the assumptions that underlie the process of textual interpretation as it is practiced by most contemporary Jewish ethicists. Specifically, I will argue that virtually all exegetes employ a model of textual interpretation that assumes first, that texts themselves contain some single determinate meaning and second, that the exegete's role is to extract this meaning from the text and apply it to contemporary problems. I suggest, however, based on the work of current literary and legal theorists, that these two assumptions regarding the character of the text and the role of the interpreter are questionable, if not altogether untenable. If, as these critics claim, the meaning of a text lies less in the words themselves than in the interpretive framework that the exegete brings to them, then most contemporary Jewish ethicists employ a very problematic methodology. In the concluding section of this chapter I suggest one way in which this methodological problem might be overcome, although not without altering significantly the way in which most people currently conceive of doing Jewish ethics.

Interpretation in Contemporary Jewish Ethics:
Description and Analysis

Translating traditional Jewish values into specific norms for ethical conduct in the modern world involves three steps: (1) identifying precedents from classical Jewish literature, (2) adducing principles from these texts, and (3) applying these principles to new sets of facts. Though the interpretive process is rarely delineated so clearly, these basic steps are implicit in the work of virtually all contemporary Jewish ethicists. Thus, while Jewish authorities differ sharply both in the ways they approach these basic interpretive tasks and in the specific conclusions they reach, the process of interpretation and the problems that it entails are shared by all. It should be noted that these three steps are in some respects closely related. Determining whether a certain text is pertinent to the issue at hand (step 1) and applying the message of that text to a contemporary situation (step 3), for example, both involve identifying the ways in which traditional cases and contemporary ones are analogous and/or disanalogous.[4] In the contemporary discussions summarized later that illustrate this interpretive process we note that these steps are not followed in a strict, chronological sequence. Nonetheless, it is helpful for analytical purposes to examine each step separately.

Let us begin by considering the difficulty of identifying precedents within the tradition for cases involving euthanasia. Traditional sources that permit people to pray for the speedy death of a dying individual who is in great pain are one striking case in point. These texts do not directly concern questions of euthanasia at all, but, in the view of some authorities, may nonetheless provide the basis for a Jewish position on such questions.

> On the day that Rabbi Judah was dying, the rabbis decreed a public fast and offered prayer for heavenly mercy [so that he would not die]. . . . Rabbi Judah's handmaid ascended to the roof and prayed [for Judah to die]. The rabbis meanwhile continued their prayers for heavenly mercy. She took a jar and threw it down from the roof to the ground. They stopped praying [for a moment] and the soul of Rabbi Judah departed.[5]

> Sometimes one must request mercy on behalf of the ill so that he might die, as in the case of a patient who is terminal and who is in great pain.[6]

> It happened that a woman who had aged considerably appeared before Rabbi Yose ben Ḥalafta. She said: "Rabbi, I am much too old, life has become a burden for me. I can no longer taste food or drink, and I wish to die." Rabbi Yose answered her: "To what do you ascribe your longevity?" She answered that it was her habit to pray in the synagogue every morning, and despite occasional more pressing needs she never had missed a service. Rabbi Yose advised her to refrain from attending services for three consecutive days. She heeded his advice and on the third day she took ill and died.[7]

> 'There is a . . . time to die' (Ecclesiastes 3:2) Why did Koheleth [the author of Ecclesiastes] say this? With respect to one

who is dying, (*goses*)[8] we do not cry out on his behalf [in the hope] that his soul will return; he can at best live only a few days, and in those days he will suffer greatly. Thus it says, 'a time to die.'[9]

Citing these sources, Solomon Freehof concludes that Jewish law sanctions passive euthanasia, at least in those cases in which the dying individual is incurable and/or in great pain. Noting that Rabbi Judah's handmaid is praised in the Talmud for her action, he writes,

> Is it the physician's duty to keep this hopeless patient (who is also in all likelihood suffering great pain) alive a little longer, maybe a day or two? Jewish law is quite clear on this question. He is not in duty bound to force him to live a few more days or hours. . . . In other words, according to the spirit of Jewish tradition, just as a man has a right to live, so there comes a time when he has a right to die. Thus, there is no duty incumbent upon the physician to force a terminal patient to live a little longer.[10]

In short, if one may pray for the death of the hopelessly ill and dying patient, one may, it is argued, take other steps that will tend to promote the inevitable end.

This same argument is stated more explicitly, and carried to a more radical conclusion, by Byron Sherwin, who argues that these texts, among others, might provide the basis for sanctioning certain forms of active as well as passive euthanasia. As Sherwin reads these texts,

> The woman's withholding of her prayers removed the cause of the extension of her life. Similarly, the removal of 'life-support' systems from a patient to whom—like this woman—life has become a burden, would be permissible. Nevertheless, it may be argued that this case underscores the inability always to make a clear-cut distinction between passive and active euthanasia. Her withholding of her prayers, or a physician or nurse's 'pulling the plug' may be considered a deliberate action aimed at precipitating an accelerated death. Once the line between passive and active euthanasia becomes so blurred, one may attempt to cross the line with care and with caution. For if the woman's withholding of her prayers is a sanctioned action deliberately designed to accelerate her own death, then other actions designed to accelerate the death of those to whom life has become an unbearable burden might also be eligible for the sanction of Jewish tradition.[11]

To others, however, such conclusions about euthanasia may not legitimately be derived from these texts. Asher Bar-Zev, for example, considers this argument but ultimately rejects it on the grounds that there is a qualitative difference between praying to God for death to come (or refraining from those prayers that presumably serve to sustain life) and taking active medical steps to hasten death.

> On the basis that prayer and medicine are considered equally efficacious in Jewish tradition, one might argue that medicinal means of hastening death would also be permitted. However, a fine distinction can be made in this case. Since one has asked God to kill oneself, it is God rather than man who is the active agent in bringing about the death. . . . We conclude, therefore, that there is a difference between prayers for a person to die and the use of a physical act in order to cause death to come.[12]

Thus, there is disagreement on the extent to which those sources that permit prayers for the death of an incurable person can be "translated" into permissive attitudes toward euthanasia. As Alan Weisbard astutely notes in this connection,

> Only a limited conclusion can be drawn from these materials on prayer. Clearly the rabbis were sympathetic to efforts to deliver incurables from their agony. They looked favourably upon and authorized behaviour inconsistent with a maximal effort to prolong life. Yet, in each instance, the process was mediated by and, presumably, consistent with, the divine will. Thus, to the extent prayer's nexus with the divine will is unique, lessons drawn from Jewish attitudes toward prayer for the dying provide only uncertain guidance with respect to medical interventions.[13]

Do texts about praying for death to come have precedential value for matters of euthanasia? The fundamental problem in answering such a question—and it is a question that must be asked by anyone who wishes to develop a position consistent with Jewish tradition—is simply that traditional sources do not come to us prelabeled to indicate which are relevant to the particular contemporary dilemma we happen to be facing. As a result, there is considerable room for contemporary authorities to differ in their choices of precedents for modern cases involving euthanasia.[14] Moreover, it is a matter of dispute among contemporary Jewish ethicists whether aggadic (nonlegal) texts can serve as valid precedents for contemporary decisions at all. This point emerges most clearly in contemporary discussions of the talmudic text describing the martyrdom of Rabbi Ḥaninah ben Tradyon, on which some rely heavily and which others dismiss as entirely irrelevant.

> They took Rabbi Ḥaninah ben Tradyon and wrapped a Torah scroll around him, and encompassed him with faggots of vine branches, to which they set fire. They brought woolen tufts, soaked them with water, and laid them on his heart, so that his soul should not depart quickly. . . . His disciples said to him: "Open your mouth that the fire may penetrate." He replied: "Better is it that He who gave the soul should take it, and that a man should do himself no injury." Then the executioner said to him: "Master, if I increase the flame and remove the woolen tufts from off the heart, will you bring me to the life of the world-to-come?" "Yes," said Ḥaninah. "Swear it," demanded the executioner. Ḥaninah took the oath. Forthwith the officer increased the flame and removed the woolen tufts from over Ḥaninah's heart, and his soul departed quickly.[15]

It is suggested by many authors that the story provides the basis for drawing a distinction between active euthanasia, which is forbidden (insofar as Ḥaninah would take no direct action to hasten his own death), and passive euthanasia, which is permitted (for Ḥaninah would allow the executioner to remove the obstacles which prolonged his death). As Byron Sherwin indicates,

> The Talmudic case of Ḥananiah ben Teradion is also used by post-Talmudic sources as a precedent for the permissibility of passive euthanasia. The rabbi permitted the tufts of wool which were 'artificially' sustaining his life to be removed. This would seem to permit both voluntary and involuntary passive euthanasia. . . . To be sure, Jewish law would not permit the removal of any and all life-support mechanisms. . . . The text of the story of Ḥaninah ben Teradion clearly relates to an individual who has no chance of survival in any case, i.e., to a terminal patient.[16]

Yet, Novak argues, such stories are not in general intended to serve as legal precedents. Presumably, they are meant rather to illustrate the rabbi's piety and willingness to die as a martyr, for the sanctification of God's name (*kiddush hashem*).[17] Moreover, Rabbi Nissan Telushkin notes that we have an obligation to preserve life by any medical means available, whereas there is no such necessity when the continuation of the status quo serves merely to perpetuate pain and suffering inflicted in order to torture (as in the case of Rabbi Ḥaninah ben Tradyon).[18] Thus, the case of Ḥaninah ben Tradyon may be irrelevant either because it is not a legal precedent at all, as Novak argues, or because it concerns a situation of torture and so is not pertinent to matters of medical care for the dying, as Telushkin maintains. Needless to say, one's decision to accept or reject one or more texts as precedential will greatly affect one's ultimate conclusion about what constitutes a Jewish view on issues such as euthanasia.

This same problem can be illustrated in connection with another body of texts often cited in contemporary discussions of euthanasia, those that concern individuals on the verge of death (*goses*) and specify what may and may not be done on their behalf.

One may not close the eyes of a dying person (*goses*); one who touches him so as to move him is a murderer. Rabbi Meir would say: "It is to be compared to a sputtering candle which is extinguished as soon as a person touches it—so too, whoever closes the eyes of a dying person is considered to have taken his soul."[19]

A dying person (*goses*) is considered to be alive in every respect. . . . To what may he be compared? To a flickering flame, which is extinguished as soon as one touches it. Whoever closes the eyes of the dying while the soul is about to depart is shedding blood. One should wait a while; perhaps he is only in a swoon.[20]

One may not prevent a person from dying quickly. For example, if there are factors preventing a speedy demise—such as a man chopping wood in the vicinity of a dying man's home, and the noise of the chopping prevents the soul from escaping—we remove the chopper from there. Likewise we do not place salt on his tongue to prevent his death. But if he is dying and he says, "I cannot die until you put me in a different place," they may not move him from there.[21]

It is forbidden to cause the dying to die quickly, such as one who is moribund (*goses*) over a long time and who cannot die, it is forbidden to remove the pillow from under him on the assumption that certain birdfeathers prevent his death. So too one may not move him from his place. Similarly, one cannot place the keys of the synagogue beneath his head [on the assumption that their presence hastens death], or move him so that he may die. But if there is something that delays his death, such as a nearby woodchopper making a noise, or there is salt on his tongue, and these prevent his speedy death, one can remove them, for this does not involve any action at all, but rather the removal of the preventive agent.[22]

Do these texts provide appropriate analogies to, and therefore precedents for, contemporary cases of euthanasia? Scholars disagree. As defined by traditional sources[23] the term *goses* refers to an individual whose death in imminent, and certain to come within seventy-two hours. Some contemporary authorities, following this definition strictly, have therefore held that terminally ill patients being kept alive on respirators do not fall within the category of *goses* at all, for it is clear that they can be kept alive for considerably longer than three days. As J. David Bleich argues,

> any patient who may reasonably be deemed capable of potential survival for a period of seventy-two hours cannot be considered a goses. . . . It would appear that Halakhah assumes axiomatically that the death process or the 'act of dying' cannot be longer than seventy-two hours in duration. . . . The implication is that a goses is one who cannot, under any circumstances, be maintained alive for a period of seventy-two hours."[24]

On this view, the texts cited here are simply irrelevant to any case in which patients could be kept alive with the help of artificial life support systems for months and even years.

Ronald Green, however, has challenged Bleich's unwillingness to apply the category of *goses* to many contemporary cases.

> Can it not be said, however, in view of the capabilities of modern medicine, that the category of the goses, as it was formerly understood, no longer exists? When the patient today begins choking on secretions, a tracheotomy is performed or the breathing passage is cleared out. When the "last breath" is drawn, the ventilator is turned on. One conclusion, of course, is that very few patients any longer are goses so that whatever permission existed in such cases for the cessation of efforts no longer applies: everything must be done to extend life. This seems to be Bleich's conclusion. But it is equally open to the halakhic scholar to conclude that medical advance forces a radical reconsideration of the classical sources in order to discern the intent of rulings that mandated life-saving ef-

forts or that created the special category of the goses. It may be that temporal limits no longer suffice to identify the imminently dying patient, for example, and that some consideration of the hopelessness of the patient's condition or continued quality of life are more relevant to the determination of this status.[25]

Others, consistent with Green's suggestion, have been inclined to interpret the category of *goses* more liberally. Marc Gellman, for example, argues,

> When therapeutic hope failed in the world of our ancestors, death was certain to come shortly, and so the category of gessisah was that short time (72 hours or less) before death when therapy failed. What has happened in our time is that a new category applies. Medical science can fail to cure and yet continue to treat for far longer than 72 hours. Is this gessisah? . . . Just as the rabbis used a time limit to define gessisah, so must we recognize that life expectancy is a crucial factor in determining whether or not to treat. This is not a quality of life argument, it is a quantity of life argument and it counts.[26]

While Gellman does not argue here that the category of *goses* must be revised in response to changing medical technology, his observation that it could be so revised is very suggestive. At very least, the way in which one interprets this traditional term could radically alter one's application of these texts to a contemporary biomedical issue. Indeed, a number of authors writing on the issue of euthanasia simply assume that the forgoing texts are applicable to any individual who is judged to be "in the process of dying" and who, without artificial assistance, would not survive for any substantial length of time. Seymour Siegel, in line with Gellman's suggestion, believed that the term should be applied to anyone who cannot be saved by medical science, for whom treatment is futile, actually a prolongation of death rather than a prolongation of life.[27] But as Weisbard notes in this connection, "Extension of that concept [goses] from the traditional three day period to a metaphoric understanding which would encompass the almost indefinite maintenance of a patient 'one moment from death' (made possible by modern medical technology) is far from universally accepted."[28]

Yet, even if all authorities could agree that traditional laws regarding the *goses* were applicable to contemporary cases of euthanasia, the principle underlying these cases is subject to several alternative interpretations. It is clear that the woodchopper is an impediment to the patient's death. But how are

we to construe the nature of this impediment—as something physically removed from the person, as something that has no therapeutic value, as something not placed there by the patient or those caring for that person, or
simply as anything whatsoever that prevents a person from dying. Similar
questions can be raised about the circumstances under which an impediment
to death, of whatever sort, can be removed. Shall we restrict the principle that
impediments may be removed to individuals who are in severe pain, to those
who are irreversibly comatose and so feel no pain at all, or to those in neither
of these categories who are terminally ill for whom medical technology can
offer only palliative care but no cure?

Answers to these questions vary widely. Immanuel Jakobovits, for one,
concludes from these sources that "Jewish law sanctions, and perhaps even demands, the withdrawal of any factor—whether extraneous to the patient himself or not—which may artificially delay his demise in the final phase."[29] This
view was also shared by the well-known Orthodox legal decisor Moshe Feinstein.[30] So too, Solomon Freehof has argued that a life-sustaining apparatus
that prevents a terminal patient from dying is the sort of impediment that the
text from Sefer Hasidim cited earlier would permit us gently to remove.[31]

Other authorities, however, question whether the impediments spoken
of in these texts are of the same character as the modern life-support equipment often in place when decisions involving passive euthanasia need to be
made. Rosner, for example, is somewhat more cautious in his application of
these sources to the discontinuation of life-supporting equipment or therapy.

> The impediments spoken of in the code of Jewish law, whether
> far removed from the patient as exemplified by the noise of wood
> chopping, or in physical contact with him such as the case of salt on
> the patient's tongue, do not constitute any part of the therapeutic ar-
> mamentarium employed in the medical management of this patient.
> For this reason, these impediments may be removed. However, the
> discontinuation of instrumentation and machinery which is specifi-
> cally designed and utilized in the treatment of incurably ill patients
> might only be permissible if one is certain that in doing so one is
> shortening the act of dying and not interrupting life.[32]

Consistent with the thrust of Rosner's view, Marc Gellman suggests that
"modern medicine can become a woodchopper when its invasive procedures
have lost their therapeutic rationale."[33] Presumably, though Gellman does not
state this explicitly, a life-supporting procedure that did have some therapeutic value would not be subject to the rule of the woodchopper.

David Novak proposes still another reading of the case of the wood-chopper's noise and so questions its applicability to cases of euthanasia on other grounds. Perhaps the author of this text wanted to distinguish between obstacles to death that were physically removed from the patient (e.g., the woodchopper) and those that were in contact with the person (e.g., the keys of the synagogue). But, Novak argues, our understanding of modern physics may not permit us to maintain this clear distinction.

> just as removing salt from the tongue was eliminated as an accept-able act because it involves the physiological result of moving the mouth, so I would argue that if one could possibly show that the sound waves caused by the woodchopper were actually life-sustain-ing in any way, then this folk remedy, [that the woodchopper should be silenced] now having an etiology, would also be elimi-nated as an acceptable act.[34]

Thus, the way in which we adduce the principle embodied in a text may de-pend, in part, on our assessment of the scientific and medical knowledge on which those traditional judgments were based.

We have seen, then, that while these traditional texts concerning treat-ment of the *goses* both proscribe taking any action that would hasten death and permit removing certain obstacles that forestall death, it is not apparent how such rules can be translated into general principles applicable to con-temporary situations. How broadly or narrowly should we construe these cases and the (unarticulated) general principles that underlie them? The sources themselves offer no guidance in this crucial respect. As Karl Llewellyn has noted, every legal precedent has not one value, but two; it can be inter-preted either broadly, so as to encompass many new cases, or narrowly, thus restricting its impact on future decisions. Both options are always open and both are equally valid.[35] In short, we have seen that quite distinct principles may be deduced logically from a single case insofar as this material is "rather opaque in terms of its underlying values."[36] As a result, these texts can be ap-plied to contemporary situations in a number of ways and, in any event, only with considerable reservation.[37]

This same methodological problem arises when authorities turn from specific cases as precedents to general principles, which, it is claimed, underlie the tradition as a whole. Many authorities, for example, base their opposition to euthanasia on the principle, derived from Scripture, that all life is a gift from God and thus sacred. This basic presupposition is most clearly articu-lated by J. David Bleich, who writes,

> In Jewish law and moral teaching the value of human life is
> supreme and takes precedence over virtually all other considera-
> tions. . . . Human life is not a good to be preserved as a condition
> of other values but as an absolute basic and precious good in its
> own stead. The obligation to preserve life is commensurately all-
> encompassing.[38]

It follows that the value of life is not quantifiable, for, having infinite value,
even the smallest fraction of life is precious.[39] On this view, the limited "quality of life" that a dying patient enjoys, and even the limited quantity of life
that such a person can anticipate, are irrelevant where questions of euthanasia
are concerned.

Others, however, would articulate the tradition's view of the sacredness
of life and apply it to cases of euthanasia quite differently. Sherwin, for example, writes:

> exceptions to the prohibition against killing and self-killing were
> condoned by classical Jewish tradition, such as cases of martyrdom
> and cases of 'justifiable homicide.' These exceptions to the rule
> lead one to the conclusion that the value of life itself is not always
> considered absolute. The permissibility and even the desirability of
> martyrdom assumes that there are occasions where life itself may
> be set aside because the preservation of life itself is not always an
> absolute moral imperative.[40]

If the value of life is conceived as relative rather than absolute, then it may be
permissible to take life in the interests of furthering some other goal, for example, the alleviation of the patient's suffering. In a similar vein, it has been
argued that "the principle of sanctity of life proscribes weakening of natural
vital forces, but does not prohibit removal of unnatural life-prolonging factors."[41] Indeed, some authors cite the "sanctity of life" principle, but appear
unable or unwilling to spell out just what this principle requires in specific
cases.[42] In short, it is not immediately obvious how these broad principles
about the value of life should be applied to questions of euthanasia, insofar as
the principles, in context, make no reference to such questions at all.

The third and final step in the interpretive process involves the application of general principles to contemporary situations. To do this the interpreter, once again, must determine the extent to which a new fact pattern does
or does not correspond to the facts underlying previous rulings. The problem,
as lawyers and journalists alike are well aware, is that facts can always be construed in more than one way. To state a set of facts is already to employ cate-

gories that shape perception, thought, and judgment. And if the "facts themselves" do not fall neatly into established categories (which they very often do not), then the very nature of the matter at hand will be difficult to determine. Indeed, much litigation in American courts involves precisely a dispute over which rule or principle should govern this particular case, that is, whether this case is more like one sort of previously decided case or another.

This, of course, is precisely the situation in many areas of biomedical ethics where unprecedented circumstances arise with the advance of medical technology. When a person pulls out a pistol and shoots someone point blank, we all recognize that as an act of murder (though, of course, the penalties imposed, if any, may vary significantly depending on the circumstances). But when a person pulls a plug on an artificial respirator, or refuses either to resuscitate a terminally ill patient or to give nutrition to a person in an irretrievably comatose state—is this murder or something else? Is letting a dying person die, even gently speeding up the inevitable end, the same as actively taking life? And to what extent, if at all, should it change our description of the situation if that individual has expressed his or her wish in advance to be allowed to die (or if that person's representative does so later)? In all these cases, the very way in which we describe the facts will influence the way in which we apply a principle to the situation at hand.[43]

Contemporary Jewish discussions of euthanasia, like all other treatments of the issue, reflect this problem. What distinguishes the Jewish discussion from others is the pool of texts and analogies from which contemporary authors draw. As we have seen, some view an artificial life-support device as analogous to a woodchopper, or to salt on a dying person's tongue, or to the woolen tufts that prolonged Ḥaninah ben Teradyon's tortured death. Some regard disconnecting a patient from such equipment as analogous to prayers offered for the death of those suffering or terminally ill. Others, as we have seen, call these analogies into question. My only point here is that all determinations of this sort entail judgments not only about the principle embodied in the case (which in many instances is difficult enough to discern) but also about the character of the act of euthanasia itself.

The Interpretation of Texts in a Legal Tradition

Thus far I have attempted to illustrate the problems inherent in the process of applying traditional texts, and the principles they embody, to contemporary moral problems such as euthanasia. We have seen that contemporary authorities have cited traditional Jewish texts to support a wide range of positions on questions of euthanasia. The permissibility of passive euthanasia has evoked the greatest diversity of response, some appearing to prohibit it in any form,[44] some arguing that only when a patient no longer responds to therapeutic treatments are we permitted to cease further life-saving efforts,[45] some permitting the removal of irreversibly comatose patients from a respirator,[46] and some inclining to permit passive euthanasia in any situation of extreme or needless suffering.[47] With respect to active euthanasia, the generally accepted view that this is "absolutely forbidden," has been challenged by Byron Sherwin, who argues for a minority view within the tradition that would permit even active intervention to cause death in certain circumstances.

But my point in exploring the interpretive process and the difficulties to which it gives rise is not primarily to note the fact that contemporary authorities, like their traditional predecessors, disagree about the meaning of specific texts. Rather, I want to stress that these differences arise within a framework of shared assumptions about the nature of the entire interpretive enterprise. Whatever other differences divide them, virtually all modern Jewish ethicists are united in their perspective on both the meaning of texts and the role of the ethicist as an exegete.

The two working assumptions that govern the entire enterprise can be stated simply as follows. First, the source of contemporary Jewish values lies within the texts and, second, the job of the modern ethicist/exegete is to extract this meaning from the texts and apply it to contemporary moral problems. The texts themselves contain meaning and the interpreter merely retrieves this meaning and draws our attention to the inherent connection between the text and the contemporary world. On this view, the interpreter's role appears to be rather limited, for it is really the texts themselves that yield fruit while the exegete is only, so to speak, the midwife. It is precisely because all the authorities cited in this study understand interpretation in this same way that they encounter similar problems in the process, though, as we have seen, they address these problems differently.[48]

But in the view of many contemporary legal and literary theorists, this represents a serious misunderstanding of the interpretive process, of the meaning of texts and of the role of the interpreter in creating that meaning. To illustrate this alternative theory of exegesis and its application to Jewish ethics, I will draw on recent discussions of the nature of textual (especially constitutional) interpretation by legal theorists.

The relationship between a text and its meaning is often discussed by legal scholars in terms of the extent to which the text (of a statute, or a constitutional clause) dictates or even constrains the meaning later interpreters can attribute to it. The question is whether the author's words, and ultimately the intentions that the author meant those words to convey, set the limits of acceptable interpretation. In constitutional interpretation, at least, some have argued that they do not. As Terrance Sandalow has claimed, the document's language plays a role in the development of constitutional law, but does not itself dictate the meaning that subsequent generations of justices see in it.

> The 'goals' and 'ideals' that Judge Wright sees 'embedded in the constitutional language' are those that subsequent generations have found there, which is not quite the same as saying that they were put there by the framers. Contemporary constitutional law does, to be sure, rest upon a conceptual framework and employ a vocabulary that is in large measure derived from the framers. . . . Decisions continue to be justified by an analysis which begins with the proposition that the exercise of power must be referable to the 'commerce' clause or one of the other heads of federal power. . . . In making these decisions, however, the past to which we turn is the sum of our history, not merely the choices made by those who drafted and ratified the Constitution. The entirety of that history, together with current aspirations that are both shaped by it and shape the meaning derived from it, far more than the intentions of the framers, determine what each generation finds in the Constitution.[49]

On this view, the meaning of a constitutional clause is not contained in its language, but rather emerges as it is applied over time by justices whose reading of the document is shaped by aspirations some of which the framers would not have shared or even understood.

By the same token, Paul Brest has noted that many constitutional provisions are inherently "open-textured," meaning that their language requires elucidation in ways that the document itself does not provide. The clause prohibiting "cruel and unusual punishment," for example, does not define the specific meaning of those terms. What we today consider "cruel" may differ significantly from the accepted definition in the eighteenth century. So the meaning of that clause is not contained in its language, but is supplied by us as we determine the perameters of what those words permit and prohibit.[50] In this way, an existing rule actually gains new meaning each time it is applied to a new set of facts.[51]

But if meaning is not fully embedded in the text itself, it follows that interpreters do not simply retrieve something that exists independent of their efforts. Indeed, many legal (and literary) theorists have argued that meaning is a product of the interaction between text and reader. James Boyd White, in an insightful comparison of legal and literary interpretation, writes,

> reading literature is an interaction between mind and text that is like an interaction between people—it is in fact a species of that— and the expectations we bring to a text should be similar to those we bring to people we know in our lives. . . .
>
> The reader, both of texts and of people, changes as he or she reads: one is always learning to see more clearly what is there and to respond to it more fully—or at least differently—and in the process one is always changing in relation to text or to friend. It is in this process of learning and changing that much of the meaning of a text or of a friendship resides; the text is in fact partly about the ways in which its reader will change in reading it.[52]

White asks us to see both law and literature as sharing a common goal of challenging the reader to become a different person, to respond to the ideals and expectations that the text articulates. The meaning of a text, then, is a function of the reaction of a reader, or a community of readers, to this challenge at a given moment. Its meaning will differ from one reader to another and even for a single reader at different points in his or her life. In sum, White argues, interpreting a text is a dialectical process; each of us plays a vital role in creating the meaning that we find in the texts we read.

These views of interpretation challenge Jewish ethicists to look at textual study and exegesis in a new light. Many of those engaged in contemporary Jewish ethics are inclined to treat the provisions of talmudic and medieval texts as if they were less open-textured than in fact they are. The Jewish legal tradition does not really constitute a body of views and precedents that "speak for themselves" to contemporary issues. Rather, it offers us categories, concepts (of life, of death, of suffering, etc.), and notions of the relationships that obtain among moral agents. It provides a rich resource of values and principles that Jewish ethicists, if they are committed to remaining within the tradition, must utilize. But the texts do not, either individually or collectively, dictate how to use or apply these resources. That is up to the interpreters, whose knowledge of the texts, of the culture that produced them, and of the history of previous exegesis, enable them to respond most fully and authentically to the textual tradition. But, as White has noted, the meaning that the interpreter finds in the text will change over time and will not be consistent from one interpreter to another.

It might appear that this hermeneutical theory turns all interpretation into pure subjectivity. If the meaning of a text is imputed to it by the interpreter, there would seem to be no limits to the possibilities, no way to distinguish legitimate from illegitimate, good from bad, readings of a text. Indeed, the deconstructionists and "reader-response" critics have adopted exactly this position.[53] But, as Owen Fiss has argued, we need not abandon all notions of objectivity in interpretation in order to acknowledge the subjective role of the reader. He writes,

> The idea of objective interpretation accommodates the creative role of the reader. It recognizes that the meaning of a text does not reside in the text, as an object might reside in physical space or as an element might be said to be present in a chemical compound, ready to be extracted if only one knows the correct process; it recognizes a role for the subjective. . . . At the same time, the freedom of the interpreter is not absolute. The interpreter is not free to assign any meaning he wishes to the text. He is disciplined by a set of rules that specify the relevance and weight to be assigned to the material (e.g., words, history, intention, consequence), as well as by those that define basic concepts and that established the procedural circumstances under which the interpretation must occur. . . .
>
> Rules are not rules unless they are authoritative, and that authority can only be conferred by a community. Accordingly, the disciplining rules that govern an interpretive activity must be seen as defining or demarcating an interpretive community consisting of those who recognize the rules as authoritative. This means, above all else, that the objective quality of interpretation is bounded, limited, or relative. . . . Bounded objectivity is the only kind of objectivity to which the law—or any interpretive activity—ever aspires and the only one about which we care.[54]

Objectivity in interpretation, according to Fiss, exists whenever there are constraints acknowledged and observed by a community of interpreters. These constraints, which are generated by communities of readers and also serve to define those communities, provide the parameters within which interpretive activity takes place. But these constraints are never wholly determinative; they never dictate in a mechanistic fashion the result of any act of interpretation. And as Fiss goes on to suggest, the nature and extent of these constraints or "rules of the game," may themselves be the subject of some disagreement within an interpretive community. This will not undermine the objectivity of the enterprise so long as there is a consensus on the framework within which interpretation takes place.

The interpretation of traditional Jewish legal texts by contemporary authorities, I would argue, proceeds in accord with Fiss's model. Here, too, as we have seen, there is latitude for considerable diversity of legitimate interpretation. Diversity results from the inescapable subjectivity of individual interpreters. These differences are legitimate because there is considerable consensus on the rules that place constraints upon the interpretive process, and so ensure that the result is objective.[55] All contemporary Jewish authorities look to the same body of literature as a source of precedents, that is, they are committed to the same canon. All would acknowledge that the history of previous interpretation of these sources must be given some weight and that the principles embodied in these sources (and not merely the words of the texts themselves) must be interpreted. It is within these parameters that each interpreter works, rendering a personal, but constrained and therefore objective, judgment as to the meaning of these texts when applied to a contemporary moral problem.

This account of the nature of interpretation demands that contemporary Jewish ethicists reexamine the sort of enterprise in which they are engaged. Let me illustrate my point once again using a passage on euthanasia. This one is taken from a handbook on Jewish bioethics and is typical of statements found throughout the literature.

> The Jewish attitude towards euthanasia as well as towards suicide, is based on the premise that 'Only He Who gives life may take it away.' . . . Any deliberate induction of death, even if the patient requests it, is an act of homicide.
>
> For Judaism, human life is 'created in the image of God.' . . . It may thus not be terminated or shortened because of considerations of the patient's convenience or usefulness, or even our sympathy with the suffering of the patient. Thus euthanasia may not be performed either in the interest of the patient or of anyone else. Even individual autonomy is secondary to the sanctity of human life. . . . In Judaism suicide and euthanasia are both forms of prohibited homicide.[56]

Rosner, like so many other scholars, writes as if the tradition relates directly to contemporary moral issues. But clearly this is not the case. For if by "Judaism" we mean that body of traditional Jewish literature that Jews cite to support their claims that some view or other is sanctioned by the tradition, then it must be acknowledged that Judaism says nothing directly at all about disconnecting artificial respirators, or about withholding antibiotics from a patient dying of cancer, or treating an anencephalic infant, or any of the other problems of euthanasia that contemporary medical science has forced upon us.[57] As we have seen, given a properly selected set of interpretive assumptions, the texts can be invoked to support a whole range of positions on such questions. We should be wary, then, of exegetes who announce that they merely discover and report what the texts say. The very process of interpretation necessitates acts of judgment on the part of the interpreter—decisions about which cases constitute precedents, what the principles of those cases are, and how they should be applied to the case at hand. And these decisions can be made responsibly and authentically in a variety of ways. It follows that the interpretive assumptions that readers bring to the literature play a decisive role in creating the very meaning that they attribute to the text. And if this is true generally, it is especially true for interpreters of classical Jewish texts, which are notoriously terse and ambiguous. Then too the creative role of the interpreter will be still more pronounced when the task at hand is to apply these classical texts to complex, wholly unprecedented dilemmas created by rapidly advancing biomedical technology.

But, it will be objected, if we view the interpretive process in this way, do we not undermine the entire enterprise of contemporary Jewish ethics? How can contemporary authorities claim to render normative Jewish judgments, in Jakobovits's words, "apply[ing] to contemporary perplexities insights that . . . are imbedded in virtually all the layers of our literature going back to earliest biblical times?" To the extent that the meaning of a text lies as much in the activity of the interpreter as in the text itself, contemporary Jewish ethics becomes at least partly a matter of reading our values into the texts rather than deriving authentically Jewish views from them. And if eisegesis replaces exegesis, what is the point of doing Jewish ethics, or rather, what makes Jewish ethics Jewish and not just the subjective judgment of an individual reader?

In attempting to answer these questions, let me turn to a model of jurisprudence suggested by Ronald Dworkin. His work addresses the very problem facing contemporary Jewish ethicists—the interplay between the constraints imposed by the textual tradition and the freedom inherent in the personal judgment of the interpreter. Dworkin suggests that judges who interpret a legal tradition are doing much the same thing as authors who interpret the literary creativity of their predecessors. Indeed, he asks us to imagine a series of authors who write a novel, each author contributing one chapter in sequence. Each author (after the first) inherits the work of earlier writers in the series and so is given a kind of limited creative license, for the author's literary imagination must work within boundaries (however fluid) that have been established by previous writers. The need to preserve a sense of coherence within the novel will provide a general framework within which successive novelists will do their work. Building upon this example, Dworkin proceeds to argue that,

> Deciding hard cases at law is rather like this strange literary exercise. The similarity is most evident when judges consider and decide common law cases; that is, when no statute figures centrally in the legal issue, and the argument turns on which rules or principles of law 'underlie' the related decisions of other judges in the past. Each judge is then like a novelist in the chain. He or she must read through what other judges in the past have written, not only to discover what these judges have said, or their state of mind when they said it, but to reach an opinion about what these judges have collectively done, in the way that each of our novelists formed an opinion about the collective novel so far written. Any judge forced to decide a lawsuit will find, if he looks in the appropriate books, records of many arguably similar cases decided over decades or even centuries past by many other judges of different styles and judicial and political philosophies, in periods of different orthodoxies of procedure and judicial convention. Each judge must regard himself, in deciding the new case before him, as a partner in a complex chain enterprise of which these innumerable decisions, structures, conventions, and practices are the history; it is his job to continue that history into the future through what he does on the day. He must interpret what has gone before because he has a responsibility to advance the enterprise in hand rather than strike out in some new direction of his own. So he must determine, according to his own judgment, what the earlier decisions come to, what the point or theme of the practice so far, taken as a whole, really is.[58]

Dworkin's conception of legal interpretation enables us to account both for the latitude and the constraints that judges in all legal traditions inevitably confront. He goes on to suggest,

> This flexibility may seem to erode the difference on which I insist, between interpretation and a fresh, clean-slate decision about what

the law ought to be. But there is nevertheless this overriding constraint. Any judge's sense of the point or function of law, on which every aspect of his approach to interpretation will depend, will include or imply some conception of the integrity and coherence of law as an institution, and this conception will both tutor and constrain his working theory of fit—that is, his convictions about how much of the prior law an interpretation must fit, and which of it and how.[59]

The function of the judge, or of the contemporary Jewish ethicist, then, is not to filter out his or her own interpretive framework, but rather to use that framework to create a coherent tradition, encompassing both the body of legal precedents and the case at hand.[60] It follows that when contemporary Jewish authorities, armed with a body of traditional Jewish sources, confront a contemporary moral problem, the decision that they reach, through interpretation and application of those sources, will be guided by a sense of what "fits" the tradition. And this sense of "fit," in turn, will be shaped by a particular way of construing the coherence of the tradition as a whole, as it relates both to the particular question at hand and, no doubt, to other aspects of the tradition as well.

This is precisely what makes contemporary Jewish ethics Jewish, the commitment of those engaged in the exercise to render a judgment that accords with their own sense of the thrust of the tradition as it has evolved. Among contemporary Jewish ethicists, of course, there are many diverse conceptions of the coherence of the tradition as a whole and it would take us too far afield to sketch them here and trace their implications for the question of euthanasia in particular. Nonetheless, Dworkin's discussion enables us to see more clearly what interpreting a tradition entails and how this activity by its nature imposes certain constraints upon the interpreter while necessitating a certain degree of "interpretive license."

Contemporary Jewish Ethics—A Reassessment

I want now to explore the implications of the hermeneutical theory sketched here for the practice of contemporary Jewish ethics. In my judgment, contemporary Jewish ethics can absorb this understanding of the interpretive process without losing its raison d'être, though the fundamental questions raised above will need to be answered in a new way. Given this understanding of the interpretive process, we need to rethink the way we conceive of

Jewish ethics. A number of semantic, methodological, and conceptual adjust-
ments appear to be in order.

On the level of semantics, Jewish ethicists should avoid talking about
what specific positions "Judaism" sanctions on contemporary issues. To do so,
as I have argued, is seriously to misrepresent the nature of the enterprise in
which one is engaged. Accordingly, the rhetoric of Jewish ethics should
change from "what Judaism teaches" to "what we, given our particular interpretive assumptions and our particular way of construing the coherence of
the tradition as a whole, find within the traditional sources."[61] The difference
is hardly a trivial one, nor is it only a matter of insisting upon a kind of "truth
in advertising." I do not suppose that contemporary Jewish ethicists have deliberately set out to deceive their readers, or that they themselves are unaware
of the spectrum of opinion that the foregoing analysis has highlighted. Yet, if
contemporary Jewish ethicists presented their views in the more precise, qualified way I am suggesting, they would be forced to confront more self-consciously than they have their own role in the interpretive process.[62]

Because this fact has been obscured by the language of contemporary
Jewish ethicists, a further important problem in this field has gone largely un-
addressed. It is the working assumption of most of the authors cited in this
study that to develop an authentic Jewish position on some contemporary
moral problem one need only cite texts and draw conclusions from them.
With rare exceptions (Novak, Weisbard), these authors have not attempted to
defend their particular way of selecting and reading the sources against other
possible or actual readings. Much less have they found it necessary to articulate
a view of the coherence of the Jewish tradition as a whole in terms of which
they have chosen to make interpretive decisions in one way as against another.
As a result, it could be said that much contemporary Jewish discourse resem-
bles a conversation in which the participants are talking past, rather than to,
one another. If the foregoing analysis is substantially correct, it follows that any
contemporary Jewish position is only as compelling as the interpretive assumptions on which it rests. To defend cogently any particular ethical position, then,
requires that one offer reasons for adopting the interpretive stance that one has.
Of course, these reasons may or may not be compelling to those who approach
the texts with other interpretive theories. But, if interpretation is to be more
than ad hoc decision making, it must rest upon a theoretical foundation. And
if one wishes to urge others to adopt a particular interpretation, that theory
must be stated explicitly and defended. In American jurisprudence, producing
a "reasoned opinion" and defending it against competing opinions is standard
procedure. Contemporary Jewish ethicists should do no less.

Moreover, given the obvious parallels between Jewish ethics as it is practiced by most contemporary authorities and Anglo-American jurisprudence,
it is most unfortunate that Jewish ethicists have largely ignored developments
in American legal theory. As I have noted throughout this chapter, contemporary Jewish ethics as practiced by all the authorities discussed here is based
on a kind of judicial model. This is most obvious when Jewish discussions of
issues like euthanasia are juxtaposed with those of philosophers and of Christian ethicists who approach the topic from an entirely nonlegal perspective.[63]
Of course, the Orthodox authorities cited here self-consciously do Jewish
ethics within the framework of halakha. Yet, even for those who do not view
themselves as operating within a strictly halakhic framework,[64] the tradition
of halakhic texts is the primary resource upon which they base their views.
Virtually without exception, they formulate their own contemporary Jewish
position in response to and in the attempt to maintain an essential continuity
with halakhic precedent. But for this very reason, theories of judicial interpretation and of legal reasoning in general have much to offer those doing
contemporary Jewish ethics. If more attention were given to the literature in
general jurisprudence, Jewish authorities might gain both a fuller understanding of the nature of legal interpretation and useful models for thinking
about the interplay between the authority of a textual tradition and the freedom inherent in the exercise of judicial discretion.

Finally, in no sense do I wish to suggest, given the subjective nature of
interpretation as I have described it, that Jewish ethicists should quit reading
traditional texts. Rather, it has been my assumption that what makes contemporary Jewish ethics Jewish is its attempt to develop positions that carry
forward the views contained within that long textual tradition. I simply wish
to spell out what is actually involved when contemporary Jewish ethicists engage in such exegesis and to suggest that, if this description is accurate, the
ways in which people currently conceptualize the field need to be reexamined. I would propose that contemporary Jewish ethics be conceived, not as
an attempt to determine what past authorities would say about contemporary
problems if they were alive today, but as a dialectical relationship in which finally no sharp distinction can be made between our voices and theirs. What
we discover through this relationship with sages of the past certainly will not
be less valid just because it cannot finally be attributed solely to the authorities of past generations. Any reading of the texts that we produce, and any
conclusions we draw from them, are as much our work as theirs. Those engaged in contemporary Jewish ethics surely need not quit reading texts, but
just as surely they need to make more modest claims on their behalf.

Chapter 9

Text and Tradition in Contemporary
Jewish Bioethics

In the preceding chapter I suggested that "doing" contemporary Jewish
ethics entails standing in a chain of tradition and interpreting classical texts
in a way that contributes to that tradition. I want here to build on that point
by sketching some of the alternative ways that contemporary Jewish ethicists
could construe the nature of their tradition and the corresponding ways in
which they would be led to interpret texts. In doing so, my goal is not to advocate any one approach over others, but to explore the range of possibilities
and the consequences of the choices that ethicists make.

Jewish Ethics in the Modern World

Modern Jewish ethics may be defined as the effort to develop positions on
contemporary moral problems continuous with the values and norms expressed in the Jewish religious tradition. As such, doing Jewish ethics involves
two distinct, but related, projects. Jewish ethicists must provide a means, first
for identifying values and norms within the Jewish tradition and then for applying them to contemporary problems.[1] Jewish ethicists can choose among
various ways of doing this, and in this chapter I explore some of these options.
Using issues in medical ethics as a basis for comparison, I illustrate the differences among three basic models for doing modern Jewish ethics. I contend
that the differences among these approaches derive from a more fundamental
difference in the way Jewish ethicists understand the very nature of their tradition. All modern Jewish ethicists have a theory, explicitly or implicitly, of what
their tradition is and how to continue it; it is this theory that guides their
interpretation of classical Jewish sources and so defines their positions on

185

contemporary problems in bioethics. While I focus here on issues in biomedical ethics, it should be noted that the basic methodological differences I want to highlight are in no way unique to these sorts of moral problems.

To understand the central problem facing Jewish ethicists in the modern context, we must begin by contrasting the modern situation with the traditional context in which Jews reflected on ethics. Before the processes of secularization transformed European society and the Jewish communities within them during the eighteenth and nineteenth centuries, Jews lived within a wholly religious framework. Their beliefs and values, their rituals and lifestyle were understood as divinely revealed. Torah was the source both of metaphysical truth and of practical wisdom. Finding the appropriate response to any moral problem, therefore, was a matter of finding within the received tradition the pertinent passages and norms and then applying them to the case at hand. While this was by no means an easy process, as anyone familiar with classical Jewish literature knows, it depended upon a fairly "simple" view of revealed truth. As Gershom Scholem expressed it,

> all this [rabbinic interpretation] was somehow part of revelation itself—and more: not only was it given along with revelation, but it was given in a special, timeless sphere of revelation in which all generations were, as it were, gathered together; everything really had been made explicit to Moses, the first and most comprehensive recipient of Torah. The achievement of every generation, its contribution to tradition, was projected back into the eternal present of the revelation at Sinai. . . . According to this doctrine, revelation comprises within it everything that will ever be legitimately offered to interpret its meaning. . . . Truth is given once and for all, and it is laid down with precision. Fundamentally, truth merely needs to be transmitted. . . . The effort of the seeker after truth consists not in having new ideas but rather in subordinating himself to the continuity of the tradition of the Divine word and in laying open what he receives from it in the context of his own time.[2]

Within this traditional religious framework, the interpretation of sacred texts was central. Because God's will was understood to be fully embodied, literally encoded, in the text of Torah, norm setting derived from a process of textual interpretation. Moreover, this textual interpretation and norm setting was understood to take place in an ahistorical context. The moral truths that people lived by were seen, not as the product of changing historical circumstances, but as expressions of God's eternal and unchanging will. Finally, as Scholem noted, this orientation to truth and revelation rests on the assumption that the divinely revealed Torah already contains all the answers to all the questions that we will ever face. If we are only skillful and diligent enough in our reading of the texts, we will discover the guidance that God has given us.

In this premodern context, it is somewhat anachronistic to speak of Jewish ethics as a distinct enterprise at all. Dealing with ethical issues was fundamentally no different from dealing with any other sort of religious question. Whether the issue was how to treat one's neighbor or how to observe a festival, how to conduct one's business or how to recite a prayer, the same corpus of biblical and rabbinic sources were cited and the same methods of logical and analogical inference were employed. Indeed, in classical sources there is no distinct category of ethical texts separate from texts concerning appropriate attitudes and behaviors in personal, family and communal life.[3] As many have noted, the primary category for Jewish ethical thinking over the ages has been "the holy," not "the good."[4] And, of course, holiness is a concept that embraces the whole of the religious life; what we call ethics is simply one subdivision within it.

This traditional approach is alive and well among contemporary orthodox rabbis writing on Jewish medical ethics. For these traditionalists, the question of maintaining continuity with the tradition of Jewish ethical reflection never arises. God has already given us the answers to all our moral problems; we need only consult the Torah and the rabbinic codes for guidance. As J. David Bleich puts it,

> To be sure, not all bioethical problems are questions of black and white. There are many gradations of gray, questions to which answers are not immediately and intuitively available. A person who seeks to find answers within the Jewish tradition can deal with such questions in only one way. He must examine them through the prism of Halakhah for it is in the corpus of Jewish law as elucidated and transmitted from generation to generation that God has made His will known to man.[5]

For traditionalists like Bleich, there is nothing arbitrary or subjective about the way this legal tradition is interpreted and applied. Neither the interpreter's volitional inclinations (toward permissiveness or stringency) nor considerations of expediency can ever consciously influence the halakhic decision-making process.[6] Moreover, since the legal process itself is an expression of God's eternal will, traditionalists see no need to examine the ways in which historical circumstances might have influenced particular decisions in the past (or present). In short, the interpretation of the law takes place in an ahistorical framework, shaped ultimately neither by the personal preferences of rabbinic decision makers, nor by the times in which they live (or lived).

But alongside this traditional method other approaches have emerged that do not share the theological assumptions of the traditional model. For these ethicists, the tradition is a resource but also a problem. They claim to stand within this tradition of Jewish religious-ethical reflection, yet they accept neither the traditional view of revelation nor the method of textual interpretation that follows from it. For them, the central problem of constructing a contemporary Jewish ethic can be phrased in terms of the meaning of tradition. They must demonstrate the authenticity of their ethics by articulating a theory of what the tradition is and showing how, through this ethic, that tradition is being perpetuated. In the following section I explore various models of modern Jewish ethics and highlight the different ways in which each approaches issues in medical ethics. I will then return to address the theory of tradition that underlies each of these models.

Models in Contemporary Jewish Ethics

The Legal Model

Investigating the literature in contemporary Jewish bioethics,[7] it appears that one model predominates. For lack of a better term, I will call this the "legal model," insofar as it approaches questions in Jewish ethics as matters for legal reflection in light of precedents found in traditional legal sources. Given a moral problem, legalists will cite classical Jewish legal sources and, through analogical reasoning and other means, attempt to distill the principles behind this line of precedents and apply them to the question at hand. To be sure, different authorities adduce these principles and apply them differently, and this accounts for the fact that they frequently differ in their opinions (as, of course, did premodern authorities). But their differences arise within a framework of common assumptions about the nature of Jewish ethics and a common method for resolving ethical problems.

This legal model may also be thought of as neotraditional. Like the traditionalists, the legalists derive answers to contemporary moral problems from the Talmuds and compendia of Jewish law, including medieval responsa, which address specific cases referred to rabbinic authorities for judgment. But while legalists share with traditionalists like Bleich the view that Jewish ethics is a legal enterprise, their methodology is more historically critical. Legalists are inclined to consider not only the substance of prior rulings but also the historical context in which they were written, the state of medical knowledge at that time, and the jurisprudential philosophy that guided those who made earlier rulings. They see the law as having developed in response to changing circumstances and so understand their role as facilitating the further development of this legal tradition.

This legal model governs much of the work in the field of contemporary Jewish bioethics, especially that done by some orthodox and most conservative rabbis.[8] Its orientation toward the law and its application to medical issues is articulated clearly by Emanuel Rackman. He begins by spelling out four "myths" concerning halakha: (1) that it is immutable, (2) that it is totally objective, (3) that it is not influenced by current conditions and circumstances, and (4) that it never transcends its own rules. Rackman, himself an Orthodox rabbi, recognizes that these myths form the cornerstone of the traditional approach to halakha and ethics, and that in challenging them he places himself in a minority position within the Orthodox camp. But, on the basis of his studies of the halakhic process he feels compelled to conclude that the law has indeed changed over time, that it has been influenced in a number of ways by historical and subjective factors.

As Rackman explains it, halakha has evolved over time for a number of reasons.

> As a matter of fact, there are three factors that play a part in all legal development: One is logic; the second is the sense of justice; and the third concerns the needs of society. All three elements play a part in Jewish law that there's no escaping. This is true of all legal systems and of the *halakhic* system as well.[9]

By "logic," Rackman means the use of analogy and definition to determine the application of an established rule to a new situation. In deciding, for example, if modern Jews could use electricity on the Sabbath, rabbinic authorities needed to determine whether electricity fell under the definition of "fire," and so was included within the biblical prohibition against lighting fires on the Sabbath. The "sense of justice" for Rackman involves humanitarian concerns and principles of equity that are not themselves legal rules, but that often shape the interpretation or application of those rules. As an example, he cites the way in which some talmudic authorities handled cases involving slaves. Because they had a deep concern to protect the humanity of the slave, they sought (and found) ways to apply the rules governing slaves to further that goal. To illustrate the final principle, that Jewish law evolves in response to social needs, Rackman cites the biblical rule that requires the cancellation of all debts every seventh year. In order to ensure that people would still be willing to lend money to the needy as the seventh year approached, the sage Hillel instituted a legal fiction that circumvented the biblical rule. In this way creditors would not lose their money every seventh year and the poor could continue to receive the loans they needed.

In the concluding section of his article, Rackman briefly indicates some of the ways in which this model of legal decision making might inform our attitudes toward certain medical issues, such as birth control and abortion. While Jewish law does not regard abortion as a case of murder (since the fetus is not regarded as a full person), it does tend to restrict abortion to cases where the mother's life (or health) is endangered. Rackman, however, suggests that responsiveness to social needs may warrant a reconsideration of that position.

> I see no possibility yet, under Jewish law, of what is called infanticide or abortion. It is fobidden [sic] by Jewish law. The question, however, is whether Jews may not come to certain conclusions with regard to restricting population growth. Such restriction may not be good for the Jewish people, and I am against zero-population growth for the Jewish people; we have had too many losses, and we have to repopulate the earth. *But at least we have an open mind with regard to it and may become more liberal with regard to planned parenthood and the circumstances under which abortions may be permitted.*[10] (emphasis added)

Rackman is suggesting that concerns about population growth may legitimately influence Jewish legal discussions about when abortion or birth control is permitted. In addition to such social concerns, Rackman also considers how humanitarian or psychological factors might influence our stance toward abortion. He notes that at least some earlier rabbinic authorities were willing to permit abortions if the child was conceived illegitimately and the birth of this child would cause its mother great distress. This leads him to suggest that, when ruling on questions of abortion, we may want to take into consideration certain "quality of life" factors, something that legal authorities until now generally have not done.

> In addition to the issue of preserving the life of the fetus, is the *quality* of the life to be preserved also a factor? . . . Today, of course, we regard the physical and psychological as interconnected.

When we speak of the quality of life, we refer to both. If one may perform an abortion to avoid a child who might suffer Tay-Sachs disease, then it may also be proper to abort a fetus that may be psychologically crippled in Jewish society.[11]

Rackman's orientation, then, represents what I have called the legal model in modern Jewish bioethics. For those authorities who employ this model, issues in Jewish ethics are legal questions and so must be dealt with in the context of the halakha. But they do not view the law as static or see this approach as formalistic. As Rackman writes,

> Thus there was always a positive response in Jewish law to social needs, together with a sense of justice, and certainly with logic playing its role as well. The principles and the underlying values do not change; the rules change. Call it innovation, call it creativity; the law is dynamic.[12]

I want now to explore two alternatives to the legal model of Jewish ethics. Neither of these has been developed as fully or applied as extensively to concrete contemporary problems as has the legal model discussed earlier. To some extent, then, what follows is descriptive of what Jewish ethicists have actually done and to some extent an effort on my part to explore possibilities that have not yet been fully worked out. In sketching the theological and methodological underpinnings of these models, my point again is not to evaluate or promote one as more successful or promising than another. Nor is this typology meant to be exhaustive of all conceivable possibilities. I want only to highlight diverse methods available for doing Jewish ethics. Once these options have been presented, I will explore the hermeneutics of each model.

A Covenantal Model

A covenantal model of contemporary Jewish bioethics has been developed in an article by Irving Greenberg, another Orthodox rabbi with liberal leanings. For Greenberg, the cornerstone of Jewish ethics, indeed of all Jewish life, is the covenant between God and Israel. This covenant has universal and messianic implications. As Greenberg puts it,

> Judaism is a commitment: what the tradition calls a covenant. Judaism is a covenant of perfection in which the Jewish people . . . are to teach the world that perfection is the end goal. The Jewish

people's mission is to teach the world not to settle for the present structure of reality, which is characterized not by the triumph of life but by sudden sickness and death, by oppression, inequity, and injustice. Judaism seeks to . . . [teach] the world that present reality is not acceptable; it is to be corrected and redeemed. Secondly, the Jewish community, as a community, is to show people how to move toward the final perfection.[13]

This messianic orientation provides the foundation for much of what Greenberg has to say about the use of power, especially in the realm of technology and medicine. Given the Jewish people's ultimate goal of bringing the world closer to perfection, we are required to use any and all means within our power to realize that goal. Indeed, the point of the covenant is that God has given us this power to use for precisely these purposes. We should not be afraid, Greenberg says, of new technologies; rather, we should welcome them as giving us new opportunities to fulfill our covenantal obligations.

But Greenberg is not so naive as to assume that the unbridled use of power always leads to moral choices. The covenant not only endorses the use of power but, equally important, establishes limits on its use.

All in all, work, productivity and medical power constitute a religious calling. But the key to constructive use of power is partnership. . . . The key is the concept of partnership and not just power for its own sake. The Bible which commands humans to shape the world and conquer it turns around and demands respect for that world. The Torah puts limits on what humans can do to that world. The classic limit is *Shabbat* (the Sabbath). The human who is commanded to work and maximize power all week long is asked to renounce that power on *Shabbat.* . . .

Thus there is a dialectic in Judaism: power is affirmed, but respect for that which already exists is also affirmed. Holiness consists of shaping and perfecting the world, of developing all the possibilities in life and eliminating sickness, and ultimately hoping to eliminate death, while at the same time respecting and enhancing the life that is.[14]

For Greenberg, then, the physician's covenantal commitment is to use power, and as much of it as possible, but only for the enhancement of life. Covenant instructs us to limit the use of our medical power to ensure that it improves the quality of life and respects the fact that all human beings are creatures in God's image.

Greenberg concludes by suggesting some of the ways in which this covenantal ethic could guide medical practice. His comments on birth control and abortion illustrate his orientation nicely.

The original birth control prohibition in Jewish law reflects the fear that human control over who shall be created, who shall be given life, is somehow robbing God of his power. What is *really* involved in birth control is an ethical trade-off: the quality of life versus the quantity of life. It is necessary to know that quantity is important. It's also essential to know that quality matters. If the marriage needs more time, if the mother needs more time or cannot handle the number of children, then it is ethical *not* to have the child rather than to have it. That is the balancing act that has to be undertaken.

The same holds true of questions of abortion. There is a profound ethical truth behind all those who oppose abortion. It is important for doctors to see it; when ending life, even during this prenatal stage, becomes casual, there will be a weakening of respect for all of life. Yet abortion can also be an act of taking responsibility for the quality of life of a mother; it can be the difference between life and a blasted life. [15]

We see here Greenberg's covenantal dialectic of power and respect for the sanctity of life. Most Jewish legal authorities would not permit an abortion in order to improve the quality of the mother's life or of the parents' marriage. For Greenberg, though, terminating a pregnancy in such cases may be preferable to bringing an unwanted child into the world. Such a choice, though by no means required, would be consistent with the goal of covenantal living: to make the world a more peaceful and perfect place.

Similarly, while most halakhic authorities permit autopsies only in cases where the knowledge gained would be of immediate medical benefit to a specific individual, Greenberg endorses a more lenient approach. He writes,

If an autopsy can lead to a medical breakthrough or to new understanding, then it is a *requirement.* A family that hesitates, or a rabbi who says no, is not being ethical or religious. This is being sacrilegious—placing a dead body ahead of a living person. [16]

Again, Greenberg believes that it is permissible (perhaps even required) to use any medical means consistent with improving the conditions of human life.

The covenantal model of Jewish ethics, then, is dialectical. It involves a constant attempt to balance the power that God has given us and the goals that God has set for us. It finds guidance, not so much in the substance of the legal tradition, as in the character of the covenantal relationship between God and Israel, between God and the world, which for Greenberg is the foundation of that legal tradition. The legal rulings of previous generations are by no means irrelevant. Through them we can discern the ways in which earlier sages defined their own obligations under the covenant.[17] But, in the last analysis, Jewish moral obligations are not determined by legal processes but by living in a covenantal relationship with God and attending to the responsibilities that are imposed by the very character of that relationship.

A Narrative Model

Narrative theology represents an important recent trend in Christian ethics, as exemplified especially in the work of Stanley Hauerwas. The essence of this approach, as Hauerwas expresses it for the Christian theologian, is that "being a Christian involves more than just making certain decisions; it is a way of attending to the world. It is learning 'to see' the world under the mode of the divine. . . . A Christian does not simply 'believe' certain propositions about God; he learns to attend to reality through them."[18] For Hauerwas, we learn to see the world in a distinctively religious way through stories. The importance of such stories is not only in their content, the principles they teach, or points they make. Rather, the narrative form is essential to the message. The very structure of the story, its characters and plot, its dramatic or tragic or comic qualities, are part and parcel of the message. Hearing these stories again and again we learn to internalize their structure, to project ourselves into the world described by the story, indeed, to see the world around us as a continuation of the story. Thus, Hauerwas says, we learn to attend to the world and act within it by means of the story.[19]

Among Jewish theologians very few have self-consciously attempted to employ this narrative approach.[20] In his book, *Jews and Christians: Getting Our Stories Straight*, Michael Goldberg contrasts Jewish and Christian ways of seeing the world through a comparative analysis of their respective "master stories," the exodus and the passion-resurrection. Following Hauerwas, Goldberg argues that for Jews the exodus narrative decisively shapes their understanding of the world and their moral responses to it. He writes, ". . . the Exodus as a master story serves as a model, a guide, for suggesting how we are to go on from here. It thus not only relates some past events in the life of one particular people, but simultaneously holds out a vision of how the life of all peoples may be sustained—and even transformed!—in the future. Hence, in the last analysis, the Exodus master story is quite literally one of *promise*, speaking of our duties and obligations as well as of the world's hopes and dreams."[21] For Goldberg, then, Jews learn what God expects of them morally by attending to the story of how God brought this people from slavery to freedom, how the Israelites participated in their own redemption, and so forth.

While Goldberg has not attempted to work out detailed analyses of contemporary problems in Jewish ethics using this approach, Hauerwas's own efforts in this respect suggest that it would certainly be possible to do so. A Jewish ethic of this sort would begin, as Goldberg does, with a detailed analysis of the themes and structure of the exodus narrative. He notes especially the themes of promise and fulfillment, of call and response, and of the mutual dependence of God and Israel. These themes would constitute the theological touchstones for developing a concept of Jewish moral responsibility. At this point I can only speculate on some of the ways in which a narrative theologian like Goldberg might analyze contemporary moral situations through the lense of this narrative.

The focus of the exodus narrative throughout is on the destiny of nations, rather than individuals. The survival of the people of Israel is threatened by the Egyptians, but their ultimate freedom has been promised by God. The tension between Pharoah's rule and God's is established early in the narrative when the Egyptian ruler demands that all male Israelite babies be killed. This focus on Israel's survival (to say nothing of the fact that the midwives are said to have defied Pharoah's decree) could underwrite a fairly conservative position on birth control and abortion. To the extent that modern Jews see their survival as threatened (as most do in the aftermath of the Holocaust), the exodus story would lead them to reject any actions that further limit the Jewish population. Moreover, since the story pays little attention to the autonomy of individuals, we would expect the narrative Jewish ethicist to reject arguments for birth control and abortion based on the rights of individuals to control their own bodies.

As Goldberg takes pains to emphasize, the exodus story is one of faithfulness and hope. Indeed, the question throughout is whether the Israelites will have faith in God's promises to redeem them and act in reliance on that promise. The need to take risks and to rely on God's power as the source of life (and death), could lead narrative ethicists to take a fairly lenient position on issues such as disconnecting life-support equipment. The Israelites in the story know that they do not have the power themselves to control their destiny; similarly, it might be argued, we must accept limitations on our power to control life and death. Indeed, a medieval pietistic work (*Sefer Hasidim*) makes precisely this point, linking it not to the exodus text but to Ecclesiastes 3:2, "There is a time to be born and a time to die."

Finally, the exodus story, according to Goldberg, tells us a good deal about what it means to be human.

> part of what it means to be human is to be fashioned in God's image; it is to be a creature that bears a certain likeness to its Creator, possessing in ways analogous to his a capacity for free, creative acts. But another part of what it means to be human—and again according to that selfsame story—is to be a limited, imperfect being who is most certainly *not* God.[22]

One might take this aspect of the story as evidence that we should be extremely wary of efforts by medical science to alter the genetic make-up of human beings. Genetic engineering potentially threatens the sacredness of human life by tampering with the divine image. Moreover, one might argue, it represents a misguided effort to "play God," to violate the limits that God has placed upon us.

It should be noted that this narrative model, if anything, is even more open-ended than the covenantal one. For Greenberg, Borowitz and other covenantal theologians, halakha represents at very least a valuable resource for understanding the history of covenantal responsibility. On the narrative model, by contrast, it appears that turning to the law as a resource for ethical reflection is looking in precisely the wrong place. The moral life is not about applying principles and rules to novel fact patterns; it operates on an entirely different level. Hauerwas expresses this orientation when he writes, ". . . our moral reasoning, especially in cases of moral doubt, is not deductive but analogical. . . . moral reason is more dependent on imagination than strict logical entailment."[23] Thus, the preoccupation with legal analysis that characterizes both traditional and much of modern Jewish ethics will strike narrative theologians as misguided, both because it looks to the wrong sources and because it appropriates them in the wrong ways.

Notwithstanding the marked differences among these various models for doing Jewish ethics, they share a few fundamental assumptions that should not escape our attention. In the first place, all would agree that Jewish ethics is distinctive in its method, if not also in its content. There is a source of specifically Jewish moral obligations separate from, though not necessarily incompatible with, whatever obligations Jews have in common with other humans. Moreover, this distinctively Jewish ethic, however it may be defined, is inescapably religious in nature. That is, it presupposes that Jews, both individually and in community, stand in relationship to God and derive their moral orientation from that relationship. Thus, modern Jewish ethicists share a commitment to affirming a transcendent source of morality, while at the same time accepting the legitimacy of some secular modes of thought.

By the same token, each of these models locates the source of transcendent moral truths in Torah, understood in the broadest sense as encompassing both sacred scripture and the rabbinic tradition that builds upon it. It follows that all these Jewish ethicists could rightly claim to derive moral guidance by reading and interpreting texts. And, given the centrality of the written word to Judaism as a whole, it is hardly surprising that this should be so. Indeed, it is difficult to imagine how one could claim authenticity for any Jewish ethic that displayed no relationship to the very body of literature that has been viewed throughout history as the authoritative source of values. But it is at this point that these models begin to diverge. For if all agree that doing Jewish ethics necessarily entails reading and interpreting Jewish texts, there is anything but agreement on which texts to read, and how. It is important then, against the background of certain shared assumptions about the centrality of God and Torah, to contrast the hermeneutics implicit in these models for contemporary Jewish ethics.

The Hermeneutics of Contemporary Jewish Ethics

We can understand how and why different "schools" of Jewish ethics read texts differently only if we first note that the ultimate purpose of this reading is far from academic. Unlike historians or literary scholars, Jewish ethicists read texts not only to understand what they say, but to orient their lives in accordance with that understanding. And since this reading and interpretation of texts is a normative exercise, the different strategies of interpretation employed reflect different ways of relating one's life to the text. It will be helpful, then, to think about how the text *functions* within each of these models, that is, what role it plays in the life of the reader. It seems to me that each model of Jewish ethics just considered offers us a distinctive way of relating ourselves to Torah, which can be characterized through a series of metaphors.

For legalists, Torah functions as a kind of blueprint for the building of an intricate structure. Like a blueprint, the goal of this text is to instruct the reader in how to produce a certain finished product. The text is utilitarian, serving as a medium for the architect to communicate a design to the builder, who will follow it for the sole purpose of actualizing this particular design. The direction that the blueprint provides is quite explicit and detailed. Reading and following blueprints is not always easy, even if one possesses the requisite skills. It demands strict discipline and extraordinary attention to detail. It also requires that the builder exercise judgment in performing all the tasks that the blueprint does not specify, but that are necessary to complete the project.

For legalists, Torah instructs us in the construction of a moral life, with certain fixed dimensions and contours. To succeed in its goal it needs fundamentally only to be followed. To be sure, the Torah on this model provides an extremely complex plan that directs us, not in how to complete a single finite task (like building a house), but rather in how to perform all our moral tasks throughout our lives. It often happens, on this view, that we find ourselves in situations for which the Torah's plan does not provide clear direction. At this point the legalists will insist that we have no choice but to study the text with the greatest care, to try to discern the intentions of the architect and to carry them out as best we can. Indeed, it may even be that the divine architect intended that the construction of a moral life entail just such ambiguities, since they force us to study the Torah ever more diligently.

The covenantal model, by contrast, views the Torah not as a blueprint but as a sort of marriage contract. Like that document, it establishes an intimate relationship between two parties but offers little in the way of concrete guidance for living in it. To be sure, this relationship requires certain personal qualities, such as trust, faithfulness, and integrity. But in the day to day business of maintaining a marriage, it helps little to consult the words of the marriage contract. That document provides the foundation for an evolving, dynamic relationship; it gives one an orientation toward one's partner, but not a specific plan of action. To the extent that the marriage contract continues to serve a function after the relationship is established, it is primarily a symbolic one. It points to the commitment and mutual respect that constitute the essence of the bond between the partners.

Torah, for the covenantal ethicist, is just such a document. If, in reality, the Torah text provides more detailed directives than a typical marriage contract, these are understood as symbolic as well. They represent some of the ways in which the essential qualities of a covenantal bond can be expressed in deeds. But it would be a mistake on this model to read the Torah as a manual for creating a successful marriage between God and Israel; that can occur only if the partners do what is necessary day by day to create the ideal world that the marriage document envisions. So it is that the covenantal ethicist rarely feels the need to engage in detailed explication of the Torah's injunctions, for they are taken as illustrative rather than definitive of one's moral responsibilities.

The narrative theologian, in turn, views the text as a work of art, a painting of sorts. Its purpose is to open our eyes to a certain way of perceiving reality. Just as viewing a work of art stimulates us to notice things about the world that we had not previously observed, the text expands our moral vision. It invites us, not only to see the world from a certain distinctive vantage point, but to carry that vision with us and to reproduce it in our responses to life. If we attend to it carefully, the text as work of art will transform us, directing us toward a new way of living in the world.

Torah, on the narrative model, instructs by guiding and stimulating our moral imagination. Its value lies, not in the rules it offers for how to behave but in the story it tells and asks us to internalize. In this sense, the text of the Torah is inherently incomplete, for it is we, the readers, who complete the story as we use it to structure our moral lives. For the narrative theologian, the text of the Torah is not meant to legislate a pattern of Jewish behavior or even to establish the relationship between God and Israel, though the story contained in Scripture surely has much to say about that relationship. It primarily provides an overarching plot for our moral lives, a meaningful structure that encompasses a conception of what the world is like and how God wants us to respond to it.

The point of the forgoing analysis should by now be clear. When Jewish ethicists read texts, they necessarily adopt a certain stance toward the text as a source of values. The way in which they appeal to the authority of the text, and consequently the way in which they read its words and apply them to their lives, all depend upon the sort of relationship they have to the text. And, as I have tried to show, several quite distinct options are viable. Builders relate to blueprints very differently from the way spouses relate to their marriage contracts, which are both very different from the way people relate to works of art. It could be said, then, that while Jewish ethicists all appear to be engaged in a common enterprise and to claim the same Torah as the source of their values, they understand that task and the role of textual interpretation within it in radically different ways. In the remainder of this chapter I suggest that these diverse approaches to the text, in turn, reflect different ways of construing what gives the tradition its coherence.

The Concept of Tradition in Contemporary Jewish Ethics

Underlying each of these models of Jewish ethics with its distinctive hermeneutic is a conception of the tradition that lends legitimacy to its methods and so to its particular way of reading Jewish texts. At bottom, what distinguishes these models of Jewish ethics from one another are their respective ways of construing the tradition and, as we shall see in a moment, each way is in a sense self-verifying. In short, modern Jewish ethicists choose among competing conceptions of tradition and the implications of that choice are very far-reaching.

What it means to construe a tradition in one way rather than another has been elucidated by the legal theorist Ronald Dworkin in a passage I cited in the preceding chapter. He discusses what it means for judges to feel bound by legal precedent and yet to make free and creative choices about how to handle the cases before them. To illustrate his point, he asks us to consider what it would be like for several authors to collaborate in the writing of a single novel, each of the authors writing one chapter in the sequence. Each novelist (after the first) enjoys a kind of constrained freedom, for their literary creativity to extend the story is necessarily limited by the parameters of the story as developed by earlier authors in the chain. So too, Dworkin argues, judges are free to render their own decisions, but in the context of an earlier legal tradition. They will need to justify any legal decision as coherent with the thrust of the legal tradition to this point as they interpret it.

Modern Jewish ethicists, I would argue, are exactly like the novelists or the judges in Dworkin's example. They are the latest link in a chain stretching back across centuries. They inherit a wealth of texts, decisions, stories, and practices that in no way form a seamless whole. Within this rich legacy the modern Jewish ethicist will find many divergent philosophies and contradictory opinions, as well as major themes and clearly articulated principles. No decision the contemporary ethicist makes can possibly be consistent with the whole of this tradition. Instead, the ethicist must (to paraphrase Dworkin) "determine what the point or theme of the tradition so far taken as a whole really is." This means coming to a conclusion about what gives this variegated tradition its coherence and then acting to preserve that coherence as one sees it. It also means recognizing that other ethicists, like other novelists in the chain, could interpret the historical record differently; they could examine the facts and legitimately reach a different conclusion about what the tradition is and how to continue it.

The most basic question for modern Jewish ethicists, then, is this: how *shall* we define the coherence of this religious tradition? What element or principle or method can provide a link between the efforts of past generations and the work that we do in this modern context? Torah is a rich and multi-faceted resource for ethical reflection. The root meaning of Torah, after all, is "to provide direction or instruction" and surely Scripture does this in a variety of ways: frequently through specific legal injunctions but also through narratives and through the depiction of a dynamic covenantal relationship between God and Israel. And, of course, this is true not only for the biblical text but for the entire corpus of rabbinic literature that flows from it. So each of these models (legal, covenantal, narrative) is firmly rooted in Jewish sources. More-over, each can provide the thread of continuity that modern Jewish ethicists need to construct a serviceable concept of tradition. And finally, once the co-herence of the tradition has been construed around any one of these elements, the relationship of the ethicist to the classical texts, and so the proper strategy for interpreting them, follow naturally.

Each of the three models of modern Jewish ethics I have explored rests upon a distinctive theory of Jewish tradition. The legalists have what we might call a "formalist" theory of coherence. On their view, the core of this religious-ethical tradition lies in its form or method, which is legal. On this model, it makes no sense to talk about Jewish moral obligations outside the context of the law. To do Jewish ethics is to stand within a legal tradition stretching back across the centuries. It is to see oneself as bound by legal precedents, and to commit oneself to extending that system of legal injunctions to an ever changing world.

For covenantal ethicists, by contrast, the law is but one expression of something more fundamental that gives the tradition its coherence. It is the covenantal relationship binding God to Israel and Israelites to one another that is central. Within this relationship one discovers one's moral obligations, partly, to be sure, by attending to legal precedents, but also by drawing upon moral wisdom expressed in other forms. On this model, the foundation of the tradition is not a body of law but an existential commitment, the com-mitment of the Jewish people to live in a covenantal relationship with God and to explore ceaselessly the moral implications of such a relationship.

For narrative ethicists, finally, the tradition's coherence is provided by the structure of its "master story." It is the task of each successive generation to remain true to that story, to add its own chapter to the unfolding plot. This concept of tradition is perhaps the most open-ended of the three. We in-herit a narrative legacy rich in possibilities; its plot gives structure and direc-tion to our moral lives but cannot fully determine how we should act in any given situation. Indeed, the narrative does not define the ethical choices we should make, so much as it shapes our moral sensitivities, provides us with a vision of what the world is and can be, and alerts us to the possibilities for living faithfully. We can perpetuate the tradition, on this view, only by internalizing the story it tells us to such an extent that our lives come to embody its many themes and messages.

It is important then that Jewish ethicists openly acknowledge that their work proceeds from some particular conception of the Jewish tradition and what gives it coherence. They should also make explicit the fact that their position, whatever it is, represents only one option among many. This does not mean that the choice is arbitrary. Indeed, one assumes that advocates of each model will have reasons for construing the tradition as they do, and that they will be prepared to articulate those reasons if asked to do so. But it is by no means self-evident that Jewish tradition is some one thing, or that there is only one way to perpetuate it. In fact, only when Jewish ethicists are explicit about the choices they have made, and also about the reasons for those choices and the implications of adopting the models they have, can there be properly speaking a "field" of Jewish ethics at all.

It remains to be noted that, just as a particular concept of tradition will ground a particular approach to Jewish ethics, each approach, if practiced consistently, will in fact contribute to the perpetuation of *a* Jewish tradition. In this sense, each model is self-authenticating. The more it is employed, and the more consistently it can demonstrate its effectiveness in providing Jewish moral guidance, the more justification there is for the claim that it truly represents a vibrant religious-moral tradition in practice. There is, then, a circular quality to the process of doing Jewish ethics. We adopt a concept of the tradition, which grounds our model of ethics and so guides our interpretations of classical texts. These interpretations authenticate our moral choices, which, in turn, reinforce our concept of tradition.

In closing, I want to quote a passage from the modern Jewish philosopher, Franz Rosenzweig. It is taken from a famous speech he gave at the opening of the Lehrhaus, a Jewish adult education institute that he helped found in Frankfort in 1920, but it touches on the heart of the matter I have been considering here.

> A new learning is about to be born. . . . It is a learning in reverse order. A learning that no longer starts from the Torah and leads into life, but the other way round: from life, from a world that knows nothing of the Law, or pretends to know nothing, back to the Torah. That is the sign of the time. It is the sign of the time

because it is the mark of the men of the time. There is no one today who is not alienated, or who does not contain within himself some small fraction of alienation. All of us to whom Judaism . . . has again become the pivot of our lives . . . know that in being Jews we must not give up anything, not renounce anything, but lead everything back to Judaism. From the periphery back to the center; from the outside, in.[24]

As modern Jews we are indeed alienated from Torah. We lack the security of possessing a divinely given center of value that can infuse the whole of our lives. In that sense we "hail from the periphery," and grope for a way back to Torah, for new ways of reading and appropriating the ancient texts. But even this is more problematic than we generally admit. For the text that we search for and draw our values from is, in large measure, a product of our own conceptualization. So too is the tradition that we hope to preserve through our moral searching and acting. Accordingly, it seems best to remember that citing classical texts in itself does not guarantee that our ethics are Jewish (as some writers appear to assume) nor does it obviate the need to make difficult theological choices or to address fundamental methodological issues.

To do modern Jewish ethics, then, is to engage in an enterprise fraught with uncertainties. Before one can take a responsible Jewish stand on any particular moral issue (in bioethics or any other area), one must first take positions on basic questions of method. Doing so is inherently risky, for there is no sure ground on which to stand, no way to ensure that the choices one makes about the very nature of the tradition are unassailable. But taking these risks and accepting their consequences is an essential part of doing Jewish ethics in the modern world.

Chapter 10

Talking Ethics with Strangers

A View from Jewish Tradition

If, as I argued in the last chapter, Jewish ethicists stand within their own tradition (albeit one of their own making), the question arises whether anything they say about moral responsibility can be intelligible to those outside that tradition. What are the resources within Judaism for addressing questions about the moral responsibilities of those outside this religious community and could these teachings contribute in any way to moral debate in a pluralistic society? These are questions that Jewish ethicists must address; how they answer them will determine the extent to which they can engage in constructive moral dialogue with other ethicists, both secularists and those from other religious traditions.

In his recently published book, *Bioethics and Secular Humanism*, H. Tristram Englehardt Jr., describes moral debate in our society as a conversation among "moral strangers."

> When one meets another as a moral stranger, one meets in circumstances where there is no commonality of moral commitment that could in principle resolve the difference. . . . To be a moral stranger to another is not to share enough of a concrete morality to allow the common discovery of the basis for the correct resolution of a moral controversy.[1]

The problem, as Englehardt and others see it, is how to create a common language in which moral strangers can discuss and resolve the moral controversies they face as members of a single society. Before turning our attention to the solution that Englehardt proposes, we should note that the problem itself reflects the multiplicity of religious commitments and communities that make up our increasingly multicultural, multiracial society. We can no longer assume (if, indeed, we ever could) that our neighbors share our moral and religious values. At times it seems that diverse communities are engaged in open conflict with one another for the right to determine legal and social policy on pressing moral issues. Insofar as religious communities have contributed to this problem—and there can be no doubt that they have—it may seem unlikely that they have a constructive role to play in solving it. In any event, it is far from obvious how they could do so. How, in speaking one's own particular, religious dialect, can one contribute to a conversation among moral strangers conducted in a neutral, secular language?

I wish to analyze just how such a conversation might proceed from within the Jewish tradition. Because every religious tradition is distinctive in many respects, each will face distinctive methodological problems as it attempts to speak about moral issues in a way that is both true to its own religious values and at the same time accessible and relevant to "moral strangers" in the larger society. The particular methodological obstacles that Jewish theologians and ethicists face derive from the unique historical circumstances and theological presuppositions that have shaped Jewish moral reflection over the centuries. These obstacles, while formidable, are by no means insurmountable. By exploring these methodological issues and the various strategies that Jewish thinkers might employ in addressing them, I hope to shed some light on the nature of Jewish ethics and the contribution it can make to public policy in a morally diverse, secular society.

Before proceeding further, it may be useful to state an obvious fact that, unfortunately, too often goes unacknowledged.[2] Modern Jewish life is characterized by a wide spectrum of views about theological and moral questions. We find traditionalists, who regard Scripture and rabbinic tradition as completely authoritative and comprehensive moral guides, and assimilationists, who look only nominally to the classic sources of Judaic tradition for moral guidance, and a wide range of positions in between. Moreover, within the classical sources themselves we can discern a remarkable range of theological and philosophical views, sometimes explicitly juxtaposed in dialectical fashion, at other times only hinted at. I cannot do justice here to the entire spectrum of classical and contemporary perspectives. I shall limit my comments to those within the contemporary Jewish community who (1) claim to base their ethical views on authoritative Jewish teachings, and (2) are willing to take up the challenge that Englehardt presents, that is, who believe Jewish ethicists can speak in authentically Jewish ways to those outside the Jewish community.[3] As we shall see, the question of how to do so is complex and open to a range of possible answers.

The Nature of Secular Bioethics

Throughout his book, Englehardt develops the distinction both historically and conceptually between two very different meanings of secular humanism and explores the implications of each for bioethics. In one sense, secular humanism is an ideological position that emphasizes the values of human well-being, rational inquiry, and individual freedom. Secular humanists in this sense view religion as misleading and perhaps even dangerous insofar as they believe it fails to promote the values of humanism, rationalism, and personal freedom. Englehardt notes that this sort of secular humanism embodies a particular moral vision with its own set of metaphysical assumptions (about the nature of human beings, the proper goals of human life, etc.). An alternative form of secular humanism is neutral, rather than antagonistic, toward religion. Making no metaphysical assumptions, it is open to all religious viewpoints and committed to none. In this latter sense, secular humanism tolerates radical differences in religious and moral perspectives without assuming that any one particular "secular" perspective ought to prevail in the social-political sphere.

Englehardt argues that a secular humanist bioethics in the first, antireligious sense is no longer tenable. That version of secular humanism rested on the assumption that a particular secular vision of humankind is universally applicable and philosophically justifiable. But Englehardt believes that the Enlightenment quest to discover a content-full moral vision based only on those things we all share as human beings has proved to be a chimera. In this postmodern age, we must confront the hard reality that our moral perspectives are incommensurable and that no ethic can be constructed solely on rational (i.e., metaphysically neutral) grounds. His goal, then, is to construct a bioethic that grows out of secular humanism in the second sense: it must recognize the rights of all groups in society to affirm their own unique metaphysical and religious views and to make moral decisions based on those views, while not permitting any group to impose its metaphysical, religious, or moral views on others. Such a bioethic would not exclude any moral-religious perspective from public policy debate, but rather would ensure that all perspectives, religious as well as secular, have a voice in that debate.

What sort of bioethic can be constructed in the context of secular humanism conceived in this way? Englehardt indicates that, making no metaphysical assumptions, it will assume only those principles necessary for civil discourse among moral strangers. He writes,

> Accepting this ground for secular ethics is equivalent to accepting the moral point of view which requires the fewest assumptions. . . . To have a morality for moral strangers, one need only refrain from using them without their consent and acknowledge them as entities that can agree or refuse to negotiate. . . .[4]

These principles—that we must not use others without their consent and that we must acknowledge their freedom to make independent moral choices—are the only ground rules for the creation of a secular humanist bioethics. They are defensible not on metaphysical grounds, as universal truths, but on pragmatic grounds, as the minimal principles necessary for moral strangers to communicate respectfully about moral disagreements at all. A secular humanist bioethics, as Englehardt conceives it, makes no assumptions in advance about what is permitted or prohibited. It only establishes a neutral framework within which individuals with different religious and moral perspectives can resolve their moral differences or, at very least, learn to live peacefully despite them.

In Englehardt's view, a secular bioethic functions in a way analogous to the post office.

> A post office of a nonauthoritarian secular pluralist society will mail both religious literature and antireligious literature, racist tracts and antiracist tracts, socialist propaganda and the publications of the John Birch Society. It asks only that the customers pay sufficient postage. . . .
>
> As the individuals from divergent moral communities stand in line at the post office, each will understand the right to use the post office, though the members of some communities will be condemning the members of other competing groups. . . . Insofar as the members of these divergent groups are willing to live peaceably and to convert others through witness, not coerce their acquiescence through force, they will understand that individuals have a secular right to use the post office, though what they are doing is morally wrong.

Similarly, Englehardt says, different religious communities with opposing views on issues such as abortion or contraception or physician-assisted suicide must acknowledge the bifurcated nature of the moral life in a pluralistic society. They will make concrete moral judgments within their own religious-moral communities, while affirming the right of others to make different (and, from their perspective, erroneous) moral judgments. In those areas where broad agreement exists, it may be possible to cooperate politically to achieve these goals. Where such agreement is not forthcoming, we will simply agree to disagree and so refrain from imposing a particular moral perspective on those who do not share it.

What role might religious communities play in a secular humanist bioethics so conceived? They will function, in Englehardt's words, as "witnesses," testifying to the meaningfulness of their own religious-moral convictions. They will succeed in "carrying the day" to the extent that they persuade those who do not share their metaphysical, religious assumptions that, nonetheless, their particular moral perspectives are worth considering and even endorsing. To do this, of course, religious people will have to demonstrate that their religious-moral perspectives make sense outside the context of their own communities and independent of the authority of their own religious leaders. This is surely a formidable task, insofar as it requires religious people to explain the value of religiously based norms in terms that are explicitly neutral and nonreligious. But unless this is possible, Englehardt's vision of a secular humanist bioethic evaporates, for religious voices that in theory have something to contribute to public policy debate will in fact be reduced to silence. The issue, then, is what sort of moral vision a religious tradition such as Judaism can offer to those outside the Jewish community and how it can articulate that moral vision in a meaningful and even compelling way. It is to these questions that I now turn.

How Judaism Can Contribute to Secular Bioethics

There are significant theological and historical obstacles that Jewish tradition must overcome in order to address itself to the larger, secular society. Theologically speaking, Judaism from its inception has seen itself as a national religion, based on a specific revelation from God to the Jews. The Torah, or law, that the Jews received from God governed their community alone, its relationship to God and to its neighbors. But Jews never viewed their religious and moral norms as binding upon the non-Jewish world; indeed, they took pride in feeling that God had imposed special restrictions on them alone that testified, they thought, to God's special relationship with them.[5] So Jewish ethics presupposes a sharp division between the norms that govern Jews and those that apply to the rest of the world. Historically speaking, Jews over the centuries have lived for the most part as a minority within a larger non-Jewish population. Moreover, their status (especially in Christian Europe) was largely that of "outsiders" with little opportunity to exercise political authority over non-Jews, even had they desired to do so. As a result of this long history of political and social disenfranchisement, Jews until relatively recently have not faced the challenge of applying Jewish legal and moral norms to the non-Jewish world.[6]

Over and above these historical and theological considerations, one further factor complicates the efforts of Jews to bring their ethical teachings into the public square. The traditional language and idiom of classical Jewish ethical teachings differ radically from those of western philosophical ethics. The Babylonian and Palestinian Talmuds, compilations of scriptural exegesis (midrash), collections of legal responsa and medieval codes of Jewish law—which are the major sources of traditional Jewish ethics—are complex bodies of literature, accessible even in translation only to those with specialized training in interpreting classical Jewish texts. Even within the Jewish community it is not apparent how these classical texts should be used to create a contemporary Jewish ethic. It is still less clear how they might be translated, both linguistically and conceptually, in ways that speak to moral problems in our pluralistic, secular society.

Despite these formidable obstacles, I want now to argue that Jewish ethical values can make an important contribution to the sort of secular humanist bioethics that Englehardt envisions. My argument rests on two suppositions. First, within this largely particularistic, nationalistic religious tradition we can find moral norms that speak of and to the human condition in general. Second, Jewish values may be compelling even to those who do not accept the theological views that underlie them. The primary issue, again, is methodological: how can Jews speak out of their own religious tradition about bioethical issues in a way that is relevant to secular society. There appear to be three basic approaches that Jewish ethicists might adopt. As we shall see, they differ from one another in the ways that each identifies and locates the "universal" ethical message within this "particular" religious-moral system.

"Noahide Laws": The Universal Alongside the Particular

Jewish ethicists searching for universal norms within Jewish tradition will be drawn first to that body of norms specifically designated as binding upon all people. Known as the "Noahide laws" (since they apply to all descendants of

Noah), these rules are enumerated in the Babylonian Talmud and elaborated upon at a number of points in rabbinic literature.[7] The standard list of Noahide laws includes prohibitions against idolatry, blasphemy, bloodshed, sexual sins, theft, eating from a living animal, and the requirement to establish law courts.[8] There is considerable disagreement among medieval and modern authorities concerning the exact status of these Noahide laws. Among the issues are the relationship of this Noahide law to Mosaic law, whether its authority is based in reason or revelation, and the degree to which Jews can enforce these laws on non-Jews within their jurisdiction.[9] Leaving aside these theoretical issues, all Jewish authorities agree that these Noahide laws are the moral norms God expects all human beings to observe. Insofar as Jewish tradition specifically identifies this moral code as universal, it would appear to offer a basis for a Jewish view of norms applicable in a pluralistic society.

Among these laws one stands out as pertinent to issues of medical ethics, namely the prohibition against bloodshed. The rationale for this prohibition is twofold. First, it represents a fundamental requirement for a stable society. Natural tendencies toward hostility and violence must be curbed to permit the flourishing of human relationships and social institutions. Second, the prohibition against murder follows from the view that all human beings are created in God's image. As one rabbinic source puts it, "whoever sheds blood it is as if he diminished the Divine likeness because . . . 'in the image of God he made man.' (Gen. 1:27)."[10] Insofar as this Noahide law is based on the needs of all societies and the nature of all human beings, its scope is clearly universal.

This prohibition against murder was understood as applying to abortion as well.[11] Relying upon a peculiar, forced reading of Genesis 9:6,[12] the rabbis concluded that abortion is categorically prohibited as a matter of Noahide law. The rabbinic sources dealing with this interpretation do not delve into the rationale behind it, though most probably it rests on a concern to preserve all human life as something sacred. Indeed, it may be that the ancient rabbis were especially concerned to instill a respect for human life among non-Jews, whom they viewed as more prone to violence than Jews. The inclusion of feticide as a form of homicide, then, would reinforce both the social and theological bases of the prohibition against murder.[13]

Certainly this Noahide principle, if applied to modern society, would warrant a strongly "pro-life" position on abortion. Arguably, our society is characterized by a growing disrespect for human life that is reflected and perhaps even promoted by the high rate of abortion. Prohibiting, or at least restricting, abortion could promote greater appreciation that human life in all its forms is sacred and so not readily expendable. Others, of course, will disagree. The point here is only that this viewpoint, based on Noahide law, has a legitimate place within the public forum, not that it will necessarily be compelling.

However we assess the applicability of this Noahide law concerning abortion to modern society, it is relevant to only one issue in contemporary medical ethics. Even if we were to extend the Noahide prohibition against murder to questions of euthanasia or contraception—and this would be to extend the rule well beyond the rabbinic understanding of it—we would still not have a basis for addressing the broad range of bioethical issues that confront our society. After all, most of the Noahide rules—against idolatry, blasphemy, theft, and the like—have no bearing on issues of bioethics. Insofar as Jewish tradition equates a universal ethic with Noahide law, and Noahide law offers limited help in dealing with bioethics, Jewish ethicists will have to look elsewhere in Judaism for material relevant to secular bioethics.

Natural Law: The Universal Within the Particular

Natural law theory has long been held to provide a system of rational and universal moral norms. While natural law theories historically have been most closely associated with Roman Catholic moral theology, in recent years there has been considerable study of the natural law elements in Jewish ethics.[14] Among Jewish ethicists, David Novak has distinguished himself as an exponent of the natural law tradition within Judaism and his reflections suggest promising avenues of research for those wishing to make a Jewish contribution to secular bioethics.[15]

As Novak understands it, natural law in a contemporary setting must jettison the Aristotelian and Thomist assumptions about a "natural" purpose for human life that prevailed throughout the medieval period. This teleological metaphysic is no longer philosophically defensible and, in any case, is not essential to a natural law theory. Novak proposes a "more modest and limited definition of natural law," according to which it constitutes "the body of elementary norms without which a society of interpersonal communion would not be possible."[16] Natural law in this sense presupposes certain views about the nature of human beings, their primary needs and desires. Novak proposes that within Judaism one can indeed discover a natural law component, consisting of a theory of human life and human society, which both emerges from and informs much of Jewish law (halakha) and scriptural exegesis. Jewish natural law could contribute substantially to a secular bioethic precisely because questions about the nature of human beings and their social needs are at the heart of so many issues in biomedical ethics.

A Jewish theory of natural law capable of contributing to a pluralistic bioethic can be found most readily in rabbinic reflections on the creation of human beings. Here the nature of humankind in general, as distinct from Jews in particular, is explored and its implications for ethics are drawn. As an illustration, consider the following rabbinic lesson drawn from the biblical story of the creation of Adam:

> Therefore [in the story of Genesis] man was created alone, to teach you that whoever destroys a single soul is regarded by Scripture as if he had destroyed a whole world, and whoever saves a single soul is regarded by Scripture as if he had saved a whole world. Also, a single man was created for the sake of peace among mankind, that no one should say to his fellow, "My father was greater than your father." . . . And again, a single man was created to proclaim the greatness of God, for a person mints many coins with one die and they are all alike, but God has stamped every man with the die of the first man, yet not one of them is like his fellow.[17]

From the simple observation that all humankind originated with one individual, the rabbis draw several important lessons about human nature: that every individual is infinitely precious, that all individuals are equal, and that all are unique.

Religious-moral reflections of this sort could ground attitudes toward biomedical issues that derive from Jewish teaching but are perceived to be universally applicable. In chapter 5 I spelled out some of the moral principles that appear to flow from such a Jewish theology of creation and will only sketch them briefly here. Jewish authorities have traditionally viewed human life as infinitely precious in and of itself. Thus, quality of life is not a significant factor in determining whether life-sustaining treatments should be initiated or terminated. Since human life is conceived as a gift from God, we are obliged to accept it, even when doing so may feel more like a burden than a blessing. Moreover, because each individual is equally precious, irrespective of age or mental state or physical condition, there are no justifiable grounds for favoring the life of one over another. Questions of triage, then, must be handled in some arbitrary fashion (e.g., on a "first come, first served" basis), rather than on the basis of a cost-benefit analysis. The uniqueness of each individual suggests that our health care delivery system should be designed to address the special needs of the few as completely as the common needs of the majority. No doubt many other values concerning human life could be derived from the foregoing passage and others like it in rabbinic literature, but the point of this exercise should by now be clear. Within Jewish tradition there exists, apart from Noahide laws, a body of teaching that pertains to human life in general. Such teachings provide distinctive Jewish perspectives on the very sorts of issues that arise in the context of contemporary biomedical ethics.

But the question remains: are such Jewish teachings convincing apart from the theological views that gave rise to them? Or, to phrase the question more pointedly, why should non-Jews in a pluralistic society incorporate such values in their bioethics when they have not adopted the religious worldview behind them (e.g., they may not believe that all humankind descends from Adam)? The first and most general reason would seem to be that the value of an idea is not restricted to the value it holds for its originator. In many areas of our lives we readily acknowledge that the purposes for which something was created and those for which it might then be used are often quite different. To take an example from the history of Anglo-American law, it has been shown that modern contract law has its roots in medieval Christian law[18] but surely no one would suggest that contract law today is meaningless or useless just because we no longer accept the religious beliefs of those who first developed it. Such a claim would make sense only if it turned out that in fact contract law was so infused with religious values that it actually made no sense outside the religious context. So the real issue at hand is whether the moral values discussed above are so intimately linked with Jewish religious beliefs that they have no real currency when divorced from their religious foundation.

I suggest that this is not the case. Certainly there is abundant historical evidence that many ethical values that are religious in origin continue to hold meaning for people long after the underlying religious beliefs are abandoned. Secular humanists, among others, have affirmed a philosophy that incorporates much of the "Judeo-Christian" ethic, while expressly rejecting the belief in a creator God. They have done so because they rightly recognize that certain values promote human well-being and preserve the basic institutions of our society. Without them we would have no society, or at least not one that most of us would care to live in. Thus, there are compelling pragmatic reasons for affirming certain moral values, even if they are rooted in a religious tradition that one does not accept.

It may yet be objected that if religiously based values are accepted on pragmatic, secular grounds, then we need not look to religious traditions to supply them. Why, in other words, turn to religions like Judaism to discover social values (in bioethics or any other area) that make just as much sense and are readily accessible outside this religious context? In response to this issue, we should note first that Judaism's contribution to ethics need not be unique in order to be valuable. A religious value system might simply reinforce or augment a set of values that society could adopt on nonreligious grounds. In this case, theology's contribution is simply to demonstrate that similar values can be (and often are) shared by people with very different religious-metaphysical views. If, as Englehardt says, we are often "moral strangers" in search of common moral ground, it will be helpful, even essential, to discover those values that are meaningful to religious and secular people alike (albeit for different reasons).

But Judaism may contribute in a more substantive way to public policy debates. A certain moral value—the ultimate significance of preserving human life—may be applied differently in religious and nonreligious contexts. Within a secular humanist framework, the value of human life may be relative to other goods that promote human well-being, such as health or happiness. In the absence of these conditions, humanists who believe in the value and uniqueness of human life may yet determine that life-preserving measures are not needed or even desirable. In a religious context, by contrast, the same value may be weighted quite differently. As I implied earlier, many scholars have suggested that in Judaism human life has absolute value, not altered by disabilities or other conditions that may make a particular individual's life less than ideal. For this reason, Jewish authorities have generally disapproved of practices such as aborting fetuses with known genetic defects, or discontinuing life support for those with irreversible, terminal conditions. Moral values, such as the importance of preserving human life, can be upheld in different ways, depending upon where this value fits within a larger system of moral principles. Thus, Judaism may offer new ways of assessing or applying moral values, ways that challenge or expand the perspectives of those who hold the same values, but for different reasons.

Thus far I have argued that within Judaism we can find principles that could apply to bioethics in a secular society. Both Noahide law and natural law have their roots in Jewish religious teaching, yet both speak to generic human issues—the nature of human beings and the requirements of human societies. But what shall we make of that substantial body of law, halakha, comprising by far the largest part of Jewish normative teaching and intended to apply only within the Jewish community? It is within halakha that we find the most sustained and detailed moral deliberation within Jewish tradition. Can these rather technical and "parochial" materials too contribute in some meaningful way to a secular bioethic? I want now to suggest that they can, provided that we see these Jewish sources as embodying general moral principles.

Halakha (Jewish Law): The Particular as Universal

Within halakha we find extensive materials pertinent to issues in biomedical ethics. Discussions of these issues typically consist of detailed analyses of legal precedents and principles as interpreted by successive generations of rabbinic authorities, discussions that, as I indicated earlier, are quite inaccessible to those without specialized training. Yet, these technical halakhic debates may have greater relevance to secular bioethics than is at first apparent.

By way of illustration, we might consider the following sources that pertain to the Jewish view of abortion.

> If men strive, and hurt a woman with child, so that her fruit depart from her, and yet no further harm ensue: he shall be surely punished, according as the woman's husband will lay upon him; and he shall pay as the judges determine. (Exod. 21:22)

> If a woman is in hard labor, the fetus is to be cut up in her womb and brought out limb by limb, because her life takes precedence over its life. If the greater part of the fetus' body has already come out, it must not be destroyed because one independent life is not to be pushed aside for another independent life.[19]

From the passage in Exodus we can infer that taking the life of a fetus is not regarded as murder. If this were so, the individual responsible would be subject to capital punishment, rather than simply liable to pay damages for loss of property (i.e., the fetus). Taken to its logical conclusion, this would imply that the fetus does not have the rights of a human being at all and can be destroyed at will. The Mishnah passage, however, views the status of the fetus somewhat differently. Again, while in utero the child's life is subordinate to that of its mother. If her life is endangered, the life of the fetus is expendable. Once the fetus has begun to emerge, however, it takes on the status of an independent life and has the same "right to life" as its mother. Some talmudic authorities understood this rule by analogy with the law of the "pursuer," according to which one has the right to take the life of an individual who is pursuing another with the intent to inflict mortal injury. In both instances, one person (whether the pursuer or the fetus) is presumed to have a right to life but is also presumed to forfeit that right if he or she is threatening the life of another. Other authorities, however, questioned this analogy, noting that if the fetus has the status of a pursuer, then it should be permitted (contrary to the Mishnah's rule) to take its life even after it emerges from the womb. At issue is the question of the fetus' status: is it dependent on its physical relationship to its mother, or is it dependent only on whether or not it constitutes a threat to its mother's life?

Now while Jewish tradition in no way suggests that these rules apply outside the Jewish community, I believe that embedded in these sources we can find principles with broad applicability.[20] Surely the issue of whether a fetus is a "person" with legal rights is at the heart of the abortion debate in this country. And while Jewish authorities also differed among themselves on this matter, some points of consensus do emerge. First, taking the life of a fetus is not ipso facto an act of murder. At least in some cases where the mother's life is threatened, it is not only permitted but mandatory. Second, although the life of the fetus is dependent upon that of its mother (one talmudic source refers to it as a "limb" of its mother), the mother does not have the right to end its life unless it is a threat to her own.[21] Thus, even though the fetus is not a person with full legal rights in Jewish law, it is nonetheless more than just an appendage of the mother that she can dispose of at will. In this sense, Jewish law's general concern to preserve human life extends to the life of the unborn. In all, Jewish law's attitude toward abortion recognizes that the mother's life takes precedence over her child's because it assigns the fetus some, but not all, the rights of a person.

Clearly, the technicalities of the talmudic debate about the status of a fetus as "pursuer" are hardly relevant to the discussion of abortion in our secular society. And yet, the principles that underlie that debate may indeed contribute to this broader discussion. The moral principles that (1) human life, in all its forms, is worth preserving and (2) an individual forfeits its right to life only when it threatens the life of another are entirely intelligible outside the context of halakha. Certainly, one need not accept the authority of the Talmud to recognize that these principles are worthy of consideration. Indeed, one could readily argue that these principles are rational and socially beneficial, that society would be more humane if we viewed unborn children as worthy of moral consideration, since they are human beings, if not quite full persons. No doubt, such a position will conflict with others in the public policy debate. But those who take this position may function, in Englehardt's words, as "witnesses" to a certain moral perspective that could influence others, by challenging them either to refine their own views or to change them.

In any event, halakhic rules intended to be normative only for the Jewish community may, if properly analyzed, contain principles that are intelligible and even compelling independent of their religious foundation.

Englehardt and Secular Bioethics Revisited

I have suggested that Judaism can make important contributions to public policy debate on specific moral problems such as abortion. In closing I want to suggest that it also offers an alternative vision of bioethics in general. Englehardt's conception of a secular humanist bioethic, while compelling in many respects, may not be entirely adequate. From the perspective of Jewish tradition, at least, some of his premises can be questioned.

Englehardt has provided a theory of secular humanist bioethics that, he claims, (1) creates a neutral context for discourse among moral strangers and (2) does so without relying on any "content-full" moral principles. His point is that bioethical decisions must be made on a "level playing field," that the game will be fair only if no metaphysical or religious presuppositions are built into the ground rules. It is for this reason that he is so concerned to distinguish secular humanism as a content-full ideology from secular humanism as a set of neutral procedural rules that require only respect for individual autonomy.

But, viewed religiously, this insistence upon autonomy, which Englehardt defends as "the one way to ground a common moral world for moral strangers without arbitrarily endorsing a particular ranking of values,"[22] may be misguided. It assumes, as a procedural matter if not as a philosophical doctrine, that individuals are autonomous beings who are free to make moral decisions by themselves for themselves. But Judaism, among other religious traditions, has taught otherwise. As the Talmud says, "All Israelites are responsible for one another."[23] As members of a common society our actions impact on one another in ways that call into question this commitment to autonomy. As a case in point, consider Englehardt's view of surrogate motherhood. At several points, he indicates that any restriction on the right of individuals to enter surrogacy contracts would violate the principle of autonomy that he believes is fundamental to a secular humanist bioethic.[24] But the practice of surrogate motherhood affects not only those who enter freely into the contract; arguably it cheapens and ultimately undermines the parent-child relationship and so has a ripple effect throughout society. Consider Paul Lauritzen's insightful comments on commercial surrogacy.

The problem with commercial surrogacy is thus not simply that it requires a woman to treat her bodily integrity as owned property available for sale to a buyer, but also that it places human relationships, indeed, one of the most intimate human relationships, in the marketplace. And the problem with commercializing relationships is that truly committed, caring relationships are not something we can simply buy and sell."[25]

My point is not to argue the merits of commercial surrogacy, but rather to point out that the effects of permitting it extend well beyond the individuals directly involved. To ignore this fact in the name of preserving the autonomy of moral decision making is to misconstrue the very nature of the moral act in question. From the perspective of Jewish tradition, moral behavior is inescapably social and so the mere fact that two consenting adults agree to a certain relationship does not, in itself, make that relationship morally acceptable.

Building on this concern for autonomy, Englehardt suggests that public policy on bioethics and health care will be determined in the marketplace, where each individual makes independent choices on the basis of his or her own values (some of which, of course, could be religious). Like a post office, the market is a neutral clearinghouse in which a multitude of moral and religious values converge. The goal is simply to ensure that the market is not biased toward a particular moral or religious set of values.

But again, from a religious perspective, this will appear a particularly inappropriate way to view decisions of a moral nature. Jewish tradition insists that there is a radical difference between laws concerning property and those concerning human lives. With respect to the former we are free to be lenient in judgment, while in the latter case we are required to scrupulously protect life. As David Novak writes in this connection, "The greater rigidity of the Jewish laws dealing with human life is, then, the result of humility rather than arrogance. Human life, in its mystery and sanctity, takes precedence over our own designs for improving its quality."[26] A neutral and free market may be the proper mechanism for delivering parcels or determining the price of a can of tuna, but it may not be appropriate at all when it comes to questions of life and death, suffering and healing. Indeed, given Judaism's persistent concern with the sanctity of human life, questions of health care are moral issues of the first order that cannot be left for resolution to the amoral forces of the marketplace. Of course, a secular, pluralistic society should not be expected to adopt a particularly Jewish view of morality. Jews living in such a society must be prepared to lead a bifurcated moral life in which their private moral judgments about life issues are at odds with the larger society's values and practices. But while individuals' moral decisions may differ, the process for finding consensus among moral strangers must itself be a moral process. From a Jewish perspective, this means, minimally, that we should begin with a moral presumption in favor of preserving life. To do otherwise would be to radically misunderstand the gravity of the moral issues involved.

Religious traditions like Judaism, I have argued, may play a constructive role in shaping public policy in a pluralistic, secular society. They do this in several ways: by offering moral principles that concern human life and society generally, by showing how principles already current in society might be weighted or applied differently, and by providing particular moral perspectives that (notwithstanding their religious roots) have appeal on pragmatic or humanistic grounds. But perhaps Judaism's most significant contribution to secular humanistic bioethics is to put the entire enterprise in a different light. At issue is not only how we can facilitate communication among moral strangers. We must attend as well to the subject of that conversation. And when the subject turns to questions of bioethics—life and death, the nature of human beings, their most basic needs and goals—then Judaism would insist that the conversation should not be conducted in a neutral, value-free language. Just as language in general presupposes the need for and value of communication, so too the language of bioethics, even in a secular society such as ours, must presuppose a basic respect for human life. Such a bioethic will not be less humanist or secular. It will, however, share with religions like Judaism a commitment to one value more fundamental than autonomy or freedom—the value of life itself.

Conclusion

New Directions in the Study of the Ethics of Judaism

The central concern of the essays collected here has been to place Jewish ethics squarely within the study of the history of Judaism. This has meant, first and foremost, that Judaism must be examined as a historical phenomenon using the tools of scholarly analysis. Projecting a research agenda for further work in this area begins from this presupposition, that Jewish ethics must be studied as one component within a system of religious thought and practice. We must ask, then, insofar as Jewish ethics is a form of religious ethics, what issues present themselves for analysis? I suggest that there are three basic lines of inquiry.

1. *Internal/systemic analysis*: what are the relationships between ethics and other aspects of this religious system?
2. *Comparative religious analysis*: how does this particular form of religious ethics compare with others, in particular, with the ethics of other western, monotheistic religions?
3. *Comparative nonreligious analysis*: how does this particular religious ethic compare with forms of secular ethics?

Each of these broad questions, of course, encompasses numerous others. It will be helpful to delve briefly into some of them in order to illustrate how the academic study of Jewish ethics might take shape.

Jewish Ethics in the Context of Judaism

In thinking about the place of ethics within Judaism, we do well to return to Clifford Geertz's frequently quoted definition of a religious system:

221

sacred symbols function to synthesize a people's ethos—the tone, character, and quality of their life, its moral and aesthetic style and mood—and their world view—the picture they have of the way things in sheer actuality are, their most comprehensive ideas of order. In religious belief and practice a group's ethos is rendered intellectually reasonable by being shown to represent a way of life ideally adapted to the actual state of affairs the world view describes, while the world view is rendered emotionally convincing by being presented as an image of an actual state of affairs peculiarly well-arranged to accommodate such a way of life.[1]

If Geertz is correct, we would expect to find links between the ethical component of Judaism and its worldview at every stage throughout its history. In a fully integrated religious system, ethics will mirror and reinforce the full range of religious beliefs, so that values about how to treat one's neighbor, or the unborn fetus, will be consistent with beliefs about the origin and destiny of human life and about the nature of religious community. One task of the academic study of Jewish ethics is to trace these linkages and, as always, to investigate their development over time.

Indeed, some of the foregoing studies have suggested that specific concepts of covenant, for example, do in fact shape classical responses to ethical questions, both theoretical and practical. Moreover, it is evident that a traditional view of human life as a divine creation leads directly to certain (often rather "conservative") positions in the area of biomedical ethics. But if studies in this regard are to proceed in a systematic fashion, rather than piecemeal, we must explore each aspect of Judaism's worldview, in all its historical complexity, as a point of departure for understanding the various dimensions of Jewish ethics.

By way of example, the relationship between ethics and eschatology has rarely been examined. In recent years, much work has been done on the various concepts of messiah in Judaism,[2] yet there has been no attempt to expose the ethical implications of each separate conception. Rather, research has focused on how various eschatologies correlate to particular conceptions of history and/or to the role and purpose of religious life in the present. In turning our attention to ethics, we would likely discover that the way in which Jews have conceptualized the end of time has affected, if only in subtle ways, their concept of how to live with one another until that time. Eschatology, in fact, may be a particularly fruitful tool for analyzing Jewish ethics, insofar as the prophetic picture of the "end of days" is one of moral harmony and universal peace. Moreover, in some places within rabbinic literature, the time preceding the days of the messiah was imagined as a period of moral depravity. How our actual moral behavior in the present relates to the coming culmination of history and how our notion of ideal moral behavior both shapes and is shaped by our conception of life in that idyllic future—these are questions that remain to be explored.

The relationship between ethics and ritual is similarly in need of systematic study. While many writers have noted the obvious places where moral considerations enter into the performance of rituals—the injunctions to break one's fast on Yom Kippur, or to violate the laws of the Sabbath, when a life is in danger, for example—there has been little effort to investigate the moral dimensions of the liturgy itself or of the liturgical calendar. Max Kadushin's *Worship and Ethics*[3] is the only full-scale work of which I am aware that attempts to examine the "value concepts" animating these two dimensions of Jewish life.[4] Perhaps because of Kadushin's reliance on the rather obscure language of "organicism" and process thought, his work has not captured the attention of subsequent Jewish ethicists (whose intellectual roots, in any case, lay mostly in the German philosophical tradition). Yet, the question of how a system of interconnected moral values is mirrored in, and communicated through, the life of prayer remains an important question.

By way of example, there is surely much to be said about the spiritual themes that pervade the liturgy and animate the cycle of holidays—dependence, thanksgiving, blessing—and the development of characteristically Jewish moral virtues, especially humility.[5] It is reasonable to suppose that the humility one experiences in supplication before a God believed to be omnipotent carries over to the humility one is expected to show in interpersonal relationships. But this connection, particularly in the context of the High Holiday liturgy with its emphasis on both our moral shortcomings and our precarious position before God, has not been the subject of sustained examination.[6]

As I suggested in chapter 9, narrative is yet another dimension of religious systems that has yet to be fully examined in relationship to Jewish ethics. In recent years, scholars of religion have drawn attention to the profound ways in which narratives—especially overarching "master stories"—shape the lives of religious communities. It is alleged that narratives are the key to understanding a religious worldview, insofar as they encapsulate a view of who we are, where we have been, and where we are headed. Narrative, in contrast to doctrine, is also alleged to be "closer to lived life," since life itself is experienced as a series of temporally sequential events—a story—while doctrines are intellectual constructs and so reflect the views of a religious elite. Whether all the claims made on behalf of narrative withstand critical scrutiny or not, there can be little doubt that it represents an important window into the world of religious experience.

Within the field of Christian ethics, Stanley Hauerwas has established himself as a major exponent of narrative approaches to theology and ethics. His formulation of the role of narrative in the ethical life of a religious community is suggestive.

> Stories are not just a literary genre, therefore, but a form of understanding that is indispensable. . . . Stories do not illustrate a meaning, they do not symbolize a meaning, but rather the meaning is embodied in the form of the story itself. Put differently, stories are indispensable if we are to know ourselves; they are not replaceable by some other kind of account.[7]

Surprisingly, in light of Hauerwas's observation, the significance of narrative for Jewish ethics has received scant attention.

It has often been noted, of course, that the Torah frequently connects the injunction to care for the stranger, and other social outsiders (the widow, the orphan, etc.), with the experience of slavery in Egypt—"You shall not oppress a stranger, for you know the heart of the stranger, seeing as you were strangers in the land of Egypt." (Exod. 23:9) And there is widespread acknowledgment that *aggadah* (narrative, lore) is both separate from and complementary to *halakhah* (law).[8] But there is almost no work analyzing the themes of the Exodus narrative—divine protection, miraculous salvation, freedom from oppression—to specific moral injunctions, or even to general features of Jewish morality.[9] There are no studies that systematically analyze the ways in which rabbinic authorities cited the Exodus story in the context of their legal-moral deliberations. And there has been no effort to explore alternative interpretations of this core narrative—the relative balance of human and divine components in the process of redemption, for example—in relation to the moral life. Until we take narrative seriously as an integral aspect of religious life, and so of Jewish ethical life, our understanding of the contours of that life will be severely limited.

Jewish Ethics in Relation to Other Religions' Ethics

Given Judaism's close historical relationship to Christianity, it is hardly surprising that Christian ethics has received by far the most attention in comparisons of Judaism and other religious traditions. At first glance, given the volume of material written on the subject, it would seem that we know a great deal about the relationship between Jewish and Christian ethics. In fact, most every attempt to describe Jewish ethics written in the past century has made comparisons to Christian ethics, sometimes en passant, but occasionally at greater length.[10] Yet, from a scholarly perspective, these comparative observations leave much to be desired. In the first place, they invariably assume a homogenized, internally consistent "Jewish" and "Christian" ethic that are nothing more than gross generalizations at best and caricatures at worst. No effort is made either to acknowledge the diversity or to trace the historical development characteristic of each tradition. Worse yet, there is all too often a polemical thrust in these comparisons, insofar as they not only compare Jewish and Christian ethics, but assess which is "superior" or "more pragmatic." Of course, the underlying purpose of such discussions is not to present a dispassionate and critical assessment of two systems of religious ethics, but to defend Jewish ethics against the charges that it is "legalistic" or "ethnocentric" or lacking in some other important respect.

There is, by the same token, another, equally uncritical, body of literature that freely describes and generally praises the "Judeo-Christian ethic." These writers are not blind, of course, to differences between the traditions, but they are persuaded that the points of divergence are less significant than the similarities. After all, both traditions affirm a transcendent, "father God" and believe that humanity is, in essence if not in fact, unified. Accordingly, the same basic body of values—justice, charity, humility, and the like—are central to both faiths. This point of view is also polemically motivated, only here the direction of the polemic has changed. Jews, anxious to enter the mainstream of American society, have felt a strong need to demonstrate that Jewish values too were "mainstream," that is, consistent with those of the Christian majority. So our common Judeo-Christian ethic was emphasized, not because scholarship on the subject confirmed its existence, but because doing so promoted integration into the surrounding, predominantly Christian, society.

Fortunately, we do have some models for the comparative analysis of religious ethics that can provide the foundation for further work in this field. David Little and Sumner B. Twiss's *Comparative Religious Ethics*[11] investigates the structures of validation for moral norms within religious systems. They suggest that each religious tradition has its own way of establishing the authority of its moral norms, leading in heirarchical fashion to a foundational, religious claim (the level of "vindication" for the entire system of norms and validations). While their book explores Christian, Buddhist, and Navaho moralities, there is no reason why the same analysis could not be extended to Jewish ethics.

A second useful analytical scheme for the comparative study of religious ethics is offered by John P. Reeder Jr. in *Source, Sanction and Salvation: Religion and Morality in Judaic and Christian Traditions*.[12] As the title suggests, Reeder argues that religion is connected with morality in three general ways: it provides a source for moral norms, a sanction for moral behavior, and a concept of salvation that grounds a vision of moral perfection (or of a world beyond morality). In a somewhat sketchy, but historically sensitive manner, Reeder outlines a number of possibilities within each of these general areas, drawing his examples from the breadth of Jewish and Christian literatures. By his own admission, he is not trained in the study of classical Jewish texts and so regards this work as preliminary to more detailed investigation. But his schema is suggestive and has yet to be taken up by Jewish ethicists as a source for questions or categories of analysis.

Finally, mention should be made of H. Richard Niebuhr's classic *Christ and Culture*,[13] which continues to be used as a textbook in Christian ethics. Niebuhr offers a typology of relationships between "Christ," representing revelation/eternity/the ideal/the spiritual, and "culture," representing world/time/the actual/the material world. Throughout the history of Christianity, this relationship between Christ and culture has been construed in numerous ways. Niebuhr constructs five models, representing five different approaches to Christian ethics, together with illuminating examples of each drawn from the history of Christian thought. Whatever one thinks of this typology, and of how well the individual figures Niebuhr chooses fit his scheme, his analysis remains a powerful heuristic devise for categorizing diverse models of Christian ethics. Again, the possibilities of such a scheme for the analysis of Jewish ethics (using "Torah and culture"?) have yet to be explored.

Each of these models (all, interestingly, developed by non-Jewish scholars) offers yet unrealized possibilities for analyzing the religious "logic" of Jewish ethics and comparing it to that of other religious/ethical systems. Nor are these the only possibilities. Modern Jewish thinkers have noted the centrality of creation, revelation, and redemption as the central theological categories of classical Judaism. As my analysis of Jewish natural law in chapter 6 suggests, these categories, and the variety of possible relationships between them, may offer yet another tool for the analysis of Jewish ethics.

Indeed, any analytical scheme that looks at ethics in relation to religious concepts and categories holds out the potential for shedding light on the distinctive aspects of Jewish ethics. Then, through careful historical comparison, we can assess points of similarity and difference among related religious traditions.

It is worth noting that, if comparisons between Jewish and Christian ethics have been drawn too facilely, comparisons between Jewish and Islamic ethics have scarcely been made at all. With the exception of some studies on comparative Jewish and Islamic law, there has been little published, at least in English, on the ethics of these two traditions. As the influence of Islam in North America continues to grow, and especially as the study of Islam becomes more widespread in the academy, we can expect that this virtually unexplored terrain will attract appropriately trained scholars with interests in comparative religious ethics.

Jewish and Nonreligious/Philosophical Ethics

The foregoing studies point in two directions vis-à-vis the relationship between Jewish and philosophical ethics. On the one hand, we can explore the ways in which Jewish thinkers, in both classical and modern times, attempted to synthesize traditional Jewish and philosophical approaches to ethics. On the other hand, we can examine the extent to which Jewish ethical discourse is compatible with and/or can contribute to moral debate in a secular society. Each set of issues deserves some further comment.

As I noted earlier, a substantial number of studies have been published that analyze the ethics of major Jewish philosophical figures, both medieval and modern. Philo, Saadia and Maimonides, Cohen, Buber and Rosenzweig have all been given due consideration. The thrust of most work in this area has been to delineate the philosophical influences present in the writings of these Jewish thinkers. As a result of these investigations in the history of Jewish philosophy, we have a fairly clear understanding of the ways in which major schools of philosophy—Aristotelianism, neo-Platonism, Hegelianism, neo-Kantianism—shaped the thought of specific figures.

What has yet to be studied in any detail is the theoretical question underlying all such efforts to synthesize Jewish and philosophical ethics. If Jewish ethics is decisively shaped by its religious foundations, then we would expect that any effort to translate it into the terms of a nonreligious system of philosophy would encounter serious difficulties. How, for example, can covenant, as the ground of Jewish moral obligation, be assimilated to a philosophical category? And to the extent that Aristotelian and neo-Platonic thought had religious components, how can these accommodate specifically Jewish religious conceptions, such as "sin" and the "kingdom of God?"

What we want is not only to know how Jewish thinkers developed their "answers" or systems of thought, but to construct a conceptual analysis of the "questions" or issues that any Jewish-philosophical system of ethics must address. Where are the points of tension between the various strains of classical Jewish thought and the various schools of philosophical thought? Which lend themselves most readily to synthesis and why? These are only some of the issues that a history of Jewish philosophical ethics would address. Ultimately, the goal would be to move beyond tracing the influence of various philosophies on specific Jewish ethicists toward a general assessment of the religious underpinnings of Jewish ethics and their compatibility with philosophical modes of thought.

A second, and closely related, line of inquiry concerns the extent to which Jewish ethics can contribute to ethical discourse in a secular, pluralistic society without betraying its own religious character in the process. Here, again, the underlying question is which aspects of Jewish ethics are intelligible and potentially persuasive when translated into nonreligious terms. In chapter 10 I argued that there is indeed a role for Jewish ethics in the "public square." But the issue deserves more extended treatment than I have offered. I noted, for example, that there are some dimensions of Jewish ethics (and of other religious ethics as well) that cannot properly contribute to secular ethical discourse. But how are these elements to be identified and distinguished from other elements of Jewish ethics that are "translatable" into a secular language? Moreover, how can we ensure that those Jewish ethical norms or principles that we bring into public discourse are not distorted in the process of their translation?

In short, the challenges of speaking from within our own religious tradition, yet in a language accessible and meaningful to those who do not share that religious worldview, are relatively new for Jewish ethicists. The problems inherent in doing so are being encountered, in many ways, for the first time in the late twentieth century. Whether Jewish ethics can successfully meet those challenges, and how, remains a theoretical issue of great significance.

I have attempted here to sketch some of the directions for further study of the ethics of Judaism. These reflections are not intended to be exhaustive of the possibilities nor do I presume to know at this juncture which of these avenues of research will prove most fruitful. Certainly, as we engage fully the work of historians of Judaism (and of other religions) they will invariably lead us to new questions, as well as new ways of approaching old ones. In short, it is clear that much work remains to be done in the academic analysis of Jewish ethics quite apart from constructive work in Jewish ethics. And it is equally clear that attending to that distinction is a prerequisite to the flourishing of Jewish ethics as a field within the history of Judaism.

Notes

Introduction

1. S. Daniel Breslauer's bibliographic survey, *Modern Jewish Morality* lists several hundred items in the area of modern Jewish morality, and is now already significantly out of date. Some more recently published works in the field include: Eugene Borowitz, *Exploring Jewish Ethics*; David Novak, *Jewish Social Ethics*; Byron Sherwin, *In Partnership with God*; David M. Feldman, *Health and Medicine in the Jewish Tradition*; Levi Meier, ed., *Jewish Values in Health and Medicine*; Ze'ev W. Falk, *Religious Law and Ethics*; and Basil F. Herring, *Jewish Ethics and Halakhah for Our Time*.

2. See Breslauer's companion bibliographic volume, *Contemporary Jewish Ethics*.

3. Examples abound. Among scholars of mysticism, one thinks of Gershom Scholem, Joseph Dan, and Moshe Idel; among scholars of theology, Paul Mendes-Flohr and Arnold Eisen.

4. Notable exceptions include Joseph Dan, *Jewish Mysticism and Jewish Ethics*, some of the historical essays in David Sidorsky, ed., *Essays on Human Rights: Contemporary Issues and Jewish Perspectives* and essays on Jewish ethics in Edwin B. Firmage, Bernard G. Weiss, and John W. Welch, eds., *Religion and Law: Biblical-Judaic and Islamic Perspectives* (Winona Lake, IN: Eisenbrauns, 1990).

5. Gershom Scholem, "Tradition and Commentary as Religious Categories in Judaism," 289.

6. Based on the popular explanation of *teiku* ("let it stand"), which the Talmud sometime appends to the end of an inconclusive legal debate, as an acronym for *Tishbi yetaretz kushyot u-ve'ayot* ("the Tishbite [Elijah] will resolve difficulties and problems").

7. Kohler, *Jewish Theology*, 8.

8. Leo Baeck, *Das Wesen des Judentums* (2nd ed.) (Frankfort, 1922), 54, as cited in Bernfeld, ed., *The Foundations of Jewish Ethics*, 33. Baeck's book appeared in English translation as *The Essence of Judaism*.

9. For a cogent critique of this view, see Ahad Ha'am's essay "The Transvaluation of Values," in Ginsburg, *Selected Essays*, 231.

10. The only significant exception to this generalization of which I am aware is Moritz Lazarus's *The Ethics of Judaism* (originally published in German as *Ethik des Judenthums* in 1898.) Lazarus purports to provide a "scientific" account of Jewish ethics and does, in fact, acknowledge the diverse tendencies within Jewish ethical literature. Yet, his work reflects throughout the apologetic purposes for which it was written: to demonstrate that Jewish ethics is essentially (if not consistently) universalist, and that it accords with Kantian conceptions of autonomous moral reason.

11. See, for example, Ze'ev W. Falk, *Religious Law and Ethics*, Haim Cohn, *Human Rights in Jewish Law*, Daniel B. Sinclair, *Tradition and the Biological Revolution*, and Boaz Cohen's lengthy study, "Law and Ethics in the Light of the Jewish Tradition," in his *Law and Tradition in Judaism*. Significantly, all of these authors are either professors of law or work primarily in that area.

12. By way of example, see Lenn E. Goodman, "Saadiah's Ethical Pluralism" and Steven Schwarzschild, "Moral Radicalism and 'Middlingness' in the Ethics of Maimonides."

Chapter 1: Law, Virtue, and Supererogation in the Halakha

1. A good bibliography of English articles on the issue can be found in Kellner, *Contemporary Jewish Ethics*.

2. The proper translation of the phrase has itself been a matter of some dispute. Some translate, "within the line . . ." in accordance with the more common meaning of *lifnim*. See, for example, Schwartzschild, "The Question", 31, Borowitz, "The Authority," and Shear-Yeshuv Cohen, "*Lifnim mishurat hadin*," 188. The sense of the phrase on this reading is that one acts (well) within the limits of the law by not exercising one's legal rights to their full extent. For this translation and explanation of the term, see Cohn, "Ancient Jewish Equity," 45. While this reading makes sense of the term in its talmudic context, the more common rendering of the phrase, as we shall show below, and the one that later rabbinic authorities appear to have adopted, is "beyond the line . . ." That is, one does more than the law requires. It should be noted that *lifnim* is sometimes used within rabbinic sources to mean "beyond;" see Mishnah Shebiit 6:1.

3. See especially the discussions of the issue by Dorff, "The Interaction," and Boaz Cohen, "Letter and Spirit."

4. This is the position taken by Lichtenstein, "Does Jewish Tradition," and Bleich, "Is There an Ethic Beyond Halakhah?"

5. Menachem Elon's view of the evolution of the term is discussed below.

6. It is interesting to note that the text most often quoted in discussions of this term (Baba Metsia 83a) concerns the damages caused by porters to wine barrels that they were transporting for Rabba son of Rabbi Huna, a text that does not in fact contain the term in question. Accordingly, I have not included this text in my study, notwithstanding the fact that Rashi's commentary on the text refers to this as an example of *lifnim mishurat hadin*.

7. My translation and discussion of the following sources is indebted to Saul Berman, "*Lifnim mishurat hadin*." Berman argues that, at least in the legal texts, the term always appears in the context of

> the attempt to resolve contradiction either between two stated laws or, more commonly, between a stated law and the behaviour of a great scholar. The sense of the resolution, and thus the legal meaning of the term *lifnim mishurat hadin*, is that the act performed was in accordance with he (sic) undifferentiated din in preference to its subsequent shurat hadin where that would produce a result more beneficial to the other party. However, in its legal usage, the term *lifnim mishurat hadin* is always a fiction, representing not the actual intent of the actor but rather the manner in which his act can be resolved within the legal order (191).

Berman, that is, claims that this is a technical term, employed in the effort by later authorities to explain why a sage at an earlier time acted in accordance with a broad legal standard rather than with the more restrictive legal standard that was in force in their own day. On Berman's interpretation, then, the term as employed in the legal sources has no particular moral force and no relevance to the issues of law and ethics, as is so often assumed. He does concede, however, that in the aggadic sources the term denotes acting mercifully in a way that is beneficial to another party. While Berman's essay represents the most detailed and systematic examination of the term in English, his understanding of the term is problematic in a number of respects. First, he ignores the fact that rabbis from Rashi and Maimonides on have consistently understood the term as representing a special ethical standard. Indeed, this is implied in the talmudic sources that list *lifnim mishurat hadin* alongside deeds of lovingkindness, visiting the sick, and so on. It seems clear then that the term in both talmudic and later usage has an ethical force and is not merely a technical term in the sense that Berman suggests. In addition, Berman's interpretation presupposes that the same term was used in legal and nonlegal sources in two quite different ways, a doubtful assumption that I avoid in the interpretation put forward here. Finally, Berman's analysis of specific passages rests in many cases on a number of problematic and unsubstantiated assumptions about the meaning of *shurat hadin* (a term that in fact appears in none of the texts he discusses) and its historic relationship to the actions described as *lifnim mishurat hadin*. For all these reasons, Berman's detailed and technical analysis of the term, while valuable and thought provoking, remains untenable.

    8. My interpretation of this passage is indebted to that of Cohn, "Ancient Jewish Equity," 60.

    9. This interpretation, suggested to me by Peter Haas, would understand Samuel's statement that the purse should be returned *lifnim mishurat hadin* not as an explication of his earlier statement that one "is obligated" (*hyb*), but as a correction to his earlier statement. Read in this way, Samuel responds to the challenge at E by retreating from his initial judgment at D that the finder was obligated to return the purse, stating now that one who does so is acting "beyond the line of the law."

    10. See Ḥullin 83a.

    11. See Sanhedrin 6a.

    12. See Boaz Cohen, "Letter and Spirit," 52, note 142, who understands the term *din torah* in this sense in the passage before us.

    13. In his responsa, Rabbi Solomon ibn Adret (Rashba) cites this passage to support the view that, in extreme circumstances, judges should actually surpass established legal sanctions by punishing criminals more severely than the law allows (the implication being that, had this been done in ancient times, law-breaking would have been discouraged and Jerusalem would not have been destroyed). This, of course, runs contrary to the understanding of this tradition presented here in the Talmud (C-D). The point here is that Jerusalem was destroyed because judges were too narrow in their enforcement of the law and instead should have enforced moral standards that go "beyond the line of the law," not, as Rashba seems to think, that courts should have imposed stricter, "extra-legal," penalties on individuals who violate the established law. For an insightful discussion of the application of this latter principle to the issue of capital punishment, see Novak, "The Image," 182–85. Notably, none of the sources that Novak cites explicitly use the term *lifnim mishurat hadin* to refer to this right of judges in a time of perceived social cri-

sis to impose stricter penalties than the law permits. This entails temporarily suspending established laws and so is quite different from the sort of activity refered to in the talmudic sources as *lifnim mishurat hadin.*

14. Bowers, *A Treatise,* 19. See also Rubin, "Toward a General Theory of Waiver," 483–84, who argues that waiver is simply relinquishment of a right, whether intentional or not.

15. This, however, does not fully support Lichtenstein's claim that the term designates a "contextual ethic."

> It goes without saying that Judaism has rejected contextualism as a self-sufficient ethic. Nevertheless, we should recognize equally that it has embraced it as the modus operandi of large tracts of human experience. These lie in the realm of *lifnim mishurat hadin.* In this area, the halakhic norm is itself situational. It speaks in broad terms: "And thou shalt do the right and the good"; "And thou shalt walk in His ways." The metaphors employed to describe it—"the ways of the good" or "the paths of the righteous"—denote purpose and direction rather than definitively prescribed acts. And the distinction from din is, finally, subtly recognized in the third source we have noted: " 'And the action'—this is the line of din; 'that they shall take'—this is *lifnim mishurat hadin*"—the reified static noun being used in relation to one and the open-ended verb in relation to the other" (Lichtenstein, "Does Jewish Tradition," 79).

While it is quite evident that *lifnim mishurat hadin* refers to a more open-ended ethical standard than the law itself, this does not imply that the term refers to a contextual ethic in general. At most, this term refers to one rather specialized instance of a contextualist ethic. The term is never applied to just any action performed in response to the demands of a specific situation, nor do the sources support Lichtenstein's contention that this is the "modus operandi of large tracts of human experience." See also Spero's discussion of this aspect of *lifnim mishurat hadin,* which he associates with Nachmanides' discussion of the term as it relates to "And thou shalt do the right and the good;" in *Morality, Halakha and the Jewish Tradition,* 175–78.

16. This position is implied by the analysis of Boaz Cohen and others (see below) who suggest that *lifnim mishurat hadin* represents the principle of equity, which is invoked when applying the established law would fail to provide a just remedy.

17. Landman, "Law and Conscience," 18–19.

18. Ibid., 20.

19. This is also the position taken by Cohn, "Ancient Jewish Equity," 50–51, who defines equity "in its widest sense" as those laws whose "enforcement depends on the fear of God and the uprightness of the individual rather than on any legal sanction administered on earth." Cohn's discussion, while focusing on many of the cases of *lifnim mishurat hadin* discussed earlier, also incorporates a range of other biblical and talmudic rules that in his view demonstrate a concern for exceptional (extra-legal) piety or righteousness.

20. Boaz Cohen, "Letter and Spirit," 51–53. See also Boaz Cohen, "Law and Ethics in Light of Jewish Tradition," 214ff.

21. Maimonides, *Mishneh Torah,* Laws of Beliefs, 1:5.

22. Maimonides, *Mishneh Torah,* Laws of Theft and Lost Property, 11:7.

23. See Maimonides, Guide for the Perplexed, III: 53, where he distinguishes the qualities of *ḥesed* and *tzedakah.*

24. See especially Urmson, "Saints and Heroes."

25. See especially Rabbi Isaac of Corbeilla's Sefer Mitzvot Katan (Semak), who includes *lifnim mishurat hadin* among the 613 commandments. See also the commentary Bayit Ḥadash on Shulhan Aruch, Ḥoshen Mishpat, 12:2 who notes that *lifnim mishurat hadin* is an actionable legal standard.

26. Lichtenstein, "Does Jewish Tradition," 83.

27. Bleich, "Is There an Ethic," 527.

28. Tosfot to Baba Metsia 24b, ad. loc., *lifnim mishurat hadin.* The comment in this case focuses on the reasons why the text of the Talmud, when presenting a case of *lifnim mishurat hadin,* sometimes cites one biblical verse as prooftext, sometimes another verse, and sometimes cites no verse at all. The Tosfot propose that the Talmud cites Exodus 18:20 ("which they shall do") in cases where one has a legal obligation to act *lifnim mishurat hadin,* cites "so that you may walk in the path of good men" when doing so constitutes a moral obligation insofar as one loses nothing by forgoing one's legal right, and cites no verse at all when one goes out of the way to find opportunities to act in this way, this being an example of supererogation. See also Spero's discussion of this passage in *Morality, Halakah,* 173–74.

29. Elon, *Ha-mishpat ha-ivri,* 176.

30. Ibid., 178.

31. Newman, *Equity and Law,* 11.

32. For a fuller discussion of the ways in which the religious nature of halakha shapes its character as a legal system, see Dorff, "Judaism."

33. This, in fact, takes the form of a talmudic principle that "they do not impose an injunction upon the community unless the majority of the community are capable of enduring it;" Baba Metsia 60b.

34. The same viewpoint is expressed in the phrase, "the spirit of the sages is pleased with him," when applied to actions that are praiseworthy, but not legally required. See, for example, M. Shebiit 10:9.

35. Cohn notes, but does not develop, this ambiguous relationship between law and equity in the biblical and talmudic sources.

> While many precepts of biblical equity have, as we have shown, been transformed by the talmudic lawgivers into rules of law, the precepts of talmudical equity have—with few exceptions—retained the character of rules of morals and ethics. But morals and ethics, insofar as they were spelled out in the context of the legal regulation of human relations, have become part and parcel of the system of law—whether or not particular rules of conduct would be formally enforceable by judicial process. ("Ancient Jewish Equity," 73).

36. M. Avot, 5:11.

37. The idea that simply fulfilling one's strictly legal duty may fall seriously short of what God demands receives perhaps its most radical and profound expression in the Gospel of Matthew. As presented in the Sermon on the Mount, Jesus' teaching requires that one do significantly more than the law requires, as conveyed in the formulation, "you have heard . . . but I say unto you . . ." Whether this stricter standard of ethical behavior is meant to supplant the established legal standards, or rather to supplement them by providing an ideal toward which the elite within the community should strive, is not clear from the text. For a more extensive analysis of Jesus' teaching as exemplifying certain "proto-rabbinic" principles in general, and *lifnim mishurat hadin* in particular, see Sigal, "The Halakah of Jesus," esp. 74–82.

38. The very fact that the halakhic literature discusses a variety of terms for moral action that is not legally required in a strict sense indicates that the halakha is not a legal system in the western secular sense. From our standpoint, as Pound has noted, the function of law is to preserve the social order and maintain general security.

39. A similar conclusion is reached by Shear-Yeshuv Cohen, "*Lifnim mishurat hadin*," 187. He goes on to suggest that *lifnim mishurat hadin* is an essential and inseparable part of the law conceived as a dynamic process, shaped by the ongoing interpretation of new situations by recognized authorities. He distinguishes law in this sense, including *lifnim mishurat hadin*, from the written or codified law.

40. A similar point is made by Kadushin:

Philosophic concepts are, in every case, formulated. Each is a summary or epitome of some kind of order. Each is complete in itself, though it may be joined with others in a system. But rabbinic concepts, as we have learned, are not given formal definition. Since only the rabbinic complex as an integrated whole exhibits an order, the single concepts are not complete in themselves. To inject an organic concept into a nicely formulated philosophical system without changing the character of the former is an impossible feat. In attempting this very thing, medieval Jewish philosophers were bound either to do violence to the rabbinic concepts or else to be inconsistent (Kadushin, "Organic Thinking," 235).

Whether or not all rabbinic concepts exhibit this character, as Kadushin claims, I would concur that the concept of *lifnim mishurat hadin* cannot be neatly analyzed using categories drawn from philosophical systems, either medieval or modern.

41. The assumption that ethical considerations, as distinct from legal ones, entered into the development of Jewish law is commonplace in discussions of Jewish ethics. See, for example, Alexander Guttmann, "The Role of Equity;" Gordis, "The Ethical Dimension;" Dorff, "The Interaction;" Spero, *Morality, Halakha*, esp. 193–200; Siegel, "Ethics and the Halakhah;" and Konvitz, "Law and Morals." By contrast, Halivni concludes that "The notion that the Rabbis of the Talmud were aware of a possible conflict between morality and religious law and consciously resolved in favor of morality, cannot be defended historically" ("Can a Religious Law be Immoral,"165). While Halivni concedes that morality played an important role in the development of the law on an unconscious level, he argues that the rabbis in no way consciously recognized the distinction between these two categories. This conclusion, of course, precludes the view common to the aforementioned discussions that *lifnim mishurat hadin* represents one instance in which the rabbis recognized the need to supplement strictly legal obligations with extra-legal moral responsibilities.

Chapter 2: Ethics as Law, Law as Religion

1. See Bleich, "Is There an Ethic;" Borowitz, "The Authority;" Boaz Cohen, "Letter and Spirit;" Dorff, "The Interaction;" Jose Faur, "Law and Justice;" Federbush, "*Al hamusar v'hamishpat*;" Gordis, "The Ethical Dimensions;" Guttmann, "The Role of Equity;" Halivni, "Can a Religious Law be

Immoral;" Konvitz, "Law and Morals;" Korn, "Ethics and Jewish Law;" Landman, "Law and Conscience;" Lauterbach, "The Ethics of the Halakhah;" Lichtenstein, "Does Jewish Tradition;" Ross, "Morality and the Law;" Siegel, "Ethics and the Halakhah;" Silberg, "Law and Morals in Jewish Jurisprudence;" Spero, *Morality, Halakha.*

2. See, for example, M. Baba Batra, 8:5.

3. Erubin 49a.

4. See, for example, Bashan, "*Lifnim mishurat*," Saul Berman, "*Lifnim mishurat hadin*," Shear-Yeshuv Cohen, "*Lifnim mishurat hadin*," Meltzer, "*Megadray lifnim mishurat hadin.*"

5. See Baba Qamma 83b.

6. For other examples, see Siegel, *Ethics and the Halakhah*, 35–36, who writes, "From these and many other examples it is clear that the sages modified the law when they saw that following another norm would result in unfavorable results. Ethical considerations and public policy were sufficient to change the decision."

7. Dorff, "The Interaction," 458.

8. Gordis, "The Ethical Dimensions," 73. A similar interpretation of these sources can be found in Guttmann, "The Role of Equity."

9. Halivni, "Can a Religious Law," 165, 168.

10. For a more extensive treatment of the traditional view that Jewish law is divine and its implications for Jewish jurisprudence, see Cohn, "Prolegomena."

11. The same view has been defended by Konvitz, whose judgment about the biblical view of law and ethics could apply to the whole of Jewish tradition. "In the Hebrew Scriptures, the distinction between law and morals does not exist; or at least, it is not articulated. Neither is there a difference between religion and morals, nor any separation between religion and law. There is a single order of values which make a total claim on the people of Israel. By covenant, they became God's people. Their rights are all subordinate to God's rights; their duties are all subordinate to their duties to him; and these duties are all commanded by God, who made the law and whose will and nature fixed what is good and what is evil" (Konvitz, "Law and Morals," 46).

12. Lichtenstein, "Does Jewish Tradition."

13. Spero, *Morality, Halakha.*

14. For a complete history of the treatment of this term by legalists over the centuries, see Elon, *Ha-mishpat ha-ivri*, 176–80.

15. An example of such harmonizing of diverse texts and viewpoints can be found in Jacobs, *A Tree of Life*, 182–92.

16. See Welch, *Law and Morality*, 1–2.

17. Little and Twiss, *Comparative Religious Ethics*, 28–31, 80–82. For a more extensive discussion of the interrelationship of law and morality, see Hart, *The Concept of Law*, 151–207.

18. Hoebel makes this point when he notes that a social norm is legal if infraction is met by physical force of a recognized authority; *The Law of Primitive Man*, 28. For a more recent discussion of the intimate connection between law and violence, see Cover, "Violence and the Word."

19. Roscoe Pound in *An Introduction to the Philosophy of Law* notes that the specific purpose of law is to preserve social order and maintain general security. In his famous essay, "On Liberty," John Stuart Mill similarly defended the view that the law should not regulate the private lives of citizens, except insofar as it prevents people from harming one another.

20. This point is nicely developed by Dorff, "The Covenant," 78–79. This article provides an extremely thoughtful and clear exposition of the concept of covenant and its implications for Jewish law.

21. See Shapiro, "The Doctrine," and Buber, "Imitatio Dei."

22. Tanna d'bei Eliyahu, 135, as cited in Montefiore and Loewe, *A Rabbinic Anthology*, 468–69.

23. For a fuller discussion of the ways in which the religious nature of halakha shapes its character as a legal system, see Dorff, "Judaism as a Religious Legal System."

24. This view is reflected in the talmudic principle that "they do not impose an injunction upon the community unless the majority of the community are capable of enduring it;" Baba Batra 60b.

25. Siegel, "Ethics and the Halakha," 33–34.

26. This is true only with regard to an analysis, like the present one, which is descriptive rather than normative. Clearly, theologians and others who claim to speak on behalf of the tradition will need and want to articulate a position on this crucial question. In doing so, however, they would do well to acknowledge the existence historically of positions other than the one they themselves have adopted.

Chapter 3: Covenant and Contract

1. See especially Levenson, *Sinai and Zion*, and *Creation and the Persistence of Evil*; Muilenburg, *The Way of Israel*; Borowitz, "The Autonomous Jewish Self;" Roth and Ruether, *The Liberating Bond*; Hartman, *A Living Covenant*.

2. This essay concerns only Israel's communal religious responsibilities and, in particular, its communal moral responsibilities. This corporate, communal relationship between God and Israel does not preclude a more personal relationship between the individual Jew and God, which may carry its own religious and moral obligations. Indeed, Jewish literature is replete with accounts of saints and holy individuals who exemplified just such an intense, personal piety. In a traditional context, however, these personal religious obligations can never supercede or supplant the religious obligations of the individual as a member of Israel. It is as a member of that covenanted community that the individual Jew has a relationship with God in the first place.

3. Hartman, *Joy and Responsibility*, 281–82.

4. Berman, "Israel and the *Oikoumene*," 51; Polish, "Covenant: Jewish Universalism and Particularism;" LaCocque, "Torah—Nomos."

5. In addition to Berman, see Lovin, "Equality and Covenant Theology;" Gardner, "Justice in the Puritan Covenantal Tradition;" Roth and Ruether, *The Liberating Bond*.

6. Harold Berman, "Religious Sources."

7. I have not attempted here to explore the many historical issues that arise with respect to the place of covenant within the biblical tradition. For surveys of the spectrum of opinion on the antiquity of the covenant concept in Israel, and for a history of the scholarly debate on these issues, the reader can consult Baltzer, *The Covenant Formulary*; Bright, *Covenant and Promise*; Nicholson, *God and His People*; Oden, "The Place of Covenant."

8. My analysis throughout this article utilizes a basic theory of contract, though one that is still current among legal scholars. I have not attempted to take into account the many subtle and complex variations among contracts. Many of these have arisen in response to our rapidly changing commercial climate and so have little if any applicability to the covenantal relationship between God and Israel.

9. As a practical matter, contracts sometimes include provisions that reiterate preexisting legal rights and duties. Still, the purpose of creating a contractual relationship is to establish the terms of a specific legal relationship that, apart from the contract, does not yet exist.

10. While it is true that certain types of contracts are void or voidable, the purpose of creating the contract is to establish a valid legal relationship that will be enforceable.

11. The fact that the Israelites enter this covenant freely is an especially salient feature of the covenant ceremony recorded in Nehemiah ch. 10.

12. See Mendenhall, "Covenant."

13. See Farnsworth, *Contracts*, 52 ff. for a discussion of agreements that fail to be legally enforceable contracts in precisely this way.

14. A third, and quite radical, view of the origins of covenant emerges in another rabbinic passage:

> When God redeemed the children of Abraham, His friend, He re-
> deemed them, not as children, but as slaves, so that if He imposed
> upon them decrees, and they obeyed not, He could say, "You are
> my slaves." When they went into the desert, He began to order
> them some light and some heavy commands. . . . They began to
> protest. Then God said, "You are my slaves. On this condition I re-
> deemed you, that I should decree, and you shall fulfill." (Sifre
> Numbers, Shelaḥ § 115; Sifre Deuteronomy, Ekeb §38)

The same view is expressed more tersely and graphically in a famous talmudic passage, Shabbat 88a. In commenting on Exodus 19:17 that Israel stood "at the foot of the mountain" or literally, "under the mountain," the rabbis state that God held Mt. Sinai over them like a barrel and said, "If you accept my Torah, well and good, but if not, this shall be your burial ground." The authors of these passages imagined the covenantal relationship, not as contractual or even moral, but as purely coercive. God is the commanding sovereign, Israel the subservient slave. This view does not appear to be represented within the biblical corpus, however.

15. See Farnsworth, *Contracts*, 374 ff. for a discussion of the Statute of Frauds, which requires that certain types of contracts are enforceable only if written.

16. See also Deuteronomy 7:9–11.

17. Similarly, Wurzburger argues that at Sinai Israel experienced primarily a revelation of God's presence, and only secondarily of specific rules as the content of revelation. There are thus covenantal imperatives "which confront us with God's demands upon us in the here and now in all their uniqueness and particularity" (Wurzburger, "Covenantal Imperatives," 11).

18. This view, which is prevalent among Christian biblical scholars, tends to contrast the covenant, which is dynamic, with the law, which is static. See, for example, McCarthy, *Treaty and Covenant*, 175–76.

19. In the nature of the case, God cannot utilize either of the classic remedies for breach of legal contract, that is, monetary damages or specific performance. There is, of course, no monetary value that could be assigned to the protection and care that God promises to bestow upon Israel, nor to the costs that God incurs in withdrawing that protection. Nor, of course, is

there any way for God to force Israel to comply with the terms of the covenant, short of turning them into automatons.

20. For a discussion of curing breaches of contract, see Farnsworth, *Contracts*, 613–18.

21. This view, of course, became a cornerstone of Christian supercessionist theology. See, for example, Hebrews 8:8–13, which interprets Jeremiah 31:31–34 as evidence that God will abandon the old covenant and create a new one.

22. It is often noted that the Abrahamic and Davidic covenants display this unconditional character, while the Sinaitic covenant, by contrast, is supposed to be conditional. See, for example, Bright, *Covenant and Promise*, 23–44; also Levenson, "The Jerusalem Temple," 48–51. Yet, insofar as the Sinaitic covenant is, from the perspective of the Torah's redactors, built upon the covenant with Abraham and extended (perhaps fulfilled) through the covenant with David, the dichotomy should not be maintained too sharply. Indeed, the Sinaitic covenant itself is, from one perspective, contractual and conditional and from another perspective, eternal and unconditional.

23. Tanna d'bei Eliyahu, 31, as quoted in Montefiore and Loewe, *A Rabbinic Anthology*, 63.

24. While I have tried to provide concrete examples of texts and thinkers that exemplify each of the tendencies I identify, I would argue that each of these options exists within the tradition, whether or not they have all been articulated and developed historically. My point, then, is to spell out the range of possibilities for a covenantal ethic in Judaism, while recognizing that it may not be possible in each instance to demonstrate explicit connections between a specific model of covenant and the ethical theory of a specific thinker.

25. See Fackenheim, "The Revealed Morality," 69–84.

26. On this analysis, Israel's obligation to observe ritual laws would likewise be a moral duty.

27. Spero, *Morality, Halakha*, 82.

28. Gordis, "A Dynamic Halakhah," and "The Ethical Dimensions of the Halakhah."

29. See Dorff, "The Interaction."

30. See Halivni, "Can a Religious Law be Immoral?"

31. Dorff, "Covenant," 79

32. For a discussion of these two models of ethical reasoning, see Ellenson, "Religious Approaches." Ellenson identifies the former approach as "legal formalism," and the latter as "covenantal," but I have tried to argue that each is really covenantal in its own way.

33. Borowitz, *Exploring Jewish Ethics*, 188.
34. Midrash Psalms on 123:1
35. Sanhedrin 44a.
36. See Schwartzschild, "On the Theology of Jewish Survival," 291–92, who notes that both these views exist within the tradition in dialectical tension with one another.
37. The most famous exponent of this view was the medieval Jewish philosopher Judah Halevi, who claims in his *Kuzari* that Jews are inherently superior to others. A similar view, expounded in a mystical context, was held by Rabbi Abraham Isaac Kook.
38. Nicholson, *God and His People*, 191–217, discerns a development within the biblical sources from an early view of covenant as a natural, familial sort of relationship that is permanent to a later view according to which the relationship is more distant and conditional. Concomitantly, Scripture presents Israel's holiness as both "indicative"and "imperative," as both a fact and a goal.
39. Goldberg, *Jews and Christians*, esp. 213–22.
40. Lovin, "Covenantal Relationships and Political Legitimacy," 16.
41. See, for example, his essay "Risk and Uncertainty in Halakhah."

Chapter 4: The Quality of Mercy

1. In this essay I deal only with the simplest case of forgiveness, where only two individuals are involved. For a provocative discussion of the issue of whether one should forgive a person for offenses that the latter committed against other people, see Wiesenthal, *The Sunflower*. Though the problems posed by this case are not discussed in this chapter, it appears to me that Abraham Joshua Heschel's response (Wiesenthal, *The Sunflower*, 130–31), that one does not have the proper standing to forgive another for offenses committed against third parties, is entirely consistent with the classical Jewish sources examined here.
2. Lauritzen, "Forgiveness," 144.
3. I have not assumed here that there is only one normative position within the Jewish tradition concerning the issue of forgiveness. With one exception, see note 6, however, it appears to me that there is a remarkable unanimity of perspective among sources that differ widely in authorship and historical period. While I am prepared to concede, then, that the conclusions I reach here about the Jewish perspective on forgiveness are not the only ones that can be gleaned from the traditional sources, I would argue that they represent by far the most dominant strain within the tradition.

4. M. Baba Qamma 8:7

5. The story of Abraham and Abimelech in Genesis 20 is somewhat incongruous with the case that the Mishnah presents. Here Abimelech's offense against Abraham, if it can be called that, is prompted by Abraham's own concealment of Sarah's true identity from him. The connection appears to be that once Abimelech is informed of his offense, he both compensates Abraham monetarily (which conforms with the Mishnah's principle) and pleads for forgiveness. Abraham's intercession with God on Abimelech's behalf, then, would be taken as an indication of Abraham's willingness to forgive.

6. I have found only one classical rabbinic source, T. Baba Qamma, 9:29, (Neusner, *The Tosefta, Fourth Division, Neziqin,* 57), which suggests that the duty to forgive could be unconditional.

A. He who injures his fellow,

B. even though the one who did the injury did not seek [forgiveness] from the injured party—

C. the injured party nonetheless has to seek mercy for him,

D. since it says, Then Abraham prayed to God, and God healed Abimelech (Gen. 20:17).

This passage, which appears to be based on a different reading of the Abraham episode, stands alone and does not alter the fact that the overwhelming majority of sources understand the duty to forgive as conditional upon the offender's prior repentance. It should be noted, of course, that the offended party might voluntarily choose to forgive in this case, but Jewish law would not regard it as his duty to do so.

7. Mishneh Torah, Laws of Repentance, 2:9–11.

8. Mishnah Avot 2:5,15.

9. Fathers According to Rabbi Nathan, 41, (Goldin, 172–73); see also Derekh Eretz Zutta 1:6.

10. Mishneh Torah, Laws of Ethical Conduct, 6:6–7.

11. See Maimonides, Mishneh Torah, Laws of Homicide and Preservation of Life, 13:14 and Laws of Ethical Conduct, 6:5; Pesahim, 113b; The Fathers According to Rabbi Nathan 16, (Goldin .86).

12. The Midrash on Psalms, XL,4; (Montefiore and Loewe, 321).

13. Pesikta Rabbati, 185a; (Montefiore and Loewe, 320).

14. Tanhuma Buber, Wayera, 47b; (Montefiore and Loewe, 325).

15. Tanna d'bei Eliyahu, p. 135 (Montefiore and Loewe, 468–69); see also Shabbat 133b).

16. Yoma 86b.

17. Fathers According to Rabbi Nathan, 39

18. It should be noted that Maimonides, (Mishneh Torah, Laws of Repentance, 3:14) presents a much expanded list of twenty-four categories of sinners who do not receive divine forgiveness. His concluding comment, however, is very telling and accords with the position that has been presented here, "All these and similar deeds, even though they hinder repentance, do not prevent it. Rather, if a person repents of them, behold, he is truly repentant and he has a share in the world to come."

19. As Lauritzen phrases the issue, there seem to be certain sins so heinous that forgiving them is, for psychological reasons, enormously difficult. As far as I can tell, the Judaic sources do not recognize such a category of offenses. I have found no texts that suggest that the duty to forgive is suspended if the offended individuals simply cannot bring themselves to do so. Indeed, the quote from Maimonides earlier supports just the opposite conclusion and it is for this reason that I stress here that forgiveness is unlimited so far as the severity of the sin is concerned, provided the sinner can and does repent.

20. It is important to note that all the sources cited here refer implicitly to the issue of one Jew's forgiving another. The reasons why this is the case should become clear in the final section of this essay. It may be that certain authorities would have extended this duty to forgiving non-Jewish offenders as well, even though they are not similarly bound by God's covenant, but this cannot be determined from the sources discussed here.

21. For an extended discussion of this issue, see Shapiro, "The Doctrine of the Image of God."

22. Ibid., 128.

23. Sotah 14a.

24. T. Baba Qamma 9:30, (Neusner, 57); see also Shabbat 151b and Rosh Hashanah 17a.

25. The contrast between these two perspectives on forgiveness can be illustrated most directly in terms of whether there can be a duty to forgive a debt. As noted earlier, there can be no general moral obligation for a creditor to forgive the debts owed to him and this in some ways underlies the view that there is no moral duty to forgive. Yet, within Jewish law there is, in fact, an obligation to forgive debts at the end of every seven-year cycle (Deuteronomy 15:1 and Mishnah Shebiit, chapter 10). The fact that maintaining a proper relationship to God entails such an obligation indicates that, for both biblical and rabbinic writers, one's duties to others are not restricted by commonly held views of moral autonomy.

26. A most cogent and sophisticated presentation of the problem faced by modern Jews who have accepted Kantian claims concerning moral autonomy but who also remain bound by the traditional covenant may be found in Borowitz, "The Autonomous Jewish Self." The very need of a contemporary liberal Jewish thinker like Borowitz to address the question in this form supports my contention here that the tension between these two models of moral responsibility is at the foundation of the difference between the approaches to forgiveness in Lauritzen and in the Jewish sources.

27. M. Yoma 8:9.

Chapter 5: Jewish Theology and Bioethics

1. As many Jewish thinkers and historians have noted, Jewish tradition contains a paucity of systematic theology. This may be, as Gershom Scholem has suggested, because for the systematic theologian the starting point is the individual's experience and so the proper form for theological expression is a treatise of one's own design. Jewish theologians, on the other hand, have tended to express themselves in the form of commentary on earlier works, which mirrors their belief that theological truths can be discovered only by subordinating oneself to a tradition of such reflection. (See Scholem, "Tradition and Commentary.") Whatever the reason, it is important to recognize that Jewish "theology" can take a variety of forms.

2. Geertz, *The Interpretation*, 126–27.

3. See Arthur Green, *Jewish Spirituality*, for a fine collection of historical–critical essays dealing with the many diverse expressions of Jewish religiosity.

4. Scholem, "Tradition and Commentary," 289.

5. Llewelyn, *The Bramble Bush*, 76.

6. For a discussion of the role of discretion in Jewish law, see Roth, *The Halakhic Process.*

7. At the same time it should be noted that often certain eminent rabbis would attract a wide following, such that other rabbis would defer to their judgments. Moreover, certain legal codes such as Maimonides' *Mishneh Torah* in the twelfth century and Joseph Karo's *Shulchan Aruch* in the sixteenth century were so widely accepted that they tended to standardize practice across communities for centuries following their publication.

8. Erubin 13b.

9. For an extended discussion of this dimension of Jewish tradition, see Novak, *The Image of the Non-Jew in Judaism.*

10. For examples of liberal Jewish theology, see Jacobs, *A Jewish Theology* and Borowitz, *Liberal Judaism.*

11. For a review and critique of current Jewish biomedical ethics, see Green, "Contemporary Jewish Bioethics."

12. Bleich, "Introduction: The *A Priori* Component of Bioethics," xix.

13. See Novak, "Judaism and Contemporary Bioethics."

14. The sole exception, to my knowledge, is one chapter on the allocation of scarce medical resources in Rosner, *Modern Medicine and Jewish Ethics.*

15. See Novak, *Law and Theology in Judaism.*

16. For fuller discussions of this, see Rosner and Bleich, eds., *Jewish Bioethics*; Bleich, *Judaism and Healing*; Rosner, *Modern Medicine and Jewish Ethics*; also Meier, *Jewish Values in Bioethics* and Feldman, *Marital Relations, Birth Control and Abortion in Jewish Law.*

17. See T. Shabbat 16:17. This principle (*pikuaḥ nefesh*) is widely invoked in rabbinic literature.

18. Feldman and Rosner, *Compendium on Medical Ethics,* 105.

19. Bleich, *Judaism and Healing,* 164.

20. As an aside it should be noted that this view of the unity of body and soul has been challenged by recent efforts to define death in terms of brain activity. The status of a person whose bodily functions continue after cerebral cortex activity has ceased is not considered in traditional sources, which define death in terms of the cessation of breathing. Some Jewish legal authorities have now accepted a brain death criterion, defined in terms of the cessation of all brain activity, though this remains controversial.

21. For an enlightening discussion of the difference in this respect between the role of principles and of rules within legal systems, see Dworkin, *Taking Rights Seriously,* especially ch. 2, "The Model of Rules I."

22. For a creative, liberal Jewish approach to the problem of euthanasia, see Byron Sherwin, "Euthanasia."

23. Stanley Hauerwas, "The Christian, Society and the Weak," 591.

24. Lisa Sowle Cahill, "Can Theology Have a Role in 'Public' Bioethical Discourse?" 11.

25. See McGowan v. Maryland, 366 U.S. 420 [1961].

26. In this respect, the theological vocabulary of Jewish ethics is more accessible to an American public than is, for example, the theology of Hinduism or Buddhism. Those traditions, too, may have important contributions to make to our moral debate, but as a practical matter the process of translation will be more difficult.

27. The claim of distinctiveness here should be qualified. I do not mean to suggest that Jewish perspectives on these matters are utterly unique. Without doubt many Christian theologians have raised similar points. My claim, rather, is that these perspectives are (a) deeply informed by Jewish thought, (b) intelligible and possibly persuasive outside of their theological context, and (c) significantly different from many views commonly expressed in public discussion of these issues.

Chapter 6: Nature and Torah, Creation and Revelation

1. A general overview of natural law theories can be found in Wollheim's excellent entry on "Natural Law" in *The Encyclopedia of Philosophy*. For a good, brief introduction to the history of natural law thinking, see Harding, *Origins*. A useful recent collection of essays on the subject can be found in George, *Natural Law Theory*.

2. Aquinas' views on natural law are expounded in his *Summa Theologica*, prima secunda, 1–2, 94.

3. Fuchs, *Natural Law*.

4. Grisez, "The First Principle."

5. Finnes, John. *Natural Law and Natural Rights*.

6. See Hittinger, "Varieties."

7. Fox, "Maimonides."

8. Faur, "Understanding the Covenant."

9. Strauss, "On Natural Law."

10. Levine, "Maimonides: A Natural Law Theorist," 11–15, 26. Levine argues that Maimonides' views are thoroughly consistent with a natural law position, even if he did not present it in those terms.

11. Bleich, "Judaism and Natural Law."

12. In chapters 5, "Natural Law for the Modern World,"and 6, "Jewish Sources of Natural Law," of his book *Judaic Ethics for a Lawless World*, Gordis argues for a modified concept of natural law in Judaism, one that is not tied to a static conception of human nature, and sees both the Decalogue and the Noahide law as instances of natural law in Judaism.

13. Novak, "Natural Law, Halakah and the Covenant," chapter 1 in *Jewish Social Ethics*, 22–44.

14. Hittinger, "Varieties," 135.

15. This appears to have been Aquinas' view. He writes, "In human matters we call something 'just' from its being right according to the rule of reason. The first rule of reason is natural law, as appears from what has been

stated. Hence in so far as it derives from this, every law laid down by men has the force of law in that it flows from natural law. If on any head it is at variance with natural law, it will not be law, but spoilt law." *Summa Theologica*, prima secunda, 1–2a, 95, 2.

16. The issue of the relationship between law and ethics generally is beyond the scope of this paper, though it obviously bears on general appraisals of natural law. For a general introduction to this issue, see Murphy and Coleman, *The Philosophy of Law*, especially chs. 1 and 2. For a discussion of the relationship between law and ethics in a Jewish context, see Dorff and Rosett, *A Living Tree*, esp. 82–123, 249–57.

17. Cicero, *De Republica*, III, xxii, 33, as cited in d'Entreves, *Natural Law*, 20–21.

18. Strauss, "On Natural Law," 137.

19. Hume, *Treatise of Human Nature*.

20. In Josef Fuchs's striking formulation, "Natural law is the superior court, so to speak, for all humanity and is independent of the changing legislation of today and tomorrow. It is the criteria of every law and of every juridical order" (Fuchs, *Natural Law*, 8). In this respect there are connections between international law and natural law with its closely related doctrine of intrinsic human rights. See, for example, the United Nations' Universal Declaration of Human Rights (1948).

21. Boyle, "Natural Law," 4.

22. Of course, natural law theorists concede that while everyone is endowed with the faculty of reason, not everyone has the opportunity or inclination to exercise it to the same degree. Accordingly, some individuals will not recognize the truth of natural law principles, but this only reflects on their own use of reason, not on the capacity of reason per se to discern natural laws.

23. See Kant, *Critique of Practical Reason*. By the same token, one could hold that there are universal moral norms, but that they have been made known to us through divine revelation. As we shall see later, Marvin Fox understands certain Jewish sources to support the view that some such universal moral norms are knowable through reason, but only ex post facto, after God has revealed them to us in the Torah.

24. Natural law theories of this type can be found in Grotius's *The Rights of War and Peace* and von Puffendorf's *Of the Law of Nature and Nations*, among others.

25. See Davitt, "St. Thomas Aquinas and the Natural Law," 40–42.

26. See Lerner, "Natural Law," 132–47.

27. See Kaddushin, *Worship and Ethics*. Perhaps the most famous instance of antiphilosophical fervor in Judaism relates to the controversy over Maimonides' rationalist philosophy; see Silver, *Maimonidean Criticism*.

28. Fox, "Maimonides and Aquinas on Natural Law," 5.

29. Ibid., 7.

30. The lofty moral injunctions in Leviticus 19 prohibiting fraud and revenge and enjoining love of others refer repeatedly to the "neighbor" (*rē'ah*) and to "your people."

31. Faur, "Understanding the Covenant," 41.

32. Strauss writes, "The notion of natural law presupposed the notion of nature, and the notion of nature is not coeval with human thought; hence, there is no natural law teaching, for instance, in the Old Testament" ("On Natural Law," 137–38).

33. Knight, "Cosmogony and Order."

34. Ibid., 143–44.

35. Novak, *The Image of the Non-Jew*.

36. This list is based on an especially fanciful homiletical exposition of Genesis 2:16 ("And the Lord God commanded man saying, 'from every tree of the garden you may surely eat.'"), which is the first explicit divine commandment given to humans.

37. Novak, *The Image of the Non-Jew*, viii.

38. It appears that the first effort to draw a connection between Noahide law and natural law can be found in the writings of Philo of Alexandria. See Wolfson, *Philo*, vol. 2,183–87.

39. See Steven Schwarzschild, "Do Noahides Have to Believe in Revelation?"

40. Mishneh Torah, Hilchot Melakhim 18:2. In part, the controversy surrounding this passage is textual, since standard versions of Mishneh Torah read in the last sentence ". . . nor is he one of . . ." rather than ". . . but he is one of . . ." The transposition of a single letter in this case completely reverses the meaning of the passage. The substantive question is whether Maimonides viewed the Noahide law as something obligatory independent of its scriptural basis, that is, on the basis of reason alone.

41. Bernard S. Jackson correctly comments on this passage, "What is clear here is that a Gentile who observes these commandments because he judges them to be rational, rather than because he wishes to obey the command of God, loses such religious merit (and reward) as is normally attendant upon observance of divine commands" ("Natural Law Questions," 2).

42. The precise nature of reason has also been a source of controversy among natural law theorists. Most often, reason includes drawing inferences from common experience, as in the case that follows, in addition to formal logic and other forms of ratiocination.

43. Other commandments that might be viewed as obligatory independent of revelation include acts of lovingkindness" (*gemilut ḥasadim*). Though one customarily recites a formulaic blessing ("Blessed are you, Lord our God . . . who has sanctified us with your commandments and commanded us to . . .") prior to the performance of a religious duty, this is not done prior to performing acts of charity. Rabbi Bahya ben Asher ben Chlava (thirteenth century) argued that this is because such acts are mandated by conscience, not divine revelation. This source is discussed by Walter Wurzburger (*Ethics of Responsibility*, 44–45).

44. Sifra, Aḥaray Mot, 86a; Yoma 67b. Interestingly, Maimonides rejects this understanding of the distinction between *mishpatim* and *ḥukim*. Relying on Deuteronomy 4:6—" When they [the nations] hear about these statutes (*ḥukim*), they will say, 'What a wise and understanding people this great nation is!' "—Maimonides argues that *ḥukim*, like *mishpatim*, are rational, for they have a purpose discernable to those who have not received God's revelation. See Maimonides, *Guide for the Perplexed*, III, 31.

45. Saadia Gaon, *Book of Doctrines and Beliefs*, 98.

46. Fox, "Maimonides and Aquinas," x–xi.

47. Bleich takes the same position, see "Judaism and Natural Law," 25.

48. Gaon, *Book of Doctrines and Beliefs*, 103–4.

49. Bleich, "Judaism and Natural Law," 12–13.

50. David Novak, *Jewish Social Ethics*, 34.

51. Ibid. This view is shared by Spero, *Morality, Halakha*, 81 and also by Daniel J. Elazar, who writes, "In its theological form, covenant embodies the idea that relationships between God and humanity are based upon morally sustained compacts of mutual promise and obligation" (*Covenant and Polity*, 23).

52. Ibid., 31.

53. Faur, "Understanding the Covenant," 44.

54. Bleich, "Judaism and Natural Law," 27.

55. Ibid., 28

56. There are probably sociological reasons, as well. Jews, at least from the outset of the rabbinic period until very recent times, never exercised legal authority over other groups. Determining the legal or moral obligations of non-Jews was, at best, a theoretical enterprise. As Novak notes, rabbinic explications of the Noahide law involve just such speculation. But this necessarily was less

urgent than determining the legal norms applicable to the Jewish community. Interestingly, it is only in modern times, as Jews become more integrated into general society, that constructing a Jewish concept of the non-Jew becomes a matter of primary importance. Similarly, I think it is no accident that David Novak, who has unquestionably provided the most extensive and sympathetic theory of Jewish natural law, has also been a leader in formulating a Jewish theology of Christianity. To the extent that circumstances necessitate developing a Jewish view of the other, natural law provides one useful tool for doing so.

57. The most complete explication of this position by a modern Jewish thinker can be found in Rosenzweig, *Star of Redemption*.

58. Genesis Rabbah 1:4

59. According to some midrashic texts, it is the oral law that distinguishes Israel from the nations. God has given Scripture to all, but the remainder of God's revelation in the form of oral tradition is communicated to Israel alone. See Tanḥuma B, Ki Tissa #17; Tanḥuma, Ki Tissa, #60; Exodus Rabbah 47:1.

60. Novak, *Jewish Social Ethics*, 15.

61. Fox, "Maimonides and Aquinas on Natural Law," 12.

62. Novak, *Jewish Social Ethics*, 74–79.

63. For a clear discussion of the tension between universalist and particularist dimensions of Israel's covenant, see Dorff, "The Covenant: How Jews Understand Themselves and Others," 481–501.

Chapter 7: Religious Faith, Historical Relativism, and the Prospects for Modern Jewish Ethics

1. For an insightful analysis of the problem of conceiving history as a science, see Berlin, "The Concept of Scientific History."

2. Troeltsch, *The Absoluteness of Christianity*, 61.

3. Hermann Cohen, *Religion of Reason*.

4. Gordis, *The Dynamics of Judaism*, 60.

5. Ibid., 29.

6. Troeltsch, "What Does 'Essence of Christianity' Mean?" 153.

7. Ibid., 141.

8. Wine, *Judaism Beyond God*, 202.

9. Cohen, *The Natural and the Supernatural Jew*, 304.

10. Baeck, "Theology and History," 281.

11. My discussion of Israel as "God-wrestlers" relies upon that of Waskow, *Godwrestling*.

12. See, in particular, books in the SUNY Series in Constructive Post-modern Thought, edited by David Ray Griffin. For a series of both constructive and descriptive essays on Jewish process thought, see Lubarsky and Griffin, *Jewish Theology and Process Thought.*

13. See Kaplan, *The Meaning of God.*

14. It is not clear to me that asserting God's transcendence is necessary in order to provide a theological foundation for a modern Jewish ethic. Moreover, while there might be philosophical reasons for positing the existence of a transcendent divine being, I remain skeptical concerning what we could know about such a God. As I read him, Franz Rosenzweig took a step in the direction I suggest here with his notion of God's revelation as nonverbal—at Sinai, Israel heard only the first letter of the first word of the Decalogue, the silent letter 'aleph.

15. Some clarification with respect to the personal nature of God is in order. The concept of God endorsed here does not preclude experiences of God in quasi-personal ways, (e.g., as being in relationship with humankind). What is disallowed by our modern, historical perspective is a God whose will has been revealed in some definitive way, thereby creating an absolute (revelation) in the midst of the relative (history). Perhaps, we can even tolerate a God who speaks, provided that, as in the biblical passages cited above, what God reveals is intentionally ambiguous, nondefinitive, and so does not fix the boundaries of divine truth over against the vagaries of human truths.

16. There is in Judaism a concept of universal moral obligations, Noahide laws, which does not rely on the covenant between God and Israel. The exact status of these obligations and their relationship to covenantal obligations has been a matter of dispute for centuries. For a thorough analysis of this material, see Novak, *The Image of the Non-Jew.*

17. Kaufman's Christian theology is intentionally noneclesial. He does not locate himself within a tradition of theological reflection that is tied to any specific denomination or any established catechism. For Jews, this second question is essential, for we stand in relationship to God not as individual souls, but as members of a people. Hence, our search for a religious grounding for our moral norms must take place in the context of community, considered both synchronically and diachronically.

18. George Mendenhall first commented on the parallels between Israelite covenant formularies and Hittite treaties in "Covenant Forms." In the intervening years, covenant has been recognized as a central metaphor in ancient Israelite religious life by many biblical scholars and theologians. Among the most important works on the covenant in ancient Israel are Hillers, *Covenant*; Nicholson, *God and His People*; Eichrodt, *Theology of the Old Tes-*

tament; Levenson, *Sinai and Zion*. See also some of the essays in Roth and Ruether's *The Liberating Bond.*

19. This has been done most extensively by Hartman in *A Living Covenant,* especially chapter 10 "Two Competing Covenantal Paradigms." Hartman himself expresses his preference for the parity model, which he believes gives Israel a greater role in determining the content of covenantal obligation, places more stock in human reason, and so undergirds a more positive attitude toward Jewish philosophy.

20. Borowitz, Choices in *Modern Jewish Thought,* 284.

21. Arthur Green, *Seek My Face,* 120–21.

22. Midrash on Psalms, 123:1.

23. By invoking this very nontraditional concept of covenant, I contribute to a tendency within contemporary Jewish thought, which Arnold Eisen has carefully documented: "The authority for covenant, more and more, will probably be the experience of meaning which the covenant provides. . . . Authority will reside within the subcommunity of Jews with which one identifies, rather than in any given, objective set of norms binding the Jewish people, ever and always, as a whole" (Eisen, "Jewish Theology in North America," 31).

24. Greenberg develops the notion of "moment faith" in his theological reflections on the Holocaust; see "Cloud of Smoke, Pillar of Fire," 27.

25. Eruvin 13b.

26. As Borowitz has written, "a living community of covenant-faithful individuals would likely create new compelling communal patterns of covenantal existence" (*Choices,* 311). Borowitz's Jewish theology and ethic are most fully articulated in *Renewing the Covenant.* I am much indebted to his thoughtful discussion of the postmodern Jewish self whose autonomy is balanced by a pervasive sense of covenantal responsibility and of postmodern Jewish ethics as inherently pluralistic. Like Borowitz, I envision contemporary Jewish notions of moral duty as necessarily covenantal, though, again, I do not imagine this God with whom we are in historic relationship as a personal, transcendent being.

27. Cited in Guenther Roth and Wolfgang Schluchter, *Max Weber's Vision of History,* frontispiece.

Chapter 8: Woodchoppers and Respirators

1. Jakobovits, "Ethical Problems," 84.

2. I say "derive," for virtually all contemporary Jewish ethicists cite biblical and rabbinic texts as the basis for what they present as the "Jewish view" on a given ethical issue. Yet, one must be cautious about taking these

contemporary discussions at face value. It could be the case that these views have not really been derived from the texts but developed quite independently and then "validated" by citing traditional Jewish sources. Notwithstanding this potential problem, we are in a position to analyze only the arguments that these authors have committed to writing. My analysis proceeds, then, on the assumption that these writers sincerely believe that the texts they cite support the conclusions they reach.

3. For a bibliography of articles in English, see Breslauer, *Modern Jewish Morality*, 67–76.

4. For a discussion of legal reasoning as "analogical," see Levi, "The Nature of Judicial Reasoning." David Novak, writing about identifying precedents within traditional sources for contemporary problems, agrees that halakhic reasoning is based on analogizing and suggests that the theological or philosophical views of the decisor will shape the way an authority selects analogies from within the tradition. ("Judaism and Contemporary Bioethics," 358).

5. Ketubot 104a.

6. Rabbenu Nissim, commentary to Nedarim 40a.

7. Yalkut Shimoni, Proverbs 943.

8. The definition of the *goses* and the problems of applying such rules to cases involving euthanasia will be discussed in greater detail later.

9. Sefer Ḥasidim 234 [ed. Margaliot].

10. Freehof, "Allowing the Terminal Patient to Die," 258–59.

11. Sherwin, "Euthanasia: A Jewish View," 47.

12. Bar-Zev, "Euthanasia," 13–14.

13. Weisbard, "On the Bioethics of Jewish Law," 353.

14. See, for example, Cytron and Schwartz, *When Life is in the Balance*, who cite and discuss some sources (notably Sanhedrin 78a and Maimonides, Mishneh Torah, Laws of the Murderer 2:7) that are discussed by none of the other authors cited in this study.

15. Avodah Zarah 18a. The text goes on to indicate that the executioner then committed suicide by leaping into the fire. A voice from heaven announced that both Ḥaninah and the executioner had been assigned a place in the world-to-come, whereupon Rabbi wept at the thought that one individual was granted immortality in a single hour, while another only after many years. The conclusion of the story, while curious in a number of respects, appears to add nothing to the discussion of euthanasia and so is generally not cited in contemporary treatments of the issue.

16. Sherwin, "Euthanasia," 42–43. So too Asher Bar-Zev argues on the basis of this text that one may remove life-support systems that are maintain-

ing the life of a terminal patient. ("Euthanasia," 14–15). Tendler cites the case of Ḥanina ben Tradyon in support of the proposition that, "if he [the patient] requests the discontinuance of therapy, emphasizing his inability to cope with his pain-filled existence, the absence of any real hope for cure makes this request binding on all who minister to him" ("Torah Ethics Prohibit Natural Death," 98).

17. It seems that Novak needs to defend this position more fully, insofar as legal authorities not uncommonly refer to biblical and talmudic narratives in their opinions. In legal discussions concerning suicide, for example, the story of Saul's death (I Sam. 31) figures prominently; see Shulchan Aruch, Yoreh Deah, 345:3 and several later sources as cited and discussed in Herring, *Jewish Ethics and Halakhah*, 75–76.

18. Cited in Herring, *Jewish Ethics and Halakhah*, 83–84.

19. Mishnah Semaḥot 1:4.

20. Maimonides, *Mishneh Torah*, Laws of Mourning, 4:5.

21. Sefer Hasidim 723 [ed. Margaliot].

22. Moses Isserles commentary to Shulchan Aruch, Yoreh Deah 339:1.

23. See Shulchan Aruch, Yoreh Deah, 339:2 and Even ha-Ezer 121:7.

24. Cited in Shapira, "The Human Right to Die," 268.

25. Ronald Green, "Contemporary Jewish Bioethics," 254–55.

26. Gellman, "Babies Doe," 108.

27. Siegel, "Biomedical Ethics," 110.

28. Weisbard, "On the Bioethics of Jewish Law," 357.

29. Jakobovits, *Jewish Medical Ethics*, 124.

30. Cited in Herring, *Jewish Ethics and Halakhah*, 84.

31. Freehof, "Allowing the Terminal Patient to Die," 259–60.

32. Rosner, *Modern Medicine and Jewish Ethics*, 200. Rosner goes on to question the possibility of making such a distinction between shortening the process of death and interrupting life. It seems that the use of the texts cited as the basis for passive euthanasia is problematic in this view.

33. Gellman, "Babies Doe," 108.

34. David Novak, *Law and Theology in Judaism*, 105.

35. Llewellyn, *The Bramble Bush*, 76.

36. Weisbard, "On the Bioethics of Jewish Law," 347.

37. The question of how to apply the values imbedded in these sources to contemporary cases becomes even more complex when we consider those individuals who are not technically in the category of *goses*. How, for example, should these sources be applied to cases of initiating life-support systems for anencephalic infants who have no hope of surviving, or of treating

infections in terminal cancer patients who are not in the final throes of death, but who, without such measures, will die much sooner. The answers are not at all apparent.

38. Cited in Shapira, "The Human Right to Die," 366.

39. Jakobovits, "Ethical Problems," 88–89.

40. Sherwin, "Euthanasia: A Jewish View," 45.

41. Shapira, "The Human Right to Die," 368.

42. Leiman, "The Karen Ann Quinlan Case," 43–50.

43. Consider, for example, the diametrically opposed ways in which antiabortion and abortion rights advocates describe the very same act—as "killing innocent life," or as "terminating an unwanted pregnancy."

44. In addition to the views of Novak cited earlier, see Federbush, "The Problem of Euthanasia," 64–68, and Weinberger, "Euthanasia in Jewish Religious Law," 99–127.

45. This position, as noted earlier, is adopted by Rosner. See also Feldman, *Health and Medicine*, 91–96.

46. This view is endorsed by Siegel, Jakobovits, and Feinstein.

47. In addition to the views of Freehof discussed earlier, see Cohn, "Natural Death," 99–101 and Halibard, "Euthanasia," 196–99.

48. These differences are attributable to a whole range of differences among contemporary Jewish ethicists, most notably, their divergent views of the very authority of the halakha. Yet, nonhalakhic perspectives may also influence a rabbi's view of euthanasia. One case in point might be Novak's essay cited earlier, which incorporates a thorough review of halakhic sources and of philosophical positions bearing on euthanasia, but then ends by connecting the practice of euthanasia with the spectre of Nazi genocide. He concludes his essay with the words, "if Judaism is not convincing, perhaps the modern Jewish experience is" (*Law and Theology in Judaism*, 117). As Dagi notes, "the spectre of genocide surrounds the entire question of euthanasia" ("The Paradox of Euthanasia," 163). The extent to which such considerations influence an author's reading of the sources is impossible to know. See also Ronald M. Green, "Contemporary Jewish Bioethics," 262–64, for an analysis of some sociological factors, which, he argues, account for the conservative drift of much contemporary Jewish literature in the area of bioethics.

49. Sandalow, "Constitutional Interpretation," 1049–50.

50. Brest relies here on Dworkin, *Taking Rights Seriously*, 134–36, who notes that the Constitution supplies us with a *concept* ("cruel"), but not with a specific *conception* of cruelty or a set of criteria for applying that concept.

51. As Freund has written, "The meaning of a rule . . . is . . . shaped in its application, which is a dialectical process that sharpens our appreciation of the rule and the facts alike" ("An Analysis of Legal Reasoning," 285).

52. White, *Heracles' Bow*, 90–91.

53. Fish, *Is There a Text*, is among the most prominent exponents of this radical view of interpretation.

54. Owen Fiss, "Objectivity and Interpretation," 744–45.

55. It could be argued that among contemporary Jewish authorities there is far less consensus on these matters than, say, within the American legal community. Perhaps liberal Jews, who have little if any commitment to the halachic process, constitute, in Fiss's terms, a different interpretive community with its own rules. Still, I would suggest that, at least those liberals like Freehof who have written responsa on contemporary problems do in fact share with more traditional authorities a common framework of interpretive assumptions. It should be remembered that the American legal community encompasses a wide spectrum of views about the rules that govern (or should govern) constitutional interpretation; for a summary of current theories, see Brest, "The Misconceived Quest," 204–38.

56. Feldman and Rosner, *Compendium on Medical Ethics*, 106.

57. Bardfelt acknowledges this implicitly when he comments, "In some cases, there may be no precedent [for contemporary cases] in Jewish law or history. . . . " ("Jewish Medical Ethics," 7).

58. Dworkin, *A Matter of Principle*, 159. Dworkin's distinction between advancing the current enterprise and striking out in a new direction has been challenged by Fish who regards meaning as wholly a function of the reader's activity ("Working on the Chain Gang," 207–8). Dworkin has responded to these criticisms, much as Fiss has, in terms of a limited notion of objectivity (*A Matter of Principle*, 167–77). For a critical review of the Fish/Dworkin controversy, see Young, "Constitutional Interpretation and Literary Theory."

59. Ibid., 161.

60. This view is consistent with the following passage taken from Joel Roth's discussion of the role of judicial discretion in halakha. He writes, ". . . widespread agreement with one position in a matter of judicial discretion puts the full weight of precedent behind that position, and, as a general rule, dictates that the arbiter abide by it. . . . Yet it must be stressed again that even the full weight of precedent does not elevate the position it favors to an absolutely definitive matter of law. . . . The right of the judge to exercise his discretion in favor of the nonprecedented position is restricted only if he is unable to offer any cogent reason or evidence for his

rejection of the precedented position. If he can offer them, his right to exercise his judicial discretion as he sees fit is, in fact, undeniable" (*The Halakhic Process*, 93).

61. A similar point has been made by Kellner, who writes, "Although many writers persist in presenting *the* Jewish position on various subjects, it very often ought more correctly to be characterized as *a* Jewish position" (*Contemporary Jewish Ethics*, 15).

62. It is striking that none of the major works in contemporary Jewish bioethics by Jakobovitz, Bleich, Feldman, or Rosner addresses the methodological or hermeneutical issues outlined in this paper.

63. For some philosophical and Christian discussions of the ethics of euthanasia, see Kohl, *Beneficent Euthanasia*; Curran, *Politics, Medicine and Christian Ethics*; Ramsey, *The Patient as Person*, especially chapter 3, "On (Only) Caring for the Dying"; and Ladd, *Ethical Issues*.

64. In the words of Hillel Cohn,

> But the conscious choice not to be bound by the halacha does not exempt me from examining as thoroughly as possible what the Jewish legal tradition says. . . . We are concerned about what the past says. We hold with Mordecai Kaplan that the past (the halacha in this case) has a vote but not a veto—or, as Solomon Freehof puts it, 'Rabbinic law is our guidance but not our governance; it is advisory but not directive' " ("Natural Death," 99–100).

See also Bardfelt, "Jewish Medical Ethics," 7, who suggests that the heritage of biblical and talmudic law should be supplemented with considerations of scientific knowledge, civil law, and our conception of individual rights when we seek to develop guidelines in the area of Jewish medical ethics.

Chapter 9: Text and Tradition in Contemporary Jewish Bioethics

1. Any Jewish ethics worthy of the name must concern itself with these methodological questions. Fortunately, there is today a growing body of serious Jewish ethical reflection; see Dorff and Newman, *Contemporary Jewish Ethics and Morality: A Reader*.

2. Scholem, "Tradition and Commentary," 288–89.

3. Medieval philosophers wrote ethical treatises, often drawing on the ethical systems of Greek philosophy. Works such as Maimonides' *Eight Chapters*, however, are not cited by subsequent legal authorities in the process of rendering decisions on ethical matters. Precisely because they deal with ab-

stract philosophical questions, they exert little influence on the tradition of practical, applied ethics.

4. Breslauer, *Contemporary Jewish Ethics*,19; Heschel, "The Meaning of Observance," 95.

5. Bleich, "Introduction," xix.

6. Bleich, *Contemporary Halakhic Problems*, xvii.

7. See Bleich, *Contemporary Jewish Ethics* and *Modern Jewish Morality*.

8. Among reform rabbis, Solomon Freehof is notable for his attempt to develop reform responsa and for the creative way in which he employed traditional legal analysis. The reform movement on the whole, however, has always been ideologically opposed to a legal definition of Jewish obligation, whether in ethics or any other area of Jewish life.

9. Rackman, "Jewish Medical Ethics and Law," 153.

10. Ibid., 166–67.

11. Ibid., 167–68.

12. Ibid., 156–57.

13. Greenberg, "Toward a Covenantal Ethic of Medicine," 127.

14. Ibid., 134–36.

15. Ibid., 145–46.

16. Ibid., 147.

17. Borowitz, *Exploring Jewish Ethics*, 165–92.

18. Hauerwas, *Vision and Virtue*, 45–46.

19. For a critique of the narrative approach, see Lauritzen, "Is 'Narrative' Really a Panacea?"

20. See also Laurie Zoloth-Dorfman, "An Ethics of Encounter."

21. Goldberg, *Jews and Christians*, 127.

22. Ibid., 56.

23. Hauerwas, *Vision and Virtue*, 22.

24. Rosenzweig, *On Jewish Learning*, 98.

Chapter 10: Talking Ethics with Strangers

1. Englehardt, xiii–xiv.

2. The field of Jewish medical ethics has been dominated by orthodox scholars who are committed to the absolute authority of Jewish law and who therefore do not accept more liberal approaches; see Green, "Contemporary Jewish Bioethics."

3. From the theological perspective of certain Orthodox writers, it may be neither possible nor desirable to extend normative Jewish teachings

into the realm of public policy debates on bioethical matters. Conversely, from the perspective of the most liberal Jewish writers, Jewish ethics is so closely identified with the general secular ethics that the issue addressed here does not arise.

4. Englehardt, 119–20.

5. The following statement from M. Makkot 3:16 is typical: "Rabbi Ḥananiah ben Aqashia says, 'The Holy One, blessed be he, wanted to give merit to Israel, therefore he gave them abundant Torah and numerous commandments, as it is said, 'It pleased the Lord for his righteousness' sake to magnify the Torah and give honor to it' (Isaiah 42:21).' "

6. The issue of Jewish jurisdiction over non-Jews arises in early rabbinic literature and has reemerged since the creation of the modern State of Israel.

7. For a full discussion of the Noahide laws, see Novak, *The Image of the Non-Jew in Judaism.*

8. T. Avodah Zarah, 8:4; Sanhedrin 56a

9. For a discussion of the disagreement over the theological underpinnings of the Noahide laws, see Schwarzschild, "Do Noachides Have to Believe."

10. Genesis Rabbah, 34:14.

11. Sanhedrin 57b.

12. The literal translation of the verse is: "Whosoever sheds the blood of a human, by a human shall his blood be shed." The word "by," however, can also be rendered "within," and so the rabbis (ignoring the final clause) render the verse "Whosoever sheds the blood of a human *within* a human . . . ," and then proceed to explain that a "human within a human" refers to a fetus.

13. It is interesting to note that Noahide law is understood to prohibit all abortion, while rabbinic law permits Jews to perform abortions in some circumstances (e.g., to save the life of the mother), making Noahide law more stringent than Jewish law in this respect. A number of rabbinic sources puzzle over this, given that Jewish law is assumed to be more stringent than Noahide law in all cases. (See Novak, *The Image of the Non-Jew in Judaism,* 185–87.)

14. Bleich, "Judaism and Natural Law;" Faur, "Understanding the Covenant;" Fox, "Maimonides and Aquinas on Natural Law."

15. Novak, *Jewish Social Ethics.*

16. Ibid., 32.

17. M. Sanhedrin, 4:5.

18. Harold Berman, "The Religious Sources."

19. M. Ohalot, 7:6.

20. See Novak, "Judaism and Contemporary Bioethics," for a rather different discussion of how these sources concerning abortion could be instructive for a non-Jewish ethic. Novak's point is that the process of analogical reasoning that characterizes the Jewish legal sources has broad application in the non-Jewish sphere as well.

21. It should be noted that many Jewish authorities have extended this rule to include threats to the mother's health, including her mental health. For a fuller discussion of the Jewish ethics of abortion, see Rosner, *Modern Medicine and Jewish Ethics*; Rosner and Bleich, *Jewish Bioethics*.

22. Englehardt, 119.

23. Shabuot 39a.

24. Englehardt, 121, 129, 131.

25. Lauritzen, *Pursuing Parenthood*, 111–12.

26. Novak, *Law and Theology in Judaism*, vol. 1, 99. Note that Novak's comments are made in connection with Jewish perspectives on euthanasia.

Conclusion: New Directions in the Study of the Ethics of Judaism

1. Geertz, The Interpretation of Cultures, 89–90.

2. See, for example, Neusner, Green, and Frerichs, *Judaisms and Their Messiahs*.

3. Kadushin, *Worship and Ethics*.

4. For a thoughtful collection of essays on Kadushin's work, see Ochs, *Essays on the Hermeneutic of Max Kadushin*.

5. For one important analysis of humility in Jewish ethics, see Ronald Green, "Jewish Ethics and the Virtue of Humility," 53–63. Green's sophisticated philosophical analysis, while valuable, does not explore humility in relation to prayer.

6. Yaffe, "Liturgy and Ethics," is a worthwhile, but limited investigation of this theme.

7. Hauerwas, *Truthfulness and Tragedy*, 76–77.

8. This theme is explored in Bialik's classic essay "Halakhah and Aggadah."

9. Some essays do explore the relationship between narrative and ethics. On the creation story, for example, see Knight, "Cosmogony and Order;" and Goldberg, "The Story of the Moral." Goldberg's *Jews and Christians* is the only effort I know of to compare Jewish and Christian ethics in relation to their "master narratives."

10. Examples of such works include Wasserzug, *The Messianic Idea*; Zwerkin, *Some Aspects of Jewish Ethics*; Meyerowitz, *Social Ethics of the Jews*; Weisfeld, *The Ethics of Israel*; Mattuck, *Jewish Ethics*; Jung, *Between Man and Man*; Priest, *Governmental and Judicial Ethics*.

11. Little and Twiss, *Comparative Religious Ethics*.

12. Reeder, *Source, Sanction, and Salvation*.

13. Niebuhr, *Christ and Culture*.

References

Rabbinic Sources

Translations from classical rabbinic texts are my own, unless otherwise noted. References to Talmudic tractates are always to the Babylonian Talmud, unless preceded by a T. (Tosefta) or M. (Mishnah). The following English translations of rabbinic sources have been consulted:

Braude, William G. *The Midrash on Psalms.* New Haven: Yale University Press, 1959.

————. *Pesikta Rabbati.* New Haven: Yale University Press, 1968.

Braude, William G., and Israel J. Kapstein. *Tanna Debe Eliyyahu.* Philadelphia: Jewish Publication Society, 1981.

Epstein, Isidore, ed. *The Babylonian Talmud.* 18 vols. London: Soncino Press, 1948.

Freedman, H. *Midrash Rabbah.* 10 vols. New York and London: Soncino Press, 1983.

Goldin, Judah. *The Fathers According to Rabbi Nathan.* New Haven: Yale University Press, 1955.

Hammer, Reuven. Sifre: *A Tannaitic Commentary on the Book of Deuteronomy.* New Haven: Yale University Press, 1986.

Neusner, Jacob. *The Mishnah.* New Haven: Yale University Press, 1988.

————. *The Tosefta.* 6 vols. New York: Ktav, 1977–86.

Maimonides, Moses. *Mishneh Torah.* 10 vols. New Haven: Yale University Press, 1949–65.

————. *Eight Chapters.* Translated by Joseph I. Gorfinkle. In Isadore Twersky, ed. *A Maimonides Reader.* New York: Behrman House, 1972.

General

Aquinas, Thomas. *Summa Theologica.* Translated by Fathers of the English Dominican Province. 5 vols. Westminster, Md.: Christian Classics, 1981.

Baeck, Leo. *The Essence of Judaism.* Translated by Victor Grubenwieser and Leonard Pearl. New York: Schocken, 1948.

———. "Theology and History." *Judaism* 13, no. 3 (1964): 274–84. This is an English translation by Michael Meyer of an essay which Baeck first published in German in 1938.

Baltzer, Klaus. *The Covenant Formulary.* Translated by David E. Green. Oxford: Basil Blackwell, 1971.

Bardfelt, Philip A. "Jewish Medical Ethics." *Reconstructionist* 42, no. 6 (1976): 7–12.

Bar-Zev, Asher. "Euthanasia: A Classical Ethical Problem in a Modern Context." *Reconstructionist* 44, no. 9 (1979): 7–15; no. 10 (1979): 7–10.

Bashan, Eliezer. "Lifnim mishurat hadin besifrut hahalakha (Hebrew)." *Deot* 39 (Spring 1970): 236–43.

Bergman, Samuel Hugo. "Israel and the *Oikoumene.*" In *Rationalism, Judaism and Universalism,* edited by Raphael Loewe, 47–65. London: Routledge & Kegan Paul, 1966.

Berlin, Isaiah. "The Concept of Scientific History." In *Concepts and Categories,* 103–42. New York: Viking Press, 1979.

Berman, Harold. "The Religious Sources of General Contract Law: An Historical Perspective." *Journal of Law and Religion* 4 (1986): 103–24.

Berman, Saul. "Lifnim Mishurat Hadin." *Journal of Jewish Studies* 26 (1975): 86–104; 28 (1977): 181–93.

Bernfeld, Simon, ed., *The Foundations of Jewish Ethics* (New York: Ktav, 1929).

Bialik, Hayim Nahman. "Halakhah and Aggadah." Translated by Leon Simon. In *An Anthology of Hebrew Essays.* Selected by Israel Cohen and B.Y. Michali. Vol. 2, 368–88. Tel Aviv: Massada, 1966.

Bleich, J. David. *Contemporary Halakhic Problems.* Vol 1. New York: Ktav and Yeshiva University Press, 1977.

———. *Judaism and Healing: Halakhic Perspectives.* New York: Ktav, 1981.

———. "Introduction: The A Priori Component of Bioethics." In *Jewish Bioethics,* edited by F. Rosner and J.D. Bleich, xi–xix. New York: Hebrew Publishing Co., 1979.

———. "Is There an Ethic Beyond Halakhah?" In *Studies in Jewish Philosophy,* edited by Norbert M. Samuelson, 527–46. Lanham, Md: University Press of America, 1987.

———. "Judaism and Natural Law." *Jewish Law Annual* 7 (1988): 5–42.

Borowitz, Eugene B. *Choices in Modern Jewish Thought.* 1st ed. New York: Behrman House, 1983.

————. *Exploring Jewish Ethics.* Detroit: Wayne State University Press, 1990.

————. *Liberal Judaism.* New York: Union of American Hebrew Congregations, 1984.

————. *Renewing the Covenant: A Theology for the Postmodern Jew.* Philadelphia: Jewish Publication Society, 1991.

————. "The Authority of the Ethical Impulse in Halakhah." In *Through the Sound of Many Voices: Writings Contributed on the Occasion of the 70th Birthday of W. Gunther Plaut*, edited by Jonathan V. Plaut, 489–505. Toronto: Lester & Orpen Dennys, 1982.

————. "The Autonomous Jewish Self." *Modern Judaism* 4, no. 1 (February 1984): 39–56.

Bowers, Renzo D. *A Treatise on The Law of Waiver.* Denver: W.H. Courtright Co., 1914.

Boyle, Joseph. "Natural Law and the Ethics of Traditions." In *Natural Law Theory*, edited by Robert P. George, 3–30. Oxford: Clarendon Press, 1992.

Breslauer, S. Daniel. *Contemporary Jewish Ethics.* Westport, Conn.: Greenwood Press, 1985.

————. *Modern Jewish Morality.* New York: Greenwood Press, 1986.

Brest, Paul. "The Misconceived Quest for the Original Understanding." *Boston University Law Review* 60 (1980): 204–38.

Bright, John. *Covenant and Promise: The Prophetic Understanding of the Future in Pre-exilic Israel.* Philadelphia: Westminster, 1976.

Buber, Martin. "Imitatio Dei." In *Contemporary Jewish Ethics*, edited by Menachem Marc Kellner, 152–61. New York: Sanhedrin Press, 1978.

Cahill, Lisa Sowle. "Can Theology Have a Role in 'Public' Bioethical Discourse?" *Hastings Center Report* 20 (4), Special Supplement (1990): 10–14.

Carney, Frederick S. "The Virtue-Obligation Controversy." *Journal of Religious Ethics* 1, no. 1 (1973): 21–36.

Cohen, Arthur A. *The Natural and the Supernatural Jew.* 2d ed. rev. New York: Behrman House, 1979.

Cohen, Boaz. *Law and Tradition in Judaism.* New York: Ktav, 1969.

Cohen, Hermann. *Religion of Reason Out of the Sources of Judaism.* Translated by Simon Kaplan. Atlanta: Scholars Press, 1995.

Cohen, Shear-Yeshuv. "Lifnim mishurat hadin." (Hebrew) In *Adam-Noah Baron Memorial Volume*, 165–88. Jerusalem, 1970.

Cohn, Haim H. *Human Rights in Jewish Law.* New York: Ktav, 1984.

———."Ancient Jewish Equity." In *Equity in the World's Legal Systems*, edited by Ralph A. Newman, 45–73. Brussels: Emile Bruylant, 1973.

———. "Prolegomena to the Theory and History of Jewish Law." In *Essays in Jurisprudence in Honor of Roscoe Pound*, edited by Ralph A. Newman, 44–81. Indianapolis: Bobbs-Merrill, 1962.

Cohn, Hillel. "Natural Death—Humane, Just and Jewish," *Sh'ma* 7, no. 132 (April 15, 1979): 99–101.

Cover, Robert. "Violence and the Word." *Yale Law Journal* 95 (1986): 1601–1629.

Curran, Charles. *Politics, Medicine and Christian Ethics*. Philadelphia: Fortress, 1973.

Cytron, Barry D., and Earl Schwartz. *When Life is in the Balance*. (New York: United Synagogue of America, 1986).

Dagi, Theodoro Forcht. "The Paradox of Euthanasia." *Judaism* 24 (1975): 157–67.

Davitt, Thomas E. "St. Thomas Aquinas and the Natural Law." In *Origins of the Natural Law Tradition*, edited by Arthur L. Harding, 26–47. Dallas: Southern Methodist University Press, 1954.

d'Entreves, A.P. *Natural Law*. London: Hutchinson's University Library, 1951.

Dorff, Elliot N. "Judaism as a Religious Legal System." *Hastings Law Journal* 29 (1977–78): 1331–1360.

———."The Covenant: How Jews Understand Themselves and Others." *Anglican Theological Review* 64 (1982): 481–501.

———. "The Covenant: The Transcendent Thrust in Jewish Law." *The Jewish Law Annual* 7 (1988): 68–96.

———. "The Interaction of Jewish Law with Morality." *Judaism* 26 (1977): 455–66.

Dorff, Elliot N. and Louis E. Newman, eds. *Contemporary Jewish Ethics and Morality: A Reader*. New York: Oxford University Press, 1995.

Dorff, Elliot N., and Arthur Rosett. *A Living Tree: The Roots and Growth of Jewish Law*. Albany: State University of New York Press, 1988.

Dworkin, Ronald. *A Matter of Principle*. Cambridge, Mass.: Harvard University Press, 1985.

———. *Taking Rights Seriously*. Cambridge, Mass.: Harvard University, 1978.

Dyck, Arthur J. "A Unified Theory of Virtue and Obligation." *Journal of Religious Ethics* 1, no. 1 (1973): 37–52.

Eichrodt, Walther. *Theology of the Old Testament*. 2 vols. Philadelphia: Westminster Press, 1961.

Eisen, Arnold. "Jewish Theology in North America: Notes on Two Decades." *American Jewish Year Book* 1991: 3–33.

Elazar, Daniel J. *Covenant and Polity in Biblical Israel.* New Brunswick, N.J.: Transaction Publishers, 1995.

Ellenson, David. "Religious Approaches to Mortal Choices: How to Draw Guidance from a Heritage." In *A Time to be Born and a Time to Die,* edited by Barry S. Kogan, 219–32. New York: Aldine De Gruyter, 1991.

Elon, Menachem. *Ha-mishpat ha-ivri.* (Hebrew) Jerusalem: Magnes Press, 1978.

Englehardt, H. Tristram, Jr. *Bioethics and Secular Humanism.* Philadelphia: Trinity Press International, 1991.

Fackenheim, Emil. "The Revealed Morality of Judaism and Modern Thought." In *The Jewish Thought of Emil Fackenheim,* edited by Michael L. Morgan, 69–84. Detroit: Wayne State University Press, 1987.

Falk, Ze'ev W. *Religious Law and Ethics.* Jerusalem: Mesharim, 1991.

Farnsworth, E. Allan. *Contracts.* Boston: Little, Brown & Co, 1982.

Faur, Jose. "Law and Justice in Rabbinic Jurisprudence." In *Samuel K. Mirsky Memorial Volume: Studies in Jewish Law, Philosophy and Literature,* edited by Gersion Appel, Morris Epstein, and Hayim Leaf, 13–20. New York: Yeshiva University Press, 1970.

———. "Understanding the Covenant." *Tradition* 9 (1968): 33–55.

Federbush, Simon. "Al hamusar v'hamishpat." (Hebrew) *Bitzaron* 6 (1942): 525–32.

———. "The Problem of Euthanasia in the Jewish Tradition." *Judaism* 1 (1952): 64–68.

Feldman, David M. *Health and Medicine in the Jewish Tradition.* Health/Medicine and the Faith Traditions series, edited by M.E. Marty and K.L. Vaux. New York: Crossroad, 1986.

———. *Marital Relations, Birth Control and Abortion in Jewish Law.* New York: Schocken, 1974.

Feldman, David M., and Fred Rosner. *Compendium on Medical Ethics.* New York: Federation of Jewish Philanthropies of New York, 1984.

Finnis, John. *Natural Law and Natural Rights.* Oxford: Clarendon Press, 1980.

Firmage, Edwin B., Bernard G. Weiss, and John W. Welch, eds., *Religion and Law: Biblical-Judaic and Islamic Perspectives.* Winona Lake, IN: Eisenbrauns, 1990.

Fish, Stanley. *Is There a Text in this Class?* Cambridge, Mass.: Harvard University Press, 1980.

———. "Working on the Chain Gang: Interpretation in the Law and in Literary Criticism." *Critical Inquiry* 9 (Sept. 1982): 201–16.

Fiss, Owen. "Objectivity and Interpretation." *Stanford University Law Review* 34 (1982): 739–63.

Fox, Marvin. "Maimonides and Aquinas on Natural Law." *Dine Israel* 3 (1972): v–xxxvi.

Frankena, William K. "The Ethics of Love Conceived as an Ethics of Virtue." *Journal of Religious Ethics* 1, no. 1 (1973): 21–36.

Freehof, Solomon B. "Allowing a Terminal Patient to Die." In *American Reform Responsa*, edited by Walter Jacobs, 257–60. New York: Central Conference of American Rabbis,1983.

Freund, Paul A. "An Analysis of Legal Reasoning." In *Law and Philosophy*, edited by Sidney Hook, 282–89. New York: New York University Press, 1964.

Fuchs, Josef. *Natural Law.* New York: Sheed and Ward, 1965.

Gaon, Saadia. "Book of Doctrines and Beliefs." In *Three Jewish Philosophers: Philo, Saadya Gaon, Jehuda Halevi*, translated by Alexander Altmann. New York: Atheneum, 1972.

Gardner, E. Clinton. "Justice in the Puritan Covenantal Tradition." *Journal of Law and Religion* 6 (1986): 39–60.

Geertz, Clifford. *The Interpretation of Cultures.* New York: Basic Books, 1973.

Gellman, Marc. "Babies Doe, an Analysis and Response." *Sh'ma* 14, no. 274 (May 11, 1984): 106–8.

George, Robert P., ed. *Natural Law Theory.* Oxford: Oxford University Press, 1992.

Ginsburg, Asher [Ahad Ha'am]. *Selected Essays of Ahad Ha-'am.* Translated by Leon Simon. Philadelphia: Jewish Publication Society, 1962.

Goldberg, Michael. *Jews and Christians: Getting Our Stories Straight.* Nashville: Abingdon, 1985.

———. "The Story of the Moral: Gifts or Bribes in Deuteronomy." *Interpretation* 38 (1984): 15–25.

Goodman, Lenn E. "Saadiah's Ethical Pluralism," in *Journal of the American Oriental Society* 100 (1980): 407–419.

Gordis, Robert. *Judaic Ethics for a Lawless World.* New York: Jewish Theological Seminary of America, 1986.

———. *The Dynamics of Judaism.* Bloomington: Indiana University Press, 1990.

————. "A Dynamic Halakhah." *Judaism* 28 (1979): 263–82.

————. "The Ethical Dimensions of the Halakhah." *Conservative Judaism* 26 (1972): 70–74.

Green, Arthur. *Seek My Face, Speak My Name.* Northvale, N.J.: Jason Aronson, 1992.

Green, Arthur, ed. *Jewish Spirituality.* Vols. 1 & 2. New York: Crossroads, 1987.

Green, Ronald M. "Contemporary Jewish Bioethics: A Critical Assessment." In *Theology and Bioethics,* edited by E.E. Shelp, 245–66. Dordrecht and Boston: D. Reidel Publishing Co., 1985.

————. "Jewish Ethics and the Virtue of Humility." *Journal of Religious Ethics* 1, no. 1 (1973): 53–63.

Greenberg, Irving. "Cloud of Smoke, Pillar of Fire: Judaism, Christianity, and Modernity after the Holocaust." In *Auschwitz: Beginning of a New Era,* edited by Eva Fleischner, 7–55. New York: Ktav and Cathedral Church of St. John the Divine, 1977.

————. "Toward a Covenantal Ethic of Medicine." In *Jewish Values in Bioethics,* edited by L. Meier, 124–49. New York: Human Sciences Press, 1986.

Grisez, Germaine. "The First Principle of Practical Reason." *Natural Law Forum* 10 (1965): 168–201.

Grotius, Hugo. *The Rights of War and Peace.* Translated by F.W. Kelley, et al., Classics of International Law. New York: Oceana, 1964.

Guttmann, Alexander. "The Role of Equity in the History of the Halakhah." In *Studies in Rabbinic Judaism,* 261–82. New York: Ktav, 1976.

Halibard, G.B. "Euthanasia." *Jewish Law Annual* 1 (1968): 11–14.

Halivni, David Weiss. "Can a Religious Law be Immoral?" In *Perspectives on Jews and Judaism: Essays in Honor of Wolfe Kelman,* edited by Arthur A. Chiel, 165–70. New York: Rabbinical Assembly, 1978.

Harding, Arthur L., ed. *Origins of the Natural Law Tradition.* Port Washington, N.Y.: Kennikat Press, 1954.

Hart, H.L.A. *The Concept of Law.* Oxford: Clarendon, 1961.

Hartman, David. *A Living Covenant.* New York: Free Press, 1985.

————. *Joy and Responsibility : Israel, Modernity and the Renewal of Judaism.* Jerusalem: Ben-Zvi Posner, 1978.

Hauerwas, Stanley. *Truthfulness and Tragedy.* Notre Dame, IN: University of Notre Dame, 1977.

————. *Vision and Virtue.* Notre Dame, IN: Fides, 1974.

————. "The Christian, Society, and the Weak: A Meditation on the Care of the Retarded." In *On Moral Medicine: Theological Perspectives in Med-*

ical Ethics, edited by S.E. Lammers and A. Verhey, 591–94. Grand Rapids, Mich.: Eerdmans, 1987.

Herring, Basil. *Jewish Ethics and Halakhah for Our Time.* New York and Hoboken, N.J.: Yeshiva University Press and Ktav, 1984.

Herzog, Isaac. *Main Institutions of Jewish Law.* 2d ed. London: Soncino, 1967.

Heschel, Abraham Joshua. "The Meaning of Observance." In *Understanding Jewish Theology,* edited by Jacob Neusner, 93–103. New York: Ktav, 1973.

Hillers, Delbert R. *Covenant: The History of a Biblical Idea.* Baltimore: Johns Hopkins University Press, 1969.

Hittinger, Russell. "Varieties of Minimalist Natural Law Theory." *American Journal of Jurisprudence* 34 (1989): 133–70.

Hoebel, E. Adamson. *The Law of Primitive Man.* Cambridge, Mass.: Harvard University Press, 1954.

Hume, David. *Treatise of Human Nature.* Book III, part 1, section 1. New York: E.P. Dutton & Co., 1949.

Jackson, Bernard S. "Natural Law Questions and the Jewish Tradition." *Vera Lex* 6, no. 2 (1986): 1–2, 6, 10.

Jacobs, Louis. *A Jewish Theology.* New York: Behrman House, 1973.

————. *A Tree of Life: Diversity, Flexibility and Creativity in Jewish Law.* Oxford: Oxford University Press, 1984.

Jakobovits, Immanuel. *Jewish Medical Ethics.* New York: Philosophical Library, 1975.

————. "Ethical Problems Regarding the Termination of Life." In *Jewish Values in Bioethics,* edited by Rabbi Levi Meier, 84–95. New York: Human Sciences Press, 1986.

Leo Jung. *Between Man and Man.* New York: Board of Jewish Education, 1976.

Kadushin, Max. *Organic Thinking: A Study in Rabbinic Thought.* Philadelphia: Jewish Publication Society, 1938.

————. *Worship and Ethics: A Study in Rabbinic Judaism.* Evanston, IL: Northwestern University, 1964.

Kant, Immanuel. *Critique of Practical Reason.* New York: Garland, 1976.

Kaplan, Mordecai. *The Meaning of God in Modern Jewish Religion.* New York: Reconstructionist Press, 1962.

Kaufman, Gordon. *In the Face of Mystery.* Cambridge, Mass.: Harvard University Press, 1993.

Kellner, Menachem Marc, ed. *Contemporary Jewish Ethics.* New York: Sanhedrin Press, 1978.

Knight, Douglas A. "Cosmogony and Order in the Hebrew Tradition." In *Cosmogony and Ethical Order*, edited by Robin Lovin and Frank Reynolds, 133–57. Chicago: University of Chicago Press, 1985.

Kohl, Marvin, ed. *Beneficent Euthanasia*. Buffalo: Prometheus Books, 1975.

Kohler, Kaufman. *Jewish Theology: Systematically and Historically Considered*. New York: Macmillan, 1918.

Konvitz, Milton R. "Law and Morals: In the Hebrew Scriptures, Plato and Aristotle." *Conservative Judaism* 23 (1969): 44–71.

Korn, Eugene B. "Ethics and Jewish Law." *Judaism* 26 (1977): 455–66.

LaCocque, Andre. "Torah—Nomos." In *The Life of the Covenant*, edited by Joseph A. Edelheit, 85–95. Chicago: Spertus College of Judaica Press, 1986.

Ladd, John, ed. *Ethical Issues Relating to Life and Death*. New York: Oxford University Press, 1979.

Landman, Leo. "Law and Conscience: The Jewish View." *Judaism* 18 (1969): 17–29.

Lauritzen, Paul. *Pursuing Parenthood: Ethical Issues in Assisted Reproduction*. Bloomington: Indiana University Press, 1993.

———. "Forgiveness: Moral Prerogative or Religious Duty." *Journal of Religious Ethics* 15 (1987): 141–54.

———. "Is 'Narrative' Really a Panacea? The Use of 'Narrative' in the Work of Metz and Hauerwas." *Journal of Religion* 67 (1987): 322–39.

Lauterbach, Jacob. "The Ethics of the Halakhah." In *Rabbinic Essays*, 259–96. Cincinnati: Hebrew Union College, 1951.

Lazarus, Moritz. *The Ethics of Judaism*. 2 vols. Translated by Henrietta Szold. Philadelphia: Jewish Publication Society, 1900.

Leiman, Sid. "The Karen Ann Quinlan Case." In *Gratz College Annual of Jewish Studies* VI (1977): 43–50.

Lerner, Ralph. "Natural Law in Albo's Book of Roots." In *Ancients and Moderns: Essays on the Tradition of Political Philosophy in Honor of Leo Strauss*, edited by Joseph Cropsey, 132–47. New York: Basic Books, 1964.

Levenson, Jon. *Creation and the Persistence of Evil*. San Francisco: Harper & Row, 1988.

———. *Sinai and Zion*. Minneapolis: Winston, 1985.

———. "The Jerusalem Temple in Devotional and Visionary Experience." In *Jewish Spirituality*, vol. 1, edited by Arthur Green, 32–61. New York: Crossroad, 1986.

Levi, Edward H. "The Nature of Judicial Reasoning." In *Law and Philosophy*, edited by Sidney Hook, 263–81. New York: New York University Press, 1964.

Levine, Michael. "Maimonides: A Natural Law Theorist?" *Vera Lex* 10 (1990): 11–15, 26.

Lichtenstein, Aharon. "Does Jewish Tradition Recognize an Ethic Independent of Halakha?" In *Modern Jewish Ethics*, edited by Marvin Fox, 62–88. Columbus: Ohio State University Press, 1975.

Little, David, and Sumner B. Twiss. *Comparative Religious Ethics*. San Francisco: Harper & Row, 1978.

Llewellyn, Karl. *The Bramble Bush*. New York : Oceana, 1960.

Lovin, Robin W. "Covenantal Relationships and Political Legitimacy." *Journal of Religion* 60 (1980): 1–16.

———. "Equality and Covenant Theology." *Journal of Law and Religion* 2 (1984): 241–62.

Lubarsky, Sandra B., and David Ray Griffin, eds. *Jewish Theology and Process Thought*. Albany: State University of New York Press, 1996.

Macmillan, Lord (Hugh Pattison). *Law and Other Things*. Cambridge: Cambridge University Press, 1937.

Maimonides, Moses. *Guide for the Perplexed*. Translated by Shlomo Pines. Chicago: University of Chicago Press, 1963.

Mattuck, Israel. *Jewish Ethics*. London: Hutchinson's University Library, 1958.

McCarthy, Dennis. *Treaty and Covenant*. Rome: Pontifical Biblical Institute, 1963.

Meier, Levi, ed. *Jewish Values in Bioethics*. New York: Human Sciences Press, 1986.

Meltzer, Tzvee Yehuda. "Megadray lifnim mishurat hadin." (Hebrew) *Hadarom* 12 (1960): 33–36.

Mendenhall, George. "Covenant." In *Interpreters Dictionary of the Bible*, vol. 1, 714–23. Nashville: Abingdon, 1962.

———. "Covenant Forms in Israelite Religion." *Biblical Archaeologist* 17 (1954): 50–76.

Meyerowitz, Arthur. *Social Ethics of the Jews*. New York: Bloch, 1935.

Montefiore, C.G., and H. Loewe, eds. *A Rabbinic Anthology*. London: Macmillan and Co., 1938.

Muilenberg, James. *The Way of Israel: Biblical Faith and Ethics*. New York: Harper and Brothers, 1961.

Murphy, Jeffrie G., and Jules L. Coleman. *The Philosophy of Law*. Totowa, N.J.: Rowman & Allanheld, 1984.

Neusner, Jacob, William Scott Green, and Ernest S. Frerichs, eds. *Judaisms and Their Messiahs.* New York: Cambridge University Press, 1987.

Newman, Ralph A. *Equity and Law: A Comparative Study.* New York: Oceana Publications, 1961.

Nicholson, Ernest W. *God and His People: Covenant and Theology in the Old Testament.* Oxford: Clarendon, 1986.

Niebuhr, H. Richard. *Christ and Culture.* New York: Harper & Row, 1951.

Novak, David. *Halakhah in a Theological Dimension.* Brown Judaic Studies. Chicago: Scholars Press, 1985.

———. *Jewish Social Ethics.* New York: Oxford University Press, 1992.

———. *Law and Theology in Judaism.* Vols. 1 and 2. New York: Ktav, 1974 and 1976.

———. *The Image of the Non-Jew in Judaism: An Historical and Constructive Study of the Noahide Laws.* New York and Toronto: Edwin Mellen, 1983.

———. "Judaism and Contemporary Bioethics." *Journal of Medicine and Philosophy* 4 (1979): 347–66.

Ochs, Peter ed. *Essays on the Hermeneutic of Max Kadushin.* Atlanta: Scholars Press, 1990.

Oden, Jr., Robert A. "The Place of Covenant in the Religion of Israel." In *Ancient Israel: Essays in Honor of Frank Moore Cross,* edited by Patrick D. Miller, Paul D. Hanson, and S. Dean McBride, 429–47. Philadelphia: Fortress, 1987.

Polish, David. "Covenant: Jewish Universalism and Particularism." In *The Life of the Covenant,* edited by Joseph A. Edelheit, 137–53. Chicago: Spertus College of Judaica Press, 1986.

Pound, Roscoe. *An Introduction to the Philosophy of Law.* New Haven: Yale University Press, 1954.

Priest, James E. *Governmental and Judicial Ethics in the Bible and Rabbinic Literature.* New York and Malibu: Ktav and Pepperdine University Press, 1980.

Rackman, E. "Jewish Medical Ethics and Law." In *Jewish Values in Bioethics,* edited by L. Meier, 150–73. New York: Human Sciences Press, 1986.

Ramsey, Paul. *The Patient as Person.* New Haven: Yale University Press, 1970.

———. "Elements of a Biblical Political Theory." *Journal of Religion* 29, no. 4 (1949): 258–83.

Reeder, Jr., John P. *Source, Sanction, and Salvation: Religion and Morality in Judaic and Christian Traditions.* Englewood Cliffs, N.J.: Prentice-Hall, 1988.

Rosenzweig, Franz. *On Jewish Learning.* New York: Schocken, 1965.

Rosenzweig, Franz. *Star of Redemption.* New York: Holt, Rinehart & Winston, 1971.

Rosner, Fred. *Modern Medicine and Jewish Ethics.* Hoboken, N.J. and New York: Ktav and Yeshiva University, 1986.

Rosner, Fred, and J. David Bleich, eds. *Jewish Bioethics.* New York: Hebrew Publishing Co., 1979.

Ross, Jacob J. "Morality and the Law." *Tradition* 10 (1968): 5–16.

Roth, Guenther, and Wolfgang Schluchter. *Max Weber's Vision of History.* Berkeley: University of California Press, 1979.

Roth, Joel. *The Halakhic Process: A Systemic Analysis.* New York: Jewish Theological Seminary of America, 1986.

Roth, Wolfgang, and Rosemary Radford Ruether. *The Liberating Bond: Covenants—Biblical and Contemporary.* New York: Friendship Press, 1978.

Rubin, Edward C. "Toward a General Theory of Waiver." *UCLA Law Review* 28 (Feb. 1981): 478–563.

Sandalow, Terrance. "Constitutional Interpretation." *Michigan Law Review* 79 (1981): 1033–72.

Scholem, Gershom G. "Tradition and Commentary as Religious Categories in Judaism." In *The Messianic Idea in Judaism,* 282–303. New York: Schocken, 1971.

Schwartzschild, Steven. "Do Noachides Have to Believe in Revelation?" In *The Pursuit of the Ideal,* edited by Menachem Kellner, 29–59. Albany: State University of New York Press, 1990.

————. "Moral Radicalism and 'Middlingness' in the Ethics of Maimonides." In *The Pursuit of the Ideal,* edited by Menachem Kellner, 137–60. Albany: State University of New York Press, 1990.

————. "On the Theology of Jewish Survival." In *Judaism and Ethics,* edited by Daniel Jeremy Silver, 289–314. New York: Ktav, 1970.

————. "The Question of Jewish Ethics Today." *Sh'ma* 7, no. 124: 31.

Shapira, Amos. "The Human Right to Die—Some Israeli and Jewish Legal Perspectives." In *The Dying Human,* edited by Andre de Vries and Amnon Carmi, 359–70. Ramat Gan: Turtledove, 1979.

Shapiro, David S. "The Doctrine of the Image of God and Imitatio Dei." In *Contemporary Jewish Ethics,* edited by Menachem Marc Kellner, 127–51. New York: Sanhedrin Press, 1978.

Sherwin, Byron. "Euthanasia: A Jewish View." *Journal of Aging and Judaism* 2, no. 1 (1987): 35–57.

Sidorsky, David, ed., *Essays on Human Rights: Contemporary Issues and Jewish Perspectives.* Philadelphia: Jewish Publication Society, 1979.

Siegel, Seymour. "Biomedical Ethics." *Sh'ma* 14, no. 274 (May 11, 1984): 109–11.

———. "Ethics and the Halakhah." *Conservative Judaism* 25 (1971): 33–40.

Sigal, Phillip. *The Halakah of Jesus of Nazareth According to the Gospel of Matthew.* Lanham, N.Y.: University Press of America, 1986.

Silberg, Moshe. "Law and Morals in Jewish Jurisprudence." *Harvard Law Review* 75 (1961): 306–31.

Silver, Daniel Jeremy. *Maimonidean Criticism and the Maimonidean Controversy, 1180–1240.* Leiden: E.J. Brill, 1965.

Sinclair, Daniel B. *Tradition and the Biological Revolution.* Edinburgh: Edinburgh University Press, 1989.

Spero, Shubert. *Morality, Halakha and the Jewish Tradition.* New York: Ktav, 1975.

Strauss, Leo. "On Natural Law." In *Studies in Platonic Political Philosophy,* 137–46. Chicago: University of Chicago, 1983.

Tendler, Moshe D. "Torah Ethics Prohibit Natural Death." *Sh'ma* 7, no. 132 (April 15, 1977): 97–99.

Troeltsch, Ernst. *The Absoluteness of Christianity and the History of Religions.* Translated by David Reid. Richmond: John Knox, 1971.

———. "What Does 'Essence of Christianity' Mean?" In *Ernst Troeltsch: Writings on Theology and Religion,* edited by Robert Morgan and Michael Pye, 124–81. Atlanta: John Knox, 1977.

Urmson, J.O. "Saints and Heroes." In *Essays in Moral Philosophy,* edited by A.I. Melden, 198–216. Seattle: University of Washington Press, 1958.

von Puffendorf, Samuel. *Of the Law of Nature and Nations.* Translated by Basil Kennett. London, 1710.

Waskow, Arthur. *Godwrestling.* New York: Schocken, 1978.

Wasserzug, D. *The Messianic Idea and Its Influence on Jewish Ethics.* London: Myers and Co., 1913.

Weinberger, Yaakov. "Euthanasia in Jewish Religious Law." (Hebrew) *Dine Israel* 7 (1976): 99–127.

Weisbard, Alan. "On the Bioethics of Jewish Law: The Case of Karen Quinlan." *Israel Law Review* 14 (1979): 337–68.

Weisfeld, Israel H. *The Ethics of Israel.* New York: Bloch, 1948.

Welch, D. Don, ed. *Law and Morality.* Philadelphia: Fortress, 1987.

White, James Boyd. *Heracles' Bow.* Madison: University of Wisconsin Press, 1985.

Wiesenthal, Simon. *The Sunflower.* New York: Schocken Books, 1976.

Wine, Sherwin T. *Judaism Beyond God.* Farmington Hills, Mich.: Society for Humanistic Judaism, 1985.

Wolfson, Harry Austryn. *Philo.* 2 vols. Cambridge, Mass.: Harvard University Press, 1947.

Wollheim, Richard. "Natural Law" In *The Encyclopedia of Philosophy,* vol. 5, 450–54. New York: Macmillan and The Free Press, 1967.

Wurzburger, Walter. *Ethics of Responsibility: Pluralistic Approaches to Covenantal Ethics.* Philadelphia: Jewish Publication Society, 1994.

———. "Covenantal Imperatives." In *Samuel K. Mirsky Memorial Volume: Studies in Jewish Law, Philosophy and Literature,* edited by Gersion Appel, Morris Epstein, and Hayim Leaf, 3–12. New York: Yeshiva University, 1970.

Yaffe, Martin D. "Liturgy and Ethics: Hermann Cohen and Franz Rosenzweig on the Day of Atonement." *Journal of Religious Ethics* 7 (1979): 215–28.

Young, R. V. "Constitutional Interpretation and Literary Theory." *The Intercollegiate Review* 23, no. 1 (1987): 49–60.

Zoloth-Dorfman, Laurie. "An Ethics of Encounter: Public Choices and Private Acts." In Elliot N. Dorff and Louis E. Newman, eds., *Contemporary Jewish Ethics and Morality,* 219–45. New York: Oxford University Press, 1995.

Zwerkin, Kenneth Carlton. *Some Aspects of Jewish Ethics.* Berkeley: Church Divinity School of the Pacific, 1936.

Index

I wish to thank Maria Den Boer for her work in preparing this index.

279